Eleven Years Afloat

From the Logbooks of TRITON 3

Peter Haase

ISBN: 978-0-9825086-5-7

Second Edition

Published by Fiction Publishing, Inc.
5626 Travelers Way
Fort Pierce, FL 34982

Printed in the United States

Contents

To all

who love the ocean, boats and sailing.

ACKNOWLEDGEMENT

When I began, many years ago, putting ELEVEN YEARS AFLOAT down on paper, I did so to have a record of these important years of my life. As I continued writing, using my logbooks as guidance, stacks of handwritten papers accumulated in my cabin and later in my house. Eventually, they became the basis for this book. In this second edition I continue to deviate little from the original logbooks and my personal notes, with the exception of some names I felt necessary to change.

In 2003, I joined a group of aspiring and accomplished writers in Port St. Lucie, Florida, the Morningside Writers Group, chaired by Sunny Serafino and later by Gene Hull. To the members of that group I owe my gratitude for their encouragement, their suggestions and their many corrections in grammar, spelling and style.
Special thanks are due to my son Carlos, who designed the cover and with patience and understanding taught me the basics of how to use a computer. My daughter, Susanne, contributed many details important for the completion of this book, and last but not least, I thank my daughter-in-law, Linda who provided the cover photo.

He who goes to the Sea

Leaves behind him all that is Solid.

He leaves behind Family and Friends,

Familiar Custom and Language.

The Rhythm of the Seasons no longer

Give him Support.

Ahead of him lie the Unknown

And the Adventure;

And ahead lie Solitude and Isolation.

A Human Being

— Alone with Himself —

Underway to ever new

And strange Places.

INTRODUCTION

My first boat was a ten-foot O'Day Sprite, which I named *TRITON*, a big name for a little boat. From 1969 to 1977, I sailed on the Hudson River with that little boat. Both my children, Susanne and Carlos learned to sail in this tiny, open boat. Born in the Hanseatic city of Rostock in Germany, I had sailed small boats when I was young and, as with a bicycle, you never forget.

Eventually I was able to buy an almost new Cape Dory Typhoon. At the length of eighteen feet, she seemed a big boat to me. There was a 4.5 HP Mercury outboard motor on her transom and I had to learn to handle this big boat and the motor. I also acquired a rigid dinghy to get to and from *TRITON II* at her mooring. My Cape Dory had a cuddy cabin and I made full use of the boat, sailing down the Hudson, staying out sometimes for a whole week. Even with my first boat, I once stayed overnight at anchor in the Hudson north of the George Washington Bridge. I woke up in the middle of the night in a puddle of rainwater. *TRITON II* was sheer luxury. Susi had developed quite an interest in sailing and she came with me when she could. Carlos did not care that much for the boat in those early years.

After a few more years on the Hudson, I moved *TRITON II* to a marina near Sheepshead Bay in Brooklyn. Although I still sailed occasionally on the river, I had now graduated to 'ocean sailing', i.e., the inner and the outer harbor of New York. I carried no electronics on my boat, no lights and no radio. I used a flashlight type red/green running light and when at anchor, I lit a kerosene hurricane lamp. I did not like engines or electronics and avoided mechanical accessories as much as I could.

In January of 1985 I sold my Cape Dory. I had made a big decision: I wanted to sail around the world. That did not happen, but I did become a cruising sailor on ocean going yachts and I gathered experience. From March, 1985 to May, 1986 I sailed as crew on five different boats: first there was the *PRI HA GOFEN*. I had given up my Manhattan apartment, flew to Guadeloupe in the Caribbean and moved on board with duffle bag and knapsack containing all of my possessions. After two months, having sailed as far as the island of Grenada, her skipper, Aaron Orbin, gave up. He had decided to return to the States and sell the boat. I had grown my sea legs in those weeks, learned to handle and live on a big yacht, got my introduction to the Diesel engine, the autohelm and the wind vane, took my first sun sights with a sextant and plotted courses; but I had no desire to return so soon to New York.

I left the *PRI HA GOFEN* as soon as we had reached San Juan, Puerto Rico and I flew to St. Thomas where I joined my friend Ken Helprin on his twenty-eight foot trimaran, the *HAPPY TIME V*. That home-built, nineteen-year old boat sank from under us in the middle of the Anegada Passage, between the British Virgin Islands and St. Maarten. The bottom of the half-rotted hull had given way under the pressure from the mast, which had worked its way little by little into the keel, and suddenly we found ourselves up to our hips in water. The boat remained barely afloat on the two outer hulls until the freighter *PACIFIC FREEDOM*, underway with grain from Montreal to South America, rescued us and we ended up in Cumaná, Venezuela.

In July I helped sail the sixty-foot *MACHETE* as paid delivery crew, nonstop to Venezuela. The owner, Francisco Hobel, a young German fellow and I started out from Newport, Rhode Island where the boat was built. This three-masted schooner was an innovative type. With her freestanding, rotating masts and brown sails, she looked like a cross between a Chinese junk and a converted speedboat. The interior was still unfinished and this was her maiden voyage. What had attracted me was that she had no engine and no electronics on board, except for a VHF radio and a tiller-mounted autohelm, powered inadequately by solar panels. The only compass on board was a handheld type like those the Boy Scouts use. The boat turned out to be inefficient in heavy weather, but very fast in good conditions. In twenty days we arrived in Puerto Azul at Naiguatá, Venezuela. Unfortunately, our third crew member, the young German, was uncooperative, unpleasant and basically dead weight throughout the whole trip.

I spent September through November of that year, on the forty-foot C+C *VAMP*, skipper Jeff Bourne. We sailed from Newport, Rhode Island via Annapolis, Norfolk and Bermuda to the Virgin Islands. We had plenty of rough weather and interrupted our voyage in Bermuda for one week.

Between Bermuda and the Virgin Islands we encountered a storm, which increased to become Hurricane Kate, with estimated sixty-knot winds and thirty-foot waves. The boat was leaky; there wasn't a dry spot on board. With a crew of four, the conditions were bad in every respect. During the worst of the storm we were all crammed in below with wet clothes and wet sails piled everywhere. Jeff and the girl who had come on board in Norfolk were all over each other, naked. Lynn Thordahl, the fourth person on board, and I got off that boat as soon as we reached St. Thomas, after stopping at Jost Van Dyke and Cruz Bay, St. John.

In the winter of 1985–86, on the cold waterfront in New York City, I worked with Nick Van Horn building a maxi-yacht. But in May, 1986 the sea fever took hold of me again. I flew to Antigua and joined Dennis O'Reilly on his cutter *CHANDELLE*. Dennis was a most disagreeable character, a stubborn Irishman who rejected everything anyone said. Of the four on board, two were inexperienced. We stopped at St. Barts and the little Dutch Island of Saba in the middle of the Anegada Passage. In St. Thomas, we lost one of the inexperienced crew over an argument with the skipper, leaving me with Dennis and Lambertus DeBoer. We docked one night at the little island of Culebra, between St. Thomas and Puerto Rico, and then headed for the Bahamas. The stubbornness and lack of common sense on the part of Dennis O'Reilly ended that trip on the reef surrounding Samana Cay in the Bahamas. We called the salvage company of Marcus Mitchell on Sampson Cay. Lambertus and I flew out with Marcus in his seaplane to Nassau and returned to the States, leaving Dennis and his stubbornness on the stranded boat with the salvage crew.

With Aaron Orbin giving up cruising, shipwreck with Ken Helprin, bad experiences with skippers and crew on the *MACHETE* and the *VAMP*, and ending up on a reef with Dennis O'Reilly, I had finally learned to steer clear of other people's boats. I was not going to sail again as a deck hand or crew member under some owner or skipper who might not have any better knowledge in navigation and seamanship than I. Yet, I say to this day, I have learned from everyone, positive or negative, what to do and what not to do. I also found out throughout my years of sailing that I would never learn it all—would never even learn enough.

In July of 1986, I found the perfect boat for me. I knew it the moment I saw her. She was docked at Lippincott's Marina in Grasonville, Maryland. Only twenty-eight feet long, she had more room than many thirty-two footers I had seen and she was in showroom condition. *SHADOWFAX* was her name, a Bristol, built in 1980. When I became her new owner on 19 August, 1986 I knew I had made one of the greatest decisions of my life.

My daughter was a driving force in the decision making. She had told me many times, "Dad, someday you will cruise in your own boat." The dream was born a few years earlier, when we had spent a two-week vacation in Tahiti. There we had met a couple who stopped at Bora Bora while on a circumnavigation in their yacht *MON AMOUR*.

Triton 3

The Saloon

Susi liked the *SHADOWFAX* immediately. "She's perfect for you, Dad!" she said and I knew it, too. The owner accepted my offer of $27,500 and I had budgeted $7,000 for additional equipment and accessories. I bought an autohelm, SatNav, knotmeter, life raft, EPIRB, inflatable dinghy with outboard motor, cruising guides, charts and much more at Goldberg's Marine in New York.

Carlos, more the pragmatist than his sister Susi, commented, "Is Dad going crazy, spending all that money on a boat?" When everything was installed, inspected and ready for launching, I renamed her *TRITON 3*.

The first trial sail was on 13 September, 1986.

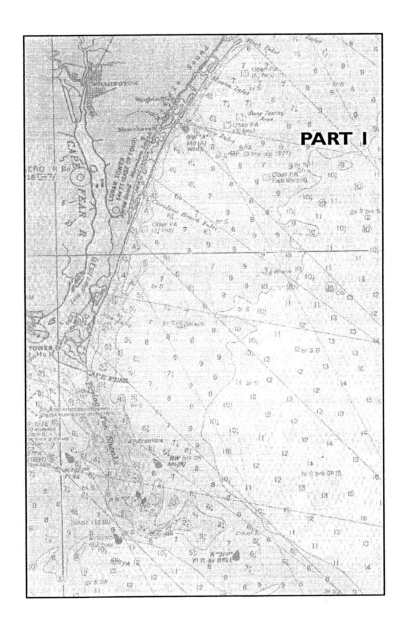

PART I

FIRST EXPERIENCE

Anchored in Spa Creek, Annapolis, I prepared for the great voyage south. Lynn Thordahl, crewmate on an earlier sailing adventure, had arrived the day before to join me on this, my first cruise in *TRITON 3*. There was, however, a delay. On the day of our planned departure, I woke up at four in the morning with a very painful and swollen right leg. With difficulty, I rowed ashore and dragged myself to the emergency room of the Anne Arundel General Hospital.

"I'll give you something for the pain," the pretty Chinese or Korean nurse said sympathetically. "The doctor will be with you in a minute."

"You're not going anywhere, said Doctor Liechtenstein. You have a staph infection in your knee. You will be in hospital for at least five days."

"My boat's anchored in the creek, ready to go. My crew just arrived. I can't do that."

"Oh yes. I put you on intravenous right away. Nurse will take you straight up to a room. You can't take another step."

Lynn Thordahl was staying at Andrea Varta's house. Lynn and Andrea had been friends for many years. I had to let her know where I was.

"I have to tell somebody what happened and where they can find me."

"I can't allow you to go anywhere. You want to risk losing the use of you leg?"

"I have to. I'll take a cab and promise to come back."

I had to sign something before I could leave the emergency room, asked the receptionist to call a taxi for me and went to Andrea 's house. I explained the situation and Lynn drove me back to the hospital. She said, not to worry. "I'm not in a great hurry. I like this town and I'm happy to spend a few days with Andrea."

While I was in the hospital, Lynn stayed at Andrea Varta's. For five straight days antibiotics were pumped into me intravenously. The pain subsided, but the swelling took much longer to go away. I still had difficulty bending my leg.

1

After a few more days recuperating at Andrea 's house, I was at last ready to begin our voyage. I was still under medication, when on 18 October Lynn and I started on the first leg down the Chesapeake Bay to Norfolk. We made overnight stops, anchoring at Solomon's Island, in Fleets Bay and the third night in Goose Creek. Despite our delayed departure we enjoyed a leisurely sail. The wide open expanse of this great bay is a fine cruising area for sailors, fishermen and powerboat enthusiasts alike. Considering that it was late October, the weather was mild in the daytime, with gentle breezes, but turned cold in the nights.

I exercised my leg and could bend it a little more every day. I was still taking antibiotics. Lynn kept a close watch on our beer supply; she did not allow me to drink alcohol until I had taken the last of my pills.

At Tidewater Marina

Norfolk harbor offered the passing sailor a terrific view of US naval power. Submarines, aircraft carriers and many kinds of warships were docked as if on display. In the afternoon of the fourth day out of Annapolis, we docked at the Tidewater Yacht

Basin, where we stayed a full day, fueling, provisioning and relaxing.

The second leg, to Beaufort, North Carolina along the Intracoastal Waterway, was a very different kind of traveling. Much of the time it was impossible to use sails. Between Great Bridge Lock and the Albermarle Sound, in the narrow canals and the creeks, the Diesel engine had to work overtime, but Albermarle Sound, the Pamlico and especially the Neuse River, notorious for stormy weather, provided us with some great sailing. In the evenings we easily found places to anchor in a protected cove or, in calm weather, an open roadstead. Usually, two or three other yachts were already at rest in those places. On the Neuse River, the fourth day out of Norfolk, we had a strong wind against us and we had to tack several times in choppy seas. We made it into Adams Creek Canal and late in the afternoon we docked at Sea Gate Marina. From there we reached Beaufort the following morning in just under two hours.

Beaufort, with its quaint maritime and yachting atmosphere, right away became one of my favorite towns. The anchorage, however, is narrow and crowded with a strong tidal current and all boats are at two anchors so that they can swing 180 degrees while remaining in the same spot. I had upgraded the ground tackle that came with the boat by adding a plow anchor, or CQR, and a hundred feet of chain, to prepare *TRITON 3* for the kind of sailing I intended to do. This boat, under her previous owner, had never left the Chesapeake Bay.

My health fully restored, we sailed out of Beaufort on 29 October in the morning for our first offshore cruise. It was a cloudy, cool and windy day. We decided to cross the Gulf Stream and took up an easterly course. The night turned rainy and miserable. At times we had no wind at all, and the following day we had a northeast breeze with intermittent rain and drizzle. The weather further deteriorated in the afternoon. It began to rain hard, the wind picked up out of the northeast and the seas built and became confused. Lynn had just settled down in the cockpit in her foul weather gear when we suffered a near knockdown and she was practically submerged for a moment. Not yet having crossed the Gulf Stream, we saw ourselves toward evening in the middle of a turbulent ocean, with seas piling up to fifteen feet and breaking, and winds of forty-five knots. With only the storm jib, we were surfing down the front of breakers at speeds of over eight knots.

By nightfall it became difficult to keep the seas at the stern quarter to avoid broaching. My leg no longer bothered me, but the pain in my shoulders from handling the wheel became too much for me. Harnessed to the life line, I crawled to the foredeck and took down the jib, hanging on to the pulpit on the rising and plunging bow. Lynn tied the helm and we went below, closing the hatch tightly. We were exhausted. I went into my bunk and took the EPIRB (emergency position indicating radio beacon) with me, while Lynn wedged herself in on the cabin sole between the table and the settee. The seas hit the boat as if with sledge hammers and banged it around like a Ping Pong ball. How much more can this boat take?

In the morning I said, "Lynn, we have to keep up our strength. See if we can make something to eat." I had eaten some Pork and Beans right from the can, but I couldn't keep it down. Later, Lynn cooked some noodles. I don't know how she managed to hold on to the pot in this turbulent sea. She tried to eat some of the pasta, but felt seasick for a while. I ate a little and recovered some of my strength.

All this time we were drifting closer to the shoals of the Frying Pan outside Cape Fear, North Carolina. On the morning of the third day, Lynn stuck her head out the hatch for a breath of fresh air. She saw, like a mirage in the drizzle and spray, a white motor yacht less than half a mile from our port side. I raised her on the VHF radio and she identified herself as the *BROWNIE III*, bound for Miami. We had a brief conversation and assured each other that we were all right. Before noon conditions allowed us to get the small jib up and we pointed the bow south, away from the shoals, which were of great concern to me. The wind, still from the northeast, abated further and we could set the reefed main. As we came closer to Charleston, South Carolina, we had radio contact with a northbound Japanese freighter and saw a lot of traffic going into and coming out of that port.

"Let's go into Charleston," said Lynn. "We need a day of rest. It's been rough."

"I agree." I was glad that she felt the same way. Lynn and I, as well as the boat, had passed the first real test.

By daybreak the following morning, in fine but cool weather, we spotted the sea buoy for the harbor entrance exactly where the SatNav, the Satellite Navigation System, told us it would be. As we entered the buoyed channel, battling a strong current, we met with a submarine. It was an ominous sight, with just the black conning tower above water and a huge bow wave ahead. I waved to the three or four personnel on the bridge but did not receive an answer. Submarines never acknowledge their presence.

That afternoon we tied up at Ashley's Marina in the harbor of Charleston and recovered from the ordeal in the Gulf Stream that had lasted three days. Confidence in ourselves as well as in *TRITON 3* had been firmly established.

We stayed for two days in beautiful and charming Charleston. Every street corner reminded us of *Gone with the Wind*. Lynn befriended a singlehander who was headed south in his Westsail. I thought she would jump ship right then and there, and she would not have hesitated if it had been to her advantage. There had been earlier occasions when she had shown her selfish side. Since our arrival in Charleston, I noticed her impatience or dissatisfaction with our slow progress.

We continued south via the Intracoastal Waterway, reached the Savannah River in three days and overcame our reluctance to go into the open ocean again. On the fifth day out of Charleston we arrived in St. Augustine.

Docked at the Municipal Marina, we met 'Mr. Westsail' again and this time Lynn did jump ship. We had been friends for some time, but I knew she was capable of grabbing an opportunity that served her purpose, without regard for anyone else. Although our separation was unpleasant, we did get together on several occasions in the years to follow. Finally, I broke contact with Lynn over an incident outrageous even for her. But I am getting ahead of myself.

After a couple of days at the city dock I moved *TRITON 3* into the yacht harbor of Camachee Cove, a very fine marina, and signed a contract for the winter months at a reasonable rate.

THE SUNSHINE STATE

Camachee Cove was my home port for the winter 1986–87. Friends and family came to visit, glad to exchange the New York winter for a few days or a weekend against some sailing in sunny Florida. I explored the waterways of the region, the Tolomato and the Matanzas rivers, and the tricky and always shifting channel through the inlet into the open water of the Atlantic. On a few rare occasions the cold northern weather came south as far as St. Augustine and a couple of mornings I found a thin sheet of ice covering the deck of *TRITON 3*.

I felt comfortable and very much at home on board my boat while living in this yacht haven, a half-hour's walk from the center of town. I bought an old, rickety station wagon to facilitate my shopping, procuring accessories, etc. but also for sightseeing and trips to the airport at Jacksonville. Several times I flew to New York, for the holidays and other occasions.

I liked St. Augustine, but I had bought the boat for cruising and was eager to feel the wind in my hair and the waves moving my world. Early in March, I invited my brother-in-law Luis and his wife Fay to accompany me sailing to Stuart, Florida. The famous Chapman School of Seamanship is located in Stuart and I thought it might be a good place to find crew for my sail to the Caribbean, my ultimate goal.

Luis has always wanted a boat to go cruising; this was his opportunity to try it out. However, Fay insisted on taking the inland waterway instead of the open ocean and so we ended up sailing, or more often motoring, south along the Intracoastal. We spent every night at a marina, interrupted our cruise one rainy, miserable day in New Smyrna Beach and arrived in Stuart on 12 March. What could have been a three-day sail, became a week-long sightseeing cruise. Luis and Fay departed seriously thinking about buying a boat. The following day I went back to St. Augustine by Greyhound to retrieve my car.

6

There is a fine anchorage in Stuart just south of the Roosevelt Bridge. *TRITON 3* joined the two or three dozen boats at anchor there. I became friends with a couple on a neighboring boat and it turned out that Frieda was from my home town, Rostock. She lived with her husband Frank Gallardo on *CIN CIN*, a 27' Albin Vega, which seemed to me half the size of my Bristol 27.7, lacking all manner of creature comforts. However, the Swedish built Vega is a seaworthy boat.

Frank Gallardo, 2nd from left, the author at right

My search for crew was unsuccessful. There were a few candidates, but I did not find anyone suitable at Chapman's or through my notes posted at conspicuous places, or an ad in the Palm Beach Post. My daughter, Susi, came to visit and we sailed on the St. Lucie River, spent a night at Club Med's Sandpiper Resort, and generally had fun in and around the anchorage with my new friends and neighbors in the anchorage.

Reluctantly, for it was to be my first solo sail, I agreed to follow *CIN CIN* to Palm Beach and Miami. We left Stuart on 21 April, with a delay of one day. It so happened that the evening before our planned departure a trawler, anchored next to me, fouled one of my anchor lines in her propeller. The skipper did not notice that he had taken *TRITON 3* in tow. I was in the galley, sauteing mushrooms for my supper, when my boat suddenly swung around and took off. In a flash I was on deck,

Susanne in Stuart

yelling after the trawler, "Hey, stop the boat!" The skipper, looked over his shoulder, surprised at what he had picked up.

My anchor line was cut and the trawler captain had to call a diver to retrieve my anchor from the bottom. Then he had to replace my seventy-five feet of 5/8th nylon 3-strand. His carelessness cost him dearly and his departure was delayed until the following day. He was in a foul mood, got mad at his wife and at me, but, I guess, mostly at himself.

My departure was also delayed by a full day settling the incident and replacing my anchor line. Frank and Frieda waited with me. We started out early the next morning and after eight hours motoring south along the ICW we anchored at Peanut Island, Palm Beach, to continue the following day offshore to Miami.

CIN CIN had been losing oil and billowed black smoke all along the waterway and I was wondering how they expected to reach Miami with an engine in that condition. I would not have gone for a day sail in that boat. We left the anchorage at Peanut Island on the evening of the following day and *CIN CIN's*

Diesel quit just outside the Palm Beach inlet. The wind was calm and so she drifted northward with the current. Talking on the radio, we agreed that I should continue on my way to Miami and that they would catch up with me. I doubted that. The next time we met was a year later.

I sailed through the night and most of the following day in light wind. My progress was slow. I reached Hillsboro in late afternoon and decided to enter through the unmarked channel against warnings that the inlet was difficult to negotiate. I was either very good at it or very lucky. Avoiding the shifting sandbanks in the inlet, I made it safely into the little cove, surrounded by luxury high-rise buildings.

Early the following morning, after a good night's sleep, I headed out through the inlet, again without touching the bottom, and continued my trip south. At the harbor entrance to Miami shortly after noon, I was confused seeing so many markers and buoys guiding ships from various directions into Government Cut. With the help of my chart I identified the ones I had to follow. Just inside the Cut a US Coast Guard vessel approached and ordered me to report for a safety check at the dock of their station. I prepared lines and fenders for docking at the concrete pier as some of the guys in blue Coast Guard uniforms called out to me and waved me away.

"It's okay," they shouted, "you're no longer required to check in with us!"

Still at a distance I yelled back, "Do they on that boat out there know this? I've been ordered to stop here at your dock."

"Go on, it's okay. You are cleared to move on!" I made a sign that I understood and continued on my course. I continued through the harbor, past docked freighters and cruise ships, until I found the junction with the Intracoastal. Here I turned hard to port and followed the markers toward Biscayne Bay, close under the skyscrapers of downtown Miami and Brickell Point. After the Rickenbacker Causeway the wide expanse of Biscayne Bay opened up before me. I steered towards Coconut Grove and rented a slip at the Dinner Key Marina.

In the predawn hour the following morning I boarded a Greyhound bus for Stuart to pick up my car, which I had left parked on a street near the town dock and drove back to Miami.

I stayed one extra day at the convenient dock of the Dinner Key Marina and then anchored *TRITON 3* in the crowded anchorage outside the yacht harbor. At the end of two weeks, and no sign of *CIN CIN*, I decided to postpone my voyage south until after the hurricane season. I met Paul Weir, a young Australian adventurer and took him on as crew for the long haul all the way back to New York.

"But I don't have any money," he told me when I picked him up at the hostel in Miami Beach. "They stole it from me right here in the hostel."

I didn't care whether the story about his money was true or not. In his early twenties, Paul was a good-natured fellow with a sense of humor. He moved on board and turned out to be an agreeable shipmate; not a sailor, but a recreational diver and that was good enough for me: he wasn't afraid of the water.

I sold my old, decrepit but mechanically sound car at a junkyard in Little Havana for two hundred bucks. On 10 May, we started for Beaufort, North Carolina, where we arrived in the evening of the 14th. There was a strong thunderstorm in the first night, but after that it was an excellent, trouble-free voyage. The Gulf Stream is a real pleasure, if you want to go north.

Paul enjoyed especially the night sailing and was not at all reluctant to take over the midnight watches. I had enough confidence in him to sleep soundly every night from twelve to six in the morning. He was a funny guy, talked dreamingly of his Vegemite, some Australian sandwich spread and praised Foster as the best beer in the world. He made fun of the Budweiser I carried on board, but drank it happily all the same.

We enjoyed quaint and charming Beaufort for two days and then took off for Norfolk via the Intracoastal Waterway, anchoring overnight at places already familiar to me. On 18 May I made this notation in the logbook:

"The best sailing ever on Alligator River! Top speed 7.7 kn., passing a ketch under power. Seldom under 7 knots, plowing NNE into Albermale Sound under main & Genoa."

We stayed two days in Portsmouth, Virginia, anchored at Hospital Point. The big yacht haven, Tidewater Marina, a short dinghy ride away, did not provide dockage for dinghies, and sailors who anchored their boats outside their facility were not welcome. Paul and I had tied up our dinghy in a remote corner of the marina and lunched at the restaurant on the premises. On leaving, we found that our dinghy had been taken to the dock in front of the marina office. I had to pay a dockage fee as if I had brought my boat in. In the ensuing argument they threatened to confiscate my dinghy. I paid the fee, but dropped supplies we were going to buy from them at their counter. On the entire eastern seaboard I have never found a more unfriendly marina than Tidewater.

We had a good time sailing along the Maryland and Jersey coasts, reached New York in the evening of 24 May and docked at the Barren Island Marina in Dead Horse Bay, Brooklyn. I was again in familiar territory.

In the morning, Susanne picked us up and drove us to her mother's house in Queens. Julia and I had been divorced for many years, but remained on friendly terms.

I introduced my shipmate to her. "Paul travels around the world on a Qantas ticket. No money, but around the world! These Australians are something else."

Julia had a nickname for everybody. "May I call you Kangaroo?" She asked, and Paul laughed. He didn't mind. He was an easygoing, likable fellow.

After a shower and a quick breakfast I drove Paul to the airport. No money, but a ticket for a round-the-world trip on Qantas, Australian Airlines.

I admired his lightheartedness, with a little bit of envy, and we said goodbye in the departure lounge. His next destination was London.

THE SUMMER OF 1987

My daughter Susanne has always had a greater interest in sailing than her brother, Carlos. She was only twelve—the age at which I started sailing—when I bought the ten-foot O'Day Sprite and she sailed with me on the Hudson. I kept the boat at a small marina in Nyack where the Tappan Zee Bridge links Westchester and Rockland counties across the wide river. Later, we enjoyed weekend trips in my Cape Dory, *TRITON II*. She was attending New York University when she enrolled as voluntary crew on the *PETREL*, an eighty-foot yawl.

The *PETREL* was built in the 1930s to defend the America's Cup and later became John F. Kennedy's favorite yacht. For a while this beautiful boat belonged to the Coast Guard, until Nick Van Horn bought her in an auction and used her for lunchtime and evening cruises in New York harbor, taking up to eighteen passengers. She was an exquisite sight under full sail, especially in the evening light of the setting sun and with the Statue of Liberty in the background. I often sailed alongside the *PETREL*; her skipper and crew named me Slocum, after the first solo circumnavigator, Joshua Slocum.

Carlos developed an interest in sailing much later, but never to the extent of his sister. I must admit that, unless you are fully dedicated, almost obsessed with it, sailing can be rather boring. It is often described as "slowly going nowhere at great expense." However, once hooked, the serenity, the feeling of freedom, the oneness with the forces of nature become the very things you don't want to give up.

It was nice to be back in New York. I was proud to show my boat to The Cat, my former girlfriend. We had remained friends after our breakup years earlier and saw each other in an on-and-off relationship. She did not like the water—hence her nickname. I was never able to persuade her to go cruising with me.

Susi, however, was enthusiastically looking forward to a summer of sailing. In June the two of us sailed to Connecticut. Ever since I had my first boat, the little open O'Day, I wanted to sail through the East River and Hell Gate. I had often watched boats struggling against the current or drifting along with it.

We left early on 12 June, and anchored for lunch in the East River, on the Queens side of Roosevelt Island, while waiting for the tide to change in our favor. It was a cold and rainy day. As we ate our prepared meal, a Coast Guard boat came alongside. The officer in charge inquired about our intentions. I declared, we were on our way to the Long Island Sound, just waiting for a favorable tide. Satisfied, they politely wished us a good trip. Late in the afternoon we sailed through Hell Gate at a slack tide, then passed the notorious prison on Rikers Island, the Whitestone and Throgs Neck bridges and came to anchor for the night in Little Bay at the north shore of Long Island.

The Long Island Sound was disappointing to me. This favorite playground for so many New York sailors, turned out to be everything I dislike: shallow water, calm or shifting winds, fog, bad currents and populated by discourteous and unseamanlike boaters

We ended this portion of our cruise at Norwalk, Connecticut. Lynn lived in Norwalk. We had stayed in touch, but never mentioned our less than amiable separation in St. Augustine the year before. Susi returned to New York while I remained for two weeks in an anchorage near Lynn's home.

Susi came back to sail with me to Newport, Rhode Island. It was a miserable day with rain and cold wind.

"Enough of this. It isn't worth it," I said to Susi. "We are hardly making any progress against the weather."

"Then let's put in at New Haven for the night."

"All right," I said and we anchored for the night in the shelter of a promontory at the entrance to New Haven. The following day we still had to fight against bad weather and got no farther than Fisher's Island.

"How will we make it into Newport for the Fourth of July under these circumstances? We have to do better than this," I said and on the third day, although in dense fog, we fought our way through the rocky passage between Watch Hill and Gangway Rock into the open waters of the Atlantic. That night we sailed into Newport Harbor and anchored next to the famed sailing vessel *SHENANDOAH*. We joined the Fourth of July celebrations, watching the fireworks over the harbor, cheering and sounding the horn at every new display of color and light soaring into the night sky, then cascading down over the waterfront.

Susi returned to New York and I took the boat up the river to Wickford, Rhode Island and hauled out for some maintenance work and bottom paint. Then I spent a few weeks sailing alone between Newport, Block Island and Montauk on the tip of Long Island. Susi and her mother visited me in Montauk. Susanne drove back to New York, leaving Julia to return with me in a leisurely night sail along the south shore of Long Island.

THE CREW QUESTION

I made a very costly mistake by putting the boat up for winter storage at Barren Island Marina in Brooklyn. Ted Monday, ruling over the marina like a despot and a tyrant, required me to insure the boat for the duration she stayed at his yard, and then the State of New York hit me with a usage tax on the value of the boat plus penalty and interest. I fought hard with the tax people of New York but lost. As much as I love New York City, I couldn't wait to leave as early as possible.

TRITON 3 was a US documented vessel with Miami as homeport, although I had purchased the boat in the state of Maryland. Under these provisions no sales tax was due in any state. But I was unaware of the New York law that, if a boat remained for six months or longer in the state, a "usage tax" in lieu of sales tax could be levied against the vessel. Ted Monday, marina manager at Barren Island, had reported boats with an out-of-state home port to the authorities, resulting in my owing New York the hefty sum of $2,688.51. Without paying this debt, I could not leave the state legally; so I paid and turned my back on New York.

It had been a long winter. *TRITON 3* was my legal residence, but I stayed with The Cat or at Julia's home most of the time. The boat was set up in the yard of Barren Island, which was not a live-aboard marina. In some milder nights I slept on board, but my electric heater was not powerful enough to keep me comfortable. The Cat's apartment was located not far from the marina in Brooklyn. It was an unsettling situation, moving between three places, not having a place of my own on tierra firma. Neither Julia nor The Cat were sure where I spent my nights, and sometimes it was not easy for me to keep track. I hated the secrecy.

Spring came and I began moving equipment and belongings, stored in Julia's garage, back to the boat in preparation for launching.

I drove to Newport, Rhode Island and to Annapolis in search of crew for an early departure and left notices at strategic places, Laundromats, nautical bookstores and ship chandlers. In the chilly weather of late March 1988, I gave the boat a fresh coat of bottom paint and I was ready to launch. To avoid incurring another month's storage fee I had to leave the marina on 1 April. Annapolis was to be my first destination. Once there, I would decide what to do next.

Johanna Klinger had responded to a note I had pinned to the bulletin board at the harbormaster's office in Annapolis. She was a young lawyer—couldn't have been more than a day out of law school—and the only boat she had ever been on was a canoe. She was a most unsuited crew for the first portion of this cruise that would take us on the open ocean, but I had received no other responses and was in a hurry to leave New York.

Perhaps it was not the best choice starting on April Fools Day. We sailed at eight in the morning, heading south along the Jersey coast. It was a cold and cloudy day, the wind was light. In twenty-four hours we had reached the entrance to the Delaware Bay where we encountered dense fog. I had stayed close to the shore, because Johanna was scared of the ocean. We were so close, we could hear the surf on the beach. At Cape May, the light tower at the end of the jetty loomed much too close out of the fog. It taught me the lesson, never to accommodate inexperienced crew. She was no help, had no sense of humor and was not good company. She found the accommodations on *TRITON 3* 'rather Spartan'. Did she expect a cruise ship?

When we anchored late in the afternoon near the eastern shore in the Delaware Bay, she was afraid of mere ripples on the water.

"Look," I explained, "a sailboat has a heavy keel which prevents it from tipping over, kind of like a pop-up doll. It's not like a canoe."

That calmed her a little, but she said, "You could have told me that earlier."

The following day we traversed the C & D Canal into the Chesapeake Bay. Before entering the canal, mariners are required to contact the authority controlling the traffic since the canal is not wide enough for two large ships to meet. The controller advised me that a big vessel was coming through from the opposite side and that I should stay close to the northern bank, my starboard side. Halfway through the canal, we met with a huge freighter, assisted by two tugboats. *TRITON 3*, with her ten-foot beam, presented no obstacle for the passage of either vessel.

We anchored for the night at the mouth of the Sassafras River, and on the fourth day we docked at the yacht harbor in Annapolis. Johanna left the boat immediately. I didn't know who was happier that the trip was over, Johanna or I.

I have always liked the nautical atmosphere of Annapolis, the bars around the harbor, filled with professional and amateur sailors, the liveliness of the town with the Naval Academy and the many art and souvenir shops. I easily felt at home in Annapolis.

It was not until the middle of May that I found a new crewmember for the continuation of my voyage south. Michael Kirk was a young engineering student, educated and well mannered. The son of a Norwegian father and Mexican mother, he was fluent in both English and Spanish. He had responded to one of my ads posted in Newport, Rhode Island. His sailing experience was minimal, yet he appeared to be potentially good company.

To accustom Michael with the boat and to living on board, and for me to get to know him before starting our long voyage south, I thought it a good idea to visit Baltimore, a day-sail away from Annapolis. We tied up for a couple of days in the inner harbor of that old city where he immediately made the acquaintances of several attractive young ladies.

Our next port was St. Michael's on the eastern shore of the Chesapeake. Before our anchor went down, he had already waved to a female watching us from land. Once ashore, he met this woman who ran a Bed & Breakfast, and that's where he stayed all day. In the evening he borrowed the dinghy and did not bring it back until the following morning, while I stayed on board without the means of getting ashore.

This behavior infuriated me. We left immediately on our trip to Washington, DC. I had always wanted to some day sail into the capital. Michael sulked all the way down the Chesapeake and up the Potomac. He had wanted to stay at least another day at St. Michaels.

We interrupted our trip at the fuel dock of Solomon's Island, where the attendant made a serious mistake. Instead of diesel, he pumped gasoline into the fuel tank. I consulted the manufacturer of my Universal engine who advised me to flush out the tank several times, until the experts deemed the ratio of gasoline residue to diesel safe enough.

Michael had friends in Washington he couldn't wait to see. Before completing our anchoring, he asked if he could go ashore. I didn't want to let him use the dinghy, so I, the skipper, rowed him, the crew, ashore and I did not see him for three days. I was fed up. The moment I ran into him in the bar of the Gangplank Marina, I asked him to get his stuff off the boat. I gathered his things and put them in the cockpit for him to pick up. In doing so, I found one of the drawers he had used full of condoms. This guy was a sex maniac!

He left me one of his books, Lust for Life, inscribed "To Peter, Buena Suerte, Michael K."

Once again I was without crew. I still did not think of sailing the boat by myself, as I intended to continue south offshore from Beaufort. I got in touch with Thomas Nagel, a young fellow who had responded earlier to one of my ads.

"Can you come down here?" I asked him. "I'm in Washington, DC. I can't pay for the air fare, but once you're here, you only need money for food."

He was staying somewhere in Vermont at the time, but immediately willing to fly to Washington and join me on the boat for a free trip to the tropics. "I'll drive to Boston day after tomorrow and catch the first flight I can get out of Logan," he said.

Thomas, in his early twenties, was from Bavaria. He had sailed boats on Chiem Lake and, as a professional truck driver, was familiar with Diesel engines.

"Good to have you on board," I greeted him when he joined me a couple of days later for the three and a half week haul to Florida. We started from Washington on 3 June, 1988. "The wind is unstable in strength and direction," I told him. "It will take us two days to get into the Chesapeake and two more to Norfolk, our first stop."

Thomas did not mind, but the last night on our way to Norfolk we had to fight a strong headwind and choppy seas, unable to make any progress toward the harbor entrance. In the rough conditions he suffered a touch of seasickness.

In the early morning hours we were tacking repeatedly, trying unsuccessfully to make some headway. "Maybe we could try Cape Charles," he suggested.

"We can do that," I acceded to his suggestion, but soon it turned out that Cape Charles was just as difficult to reach. By midmorning the wind had increased to twenty-five knots. The tide changed in our favor and again we took up course for Norfolk. Thomas hanked on the smaller jib and I reefed the mainsail. Finally we made it into Hampton Road and the harbor of Norfolk. In the shelter of the land on both sides, we ran past the aircraft carriers, submarines and other warships docked at the Navy port.

We anchored in the small cove right next to the Tidewater Yacht Harbor, at Hospital Point in Portsmouth. I remembered how rudely they had treated me the year before at that marina, when I had to pay for docking my dinghy, as if it had occupied a whole slip.

Without having set foot ashore, we started the next morning on our way along the ICW, my second trip south, and anchored overnight at places already familiar to me. The third night, however, we left the waterway and sought shelter from a strong thunderstorm in Belhaven, North Carolina. At the little marina the water was too shallow and we had to anchor. The storm passed us with torrential rain but did no harm.

Before entering the Neuse River, we stopped at the fish pier at Hobucken where a Canadian boat was tied up. The skipper told us his boat had hit a submerged log, lost the rudder and bent the propeller. He was waiting for spare parts. "It's rough on the Neuse River today," he said, but we headed out and had a great time with strong wind on the port quarter and following seas.

We stayed for two days anchored in Beaufort, North Carolina. I love the waterfront, the boardwalk along the docks with the bars and restaurants, the ship stores, the harbormaster's office with the attached snack bar, the many boats of all kinds and sizes and home ports. There is a free dinghy dock. Shops and the post office are nearby and for provisioning the harbormaster lets boaters use a courtesy car, an old beat up van, to drive to the supermarket. The friendliness at the Beaufort dock was in sharp contrast to the nasty attitude of the people at Tidewater in Portsmouth.

Anchoring in Beaufort was tricky. It was difficult to find a spot in the crowded harbor. There was not much room between the channel along the docks and the shallows close to an outer island, on which wild horses roam free. Sometimes the horses come to the beach facing the harbor front as if begging for attention. People occasionally ferry straw and hay over to them.

On the second day we moved to the dock to have Bob Miller change the oil. Bob, however, sent us Drew, a burned out pothead, to do the job. Drew didn't know an oil filter from a fuel filter. I had an argument over that with Bob, but Beaufort did not lose its charm for me over that incident.

When we left Beaufort, I was hoping for a better experience than on my first voyage to Florida. I told Thomas about the storm Lynn and I had endured almost two years earlier in the Gulf Stream. "We are going to do it differently this time," I said to him.

"How can we avoid bad weather?" He challenged me. "You never know what we may run into." He argued a lot, and not always logically. He had annoyed me a few times with useless contradictions and stubborn quarreling.

"We can't," I said, "but we don't have to get caught in a northeaster in the Gulf Stream." I had decided to stay closer to the coast, leaving the Stream and the ship traffic far to our port side. Thomas did not know how dangerous a northeaster in these waters could be, so I told him what I had read somewhere. "Many a foolish captain has survived a storm in the Gulf Stream, while many experienced ones have perished in it."

On the third morning we passed Charleston. We heard the whistle of the sea buoy marking the harbor entrance, but did not see it. The days became summery hot and the wind was often light. Thomas and I enjoyed watching dolphins playing at the bow, jumping high out of the water and splashing down, like in a show at Sea World. We took turns showering on the foredeck with water warmed by the sun. At night we could see the glare from the coast on one side and the lights of freighters far offshore on the other. In the afternoon of the fourth day out of Beaufort, we anchored at the Bridge of Lions in St. Augustine.

A whole week we remained in this oldest town of the United States so familiar to me since I had spent my first winter there living on my boat. On Saturday evening, 25 June, we headed out for our next destination, Palm Beach. Our progress was slowed by the Gulf Stream, only a few miles from the shore. On the evening of the second day, one anchor chain slid off the deck dragging about fifty feet of line with it. I sent Thomas over the side to make sure the line was not caught in the propeller. He actually enjoyed swimming in the warm water of the Gulf Stream. This little incident had happened just outside the restricted area of Cape Canaveral, a zone for the recovery of debris and jettisoned fuel tanks from rockets and shuttle launches, which may not be traversed by any vessels.

On the third night out of St. Augustine, frustrated by the slow progress against the Gulf Stream, we closed in on the shore and saw first the lights of Fort Pierce, then Stuart, Hobe Sound and Jupiter. At last, at noon of 28 June we sailed through the Lake Worth inlet and anchored at Peanut Island. Sailing in the opposite direction, going north with the Gulf Stream, I had covered the same distance in half the time.

After one night at anchor, we moved to a dock at the Municipal Marina in Riviera Beach to do some routine maintenance work on the boat. Thomas had been difficult to keep in line throughout the entire voyage, headstrong and stubborn Bavarian that he was. Unruly, he contradicted me, questioned my authority and argued about every little thing. I finally had to ask him to pack his bags over an argument of how to tie a bowline.

Susanne came for a five-day vacation cruise to West End, Grand Bahama for the Fourth of July. It was my first visit to the Bahamas in *TRITON 3*. We sailed through the mild night in a fine southerly breeze and reached West End by morning. At the entrance, we encountered such turbulent seas that I had Susi stand on the bow, holding on tightly to the forestay, alternately dipping into the water and then again almost airborne. She directed me with hand signals between the boulders clearly visible on the bottom as we plunged into the breakers. I was not at all sure how much water we had under the keel in that poorly marked channel and, I must say, I was more than a little nervous. I had not experienced such a tight situation before.

We had much fun at the resort of the Jack Tar Marina, sipped drinks at the pool and had a dinner of fried fish at a rustic local kitchen in the village. We played volleyball on the beach and swam in the clear water. One afternoon I took out one of the little Sailfish for some sailing along the beach.

We headed back to Palm Beach in a totally dark night, with no moon and no stars, and encountered heavy freighter traffic in the Gulf Stream. The wind had come around to the north and the sea became choppy. Susi accompanied me in the cockpit throughout the night and we enjoyed the brisk sail. At eight in the morning we were back at the dock in Riviera Beach. I telephoned Customs to report our return from West End, Grand Bahama Island. Susi flew home to New York, and I brought the boat for some minor repair over to Florida Diesel & Marine. I had to replace the leaking water pump of my Universal Diesel.

A few days later I sailed to Miami. I was now quite confident and competent handling the boat by myself. After all, it was only little more than an overnight sail along the coast from Palm Beach to Miami.

When I arrived at Dinner Key, Coconut Grove, I looked for a place in the crowded anchorage for *TRITON 3*, where I could put two anchors down for safety. There I found *CIN CIN* happily bopping on the small waves in this semi-protected cove, among all kinds of craft imaginable: houseboats, pontoon boats, fit and unfit sailboats, cabin cruisers and some derelict wrecks. It had been over a year since we were separated outside Palm Beach. With Frank's help I squeezed *TRITON 3* between *CIN CIN* and a pontoon boat with a pet monkey, some parakeets and a black Labrador on board. To make sure not to swing into neighboring boats in this tightly packed anchorage, I carried a third anchor out in my dinghy. Better safe than sorry.

Frank watched me. "You are paranoid," he called out to me. "What are you so worried about?" He always thought I was overly careful, while I thought that he was rather haphazard in the way he handled his boat.

"Remember what happened to me in Stuart?" I replied. "That trawler that cut my anchor line? Shit happens! And what about you, with that burned out engine of yours?"

Frieda stuck her head out the hatch and we all had a good laugh. Later we sat in my cockpit and celebrated our reunion with plenty of beer and told our stories.

While I had spent the remaining summer months of the previous year around New York and Long Island, Frank and Frieda had a new engine installed in *CIN CIN* and then they cruised between Miami and Key West. They had stayed for long periods of time in Marathon. I told them of the costly mistake I had made leaving the boat in New York for the winter. "I can still taste the bitter pill I had to swallow," I said.

"My new Perkins Diesel cost less than what you had to pay the State of New York," Frank laughed, rubbing it in.

I wanted to get off that subject and continued with my story. I told them about Johanna and how scared she was, about Michael and his condoms, Thomas Nagel, the Bavarian truck driver and finally my visit to West End, Grand Bahama with my daughter whom they had met when Susi visited me in Stuart.

In the days that followed, I could not persuade Frank to do some sailing, *CIN CIN* and *TRITON 3* together, to the Bahamas, the Keys or anywhere. He and Frieda were too content just hanging out at Dinner Key and, especially Frank liked the vagabond lifestyle. They were quite at home there, happy and without a care.

THE INTRACOASTAL WATERWAY

After two weeks at the same spot, among all those boat bums and derelicts, I felt the need to get underway again. I had not yet become one of them, like Frank and Frieda.

Again it was the height of the hurricane season and I decided to go north; it would be the last time. New York, however, was out of the question. I intended to rent a slip in Grasonville, Maryland and sail on the Chesapeake, a body of water full of charming coves, with alluring ports and quaint villages to be explored. The Caribbean could wait one more year.

A young Dutch girl looking for a free ride to Washington, DC had answered my notice, which I had pinned to the bulletin board in the laundry room of the Dinner Key Marina, but in the meantime I had already talked to Julia and surprisingly she was interested in coming to Miami to sail with me on the condition that we take the Intracoastal Waterway all the way. Julia had been a good shipmate on our short overnight trip last summer from Montauk to Brooklyn. The idea of sailing the full length of the "ditch," as the ICW is often referred to, rather appealed to me, although it would take us a whole month. I asked Julia to fly down; I knew she would be an excellent companion without having the slightest idea about anything to do with boats.

The Cat never had an interest in boats. "You know, I can't swim," she had told me. I never understood what swimming had to do with being in a boat.

Frank kidded me, "You screwed up! You had the chance to take a beautiful Dutch girl on board, but you had no patience. Could have waited another day for someone to answer your ad, but no, you called your ex-wife!"

"First of all, that girl was not so pretty, kind of plump; and secondly, Julia will be an excellent shipmate."

Julia arrived promptly and we spent the evening until past midnight with Frank and Frieda on my boat, drinking beer and talking. Early in the morning of 27 July, we weighed anchors. We said goodbye to *CIN CIN* and made our way out of the anchorage. I convinced Julia that it was only a short stretch along the coast to Ft. Lauderdale to avoid the twenty-seven bridges between Miami and Ft. Lauderdale. The weather was fine and she did not object. We exited through the Government Cut to the open ocean and six and a half hours later we sailed into Port Everglades.

The first day got us past Hillsboro into Riviera Beach. At times it was possible to use the Genoa and give the engine a rest. What a relief it was for the ears to hear the soft swoosh of the bow wave instead of the monotonous hammering of the Diesel. On day two we arrived in Fort Pierce, where we tied up at the Municipal Marina.

We reached New Smyrna Beach on 31 July and anchored in a quiet cove. The weather was fine in the morning, and it seemed logical to take another turn on the ocean. It was a day's sail from Ponce de Leon inlet to St. Augustine and we enjoyed sailing on the open ocean, a couple of miles from the beach. We got into St. Augustine by sundown and anchored just outside the Bridge of Lions. The Municipal Marina, a short dinghy ride away, offered cruising sailors a dinghy dock and the right to use showers and laundry facilities for a small fee.

In quaint but touristy St. Augustine we enjoyed a couple of days of rest and relaxation, then sailed on through Jacksonville, crossed the busy St. Johns River and arrived late in the evening at Fernandina Beach. Suddenly, the engine stalled while in the process of anchoring in Jack's Creek. A big, black plastic bag, like those the fishermen use, had wrapped itself around the propeller. I had to get into the water to cut it loose, which was no easy feat. The thick, heavy duty plastic had wound itself tightly around the shaft. It took me half an hour to cut it to shreds.

Getting underway the next morning, we spotted two alligators. "Was I in the water with alligators last night? Holy mackerel! I could have lost a leg." I shook my head. "I didn't think of that at all."

"Then I would call you Captain Ahab now," Julia laughed.

We entered Georgia and the weather was stifling hot. Almost every evening we had thunderstorms, some of them very heavy. Several nights we spent at anchor in lonely coves or, where possible, along the edge of the ICW outside the marked channel.

On 9 August we got into Charleston, South Carolina and docked at the Lockwood Marina. A full day and two nights we stayed in this old southern town, interrupting our northward cruise for some sightseeing. I had been here two years ago with Lynn Thordahl and could act as a tour guide for Julia. We enjoyed walking the charming streets, seeing the colonial architecture and the market halls with their great variety of artifacts and souvenirs, pottery, baskets, as well as fruit and vegetable.

The heat during the next days became almost unbearable. The thermometer reached 104 degrees, hardly cooling off at night. But worse than the heat were the flies. These small, black, biting flies had been with us since the swamps and marshes of Georgia, but in South Carolina they became a real pest. There were hundreds and thousands of them. I wore a T-shirt against the burning sun as much as against the flies. Standing at the wheel, watching out for the channel markers and following them on the chart, the bastards wouldn't leave me alone. We threw water on each other to cool us down and hit ourselves constantly with rags or towels to get the flies off.

"They're driving me crazy. I can't take it anymore!" I got so desperate, I jumped up, left the helm, doing some sort of a dance in the cockpit, like in a frenzy.

Julia, overcome with laughter, blurted out, "The captain is abandoning the helm, dancing with flies!" Although she was beset by the annoying pest as much as I was, she found my ridiculous antics a good source for amusement.

We kept the cabin closed with screens as much as we could, but from time to time we had to get in—and so did the flies. In the evenings at anchor or at the dock of some rustic marina, we sprayed the cabin thoroughly with bug spray. Before retiring, we literally removed dustpans full of dead flies, which had collected everywhere among our bedding and seat cushions.

Every night, thunderstorms brought a little relief from the heat, but then we had to deal with the mosquitoes. Screens in the companionway and over the hatches helped, but they decreased the wind flow through the cabin. I had only one small fan that operated on the boat's batteries; when docked, I could usually plug into shore power and turn on my big 110 Volt fan.

One entire day we sailed along with three US Navy mine sweepers. Some of the sailors on board had shed all their clothes and, to Julia's amusement, were lying on deck or walking around in the nude. That evening we tied up at a rustic pier in the small, rural town of Bucksport and had supper at a "greasy spoon". Some of the young guys were eating there, too. They recognized us, seemed a little embarrassed and snickered among them and avoided to look in our direction.

Late the next afternoon we arrived in Shallotte, North Carolina after hours of negotiating the narrow channel leading toward Enterprise Landing and Nixon Crossroads. All day long, in light rain, we had been battling a stiff breeze from the northeast.

On Sunday, 14 August in the evening I made this entry in the logbook:

"A particularly tough day. Struggling in rainsqualls and gusty winds against the tide in the Cape Fear River. Julia supplied me with coffee and was able to heat up a can of Campbell's soup for lunch while choppy seas coming in from the ocean through the inlet pounded the boat. By six o'clock we found a place to anchor in a shallow cove at Carolina Beach."

The next night we anchored in the New River. In gusty winds and a strong current we found little rest. Then, starting at five o'clock in the morning, one fishing boat after another passed us at close quarter on their way to the inlet. Their wakes kept me up, making sure the anchor was holding.

We were glad when we docked in the afternoon of 16 August at my favorite port, Beaufort, North Carolina. We treated ourselves to the luxury of taking a slip at the City Dock. I did some maintenance work, changed oil and filters and adjusted hose clamps, tightened the stuffing box and checked all through-hulls. The courtesy car was available for our grocery shopping to refurbish our dwindling food stores. We enjoyed walking along the boardwalk past the docks, seeing the yachts of many different homeports and nationalities, and stopping in at one of the restaurants for dinner or at a bar for drinks.

Julia, too, fell in love with Beaufort. In the evenings, at sundown, all along the docks people stopped in their tracks and, with their right hands on their hearts, listened to the trumpet sound as the flag was lowered.

We stayed for two full days and then, well rested and with fresh energy, continued our voyage. The Intracoastal Waterway from Beaufort to Norfolk, already well known to me, was new and interesting for Julia. On the Neuse River we had a few hours of fine sailing in light but favorable wind. Then the heat of the previous days returned—and with it came the flies. I wrote in the logbook:

"The days are hot, the pest of flies unbearable," and again, at anchor in Goose Creek, *"Thousands of flies."*

In the Pamlico River and the Albermarle Sound, the wind was also right for us and we could turn off the engine until we reached the canal between the Pungo and Alligator rivers. The second night out of Beaufort we anchored at Deep Point where I had already been three times, and the last night before Norfolk we docked at Harrison Marina in Coinjock. At last we reached Portsmouth, Virginia on the afternoon of 21 August and anchored near the Tidewater Marina.

Julia was disappointed when I said, "We're just staying overnight."

"Why can't we go ashore here? There seems to be a nice place across the river, like South Street Seaport in Manhattan."

I was not going to give the rude people at the Tidewater Marina another opportunity to harass and insult me. I told her of my previous experience. "These are the meanest people on the entire eastern seaboard. I'm not going to reward them by renting dock space." We had provisioned ourselves sufficiently with food and water in friendly Beaufort.

Without delay, we got underway the following morning for the last leg of our long journey: the Chesapeake Bay. It was to be the first overnight sail for Julia, as I wanted to continue nonstop to Solomon's Island.

"You better take one of these Dramamine pills. The Chesapeake can be quite rough sometimes," I said to Julia.

The pill knocked her out and she slept through the night, as I dodged freighter after freighter coming down the waterway.

I liked having the cockpit to myself for a change and it was a smooth ride through the night. The Dramamine had not been necessary at all.

Solomon's Island, one of my favorite places on the Chesapeake, was our last stop before Grasonville. We enjoyed a good lunch under the roof of a tiki hut at the quaint harbor front. For dinner we had of a big bucket of steamed clams and several beers. After a calm night at anchor, we were ready for the very last day sail to Grasonville on the Eastern Shore of Maryland. We entered Lippincott's Marina on 24 August, four weeks to the day since weighing anchors at Dinner Key in Miami.

We spent one last night on the boat and in the morning we boarded a Greyhound bus for the long and not too pleasant ride to New York.

Julia had been a most agreeable shipmate. We had a lot of fun and she took the entire trip in stride, never complaining about anything—except the heat and the flies.

Initially she had some difficulty handling the wheel. She used to call out, "Peter, ven! El bote se me va!" her way of saying, the boat keeps drifting off course.

I told her, "that's why you are at the helm, to prevent that. Turn the wheel, like in a car." She did learn to steer a compass course and enjoyed handling the wheel when I was busy with the charts or in the galley, took a break or changed sails.

Johanna Klinger, who was scared of mere ripples on the water, came to my mind. Julia was brave and she never questioned any of my decisions, like quarrelsome Thomas Nagel, the Bavarian truck driver. What about the others? Paul Weir, my Australian shipmate on my first voyage north from Miami, never gave me any trouble; on the contrary, he was good-natured, funny and always willing and ready for any task on board. And Susi? Well, she's a sailor, quite competent and fearless, practical and adventurous, with good common sense and a great sense of humor. What about Michael Kirk? He, of course, is best remembered for his box of condoms. Oh, did I forget Lynn? There will be more about her later.

I signed a dockage contract with Lippincott's Marina for the rest of the summer and the following winter.

THE CHESAPEAKE BAY

Lippincott's Marina did not normally accommodate live-aboard residents. I was the exception. I had bought the boat, then named *SHADOWFAX*, through Lippincott Brokerage and I had all the accessories installed and maintenance work done at their yard, so they had nothing against me living on my boat as the sole resident in their marina.

The rest of the summer and in the fall of '88 I sailed on the Chesapeake, exploring the little islands, coves and sheltered bays on the eastern shore of Maryland and Virginia. The weather was hot and sultry and there were days with practically no wind at all. On such days I remained anchored, hidden away in some remote creek, or in Annapolis, one of my favorite harbors. Annapolis, capital of Maryland and home of the Naval Academy, is a lively town. I especially enjoyed the nautical atmosphere; the quaint, little streets lined with art and antique shops; the market hall right next to the inner harbor; the many bars and restaurants, meeting places of skippers and crews of the yachts anchored in the harbor.

I felt quite at home on the Chesapeake on those lazy days of late summer and fall of 1988. My dinner often consisted of the famous blue crabs, so abundant in these waters. Armed with my net, I walked on the docks or the seawall and on a good day I caught a dozen crabs in an hour. Sometimes, on calm days, I sat on the bow of my boat and caught them while slowly motoring along.

On some weekends, Susi or Carlos drove down from New York, bringing friends with them, and we sailed, swam and fooled around with the dinghy at Gibson Island, the Megothy River, Solomon's Island or St. Michael's. On Sunday evenings, before they headed back home, we had dinner in one or another of the rustic taverns, noisy with bragging, drunken sailors.

Winter approached. It often became too cold for me to stay on the boat. My little electric heater, which I used when connected to shore power, gave but little comfort. Some cold nights I spent in New York with The Cat or in the basement apartment of Julia's home.

One cozy evening, as Julia, Susi, Carlos and I were sitting around the dining room table, the conversation, as usual, came around to sailing and to boats.

Carlos asked, "Dad, you never told us why you named the boat TRITON. I mean, there must be a reason for you to pick a name from Greek mythology."

"Yes, there is," I said, "and it has really nothing to do with the Greek god, son of Poseidon," and I began to tell the story.

"It was the last year of the war, fall of '44. I stood with my friend Konnie Sperlich on the dock of our Yacht Club and we admired a sleek racing sloop, about thirty-two feet long. Her hull was painted black, the deck light blue. She had a long, flush foredeck and a narrow cockpit. The mast was tall and slightly raked back. We had not seen this boat before and did not know to whom it belonged. As we stood there and commented on the boat's elegant lines, a gentleman approached us. We did not know him, but for some reason he knew me. 'You know,' he said to me, 'this boat once belonged to your father.' He further explained that he was not the owner, only taking care of the boat.

"I knew that my father's first boat was one of two identical ones built at the local shipyard Neptun. The other one was built for his friend Grafunder. I said to the man, 'Are you sure? This must be Grafunder's boat; my father's was called ALBATROSS.' But it seemed he knew a lot about the history of these two boats. 'Grafunder's boat was called the SEEHUND (Seal), this is the original ALBATROSS. She went through several hands and was renamed TRITON along the way.' "

"And you picked up on the tradition, but why not ALBATROSS?" asked Susi.

Carlos knew the answer. "It is the belief of seafaring people that every albatross represents the soul of a drowned sailor. Maybe in Germany they don't know that. Opa (as the kids called their grandfather) wouldn't have named his boat after a dead sailor."

32

"I have also always wondered, why TRITON," Julia put in. "It's a connection to your past. I like that you continued the tradition."

I interrupted, "Wait, the story is not finished. As we stood talking, this stranger who knew so much about this boat said, 'you would like to take her out for a sail, huh? Well, I'll fix her up for you. The sails are in the shed. Come tomorrow morning'. We were thrilled, I tell you!"

It had become quiet around the table. This they wanted to hear. "Next morning," I continued, "there she was, mainsail on the boom, jib in the sail bag on the foredeck. We backed her out of the slip and put the sails up. It was a blustery day with sharp, gusty winds and intermittent rain. We didn't care. We sailed with gusto, heeling her over, with close-hauled sheets, putting the rail under. This was real sailing. What a boat!

"We sailed downstream on the Warnow. At Oldendorf there was a dilapidated old pier where we tied up briefly to bail out because we had taken on a lot of water by the reckless way we sailed in the choppy seas. The boat rocked in the choppy water, the port shroud got stuck on a protruding plank and we heard a light snap. 'What was that?' Konnie asked. 'The mast?' I asked back. This was a glued mast, meaning it's hollow, made of narrow pieces of wood wedged and glued together. Very strong. Stronger than solid masts.

"Konnie managed to get up on the pier and called down to me, 'There seems to be a small crack, but it could have been there before.' I said, 'Come down, let's get back. It probably was there.'

"We reefed the mainsail so that there would be less stress on the mast above the crack and sailed home. Never said a word about the whole thing. Nobody ever found out, as far as I know."

"What happened then? I mean, this was during the war, where did this TRITON or ALBATROSS end up?" Susi wanted to know.

"I have no idea," I said. "As mysteriously as she had appeared, one day she was gone. The last winter of the war came, in the spring the Russian front drew closer and closer, many boats disappeared. They went west, or to Denmark or Sweden. Who knows? I never saw the boat or this man again."

"Fascinating. What a memory for you," Julia said. "What a story!" Yes, it was.

The following morning I drove back to Grasonville. There was always some repair and maintenance work to be done on the boat. I continually upgraded my anchor chains and lines. The last time I had been at Dinner Key in Miami, I had "confiscated" a cinder block at a construction site, which I used as a so-called piglead. I devised a system by which I let the block slide down the anchor rode one half or three quarters of the way. This worked very well in certain conditions, holding the chain down, preventing the anchor from breaking out. When I had the boat on more than one anchor, however, it could happen that the piglead got fouled with the rode of another anchor, as the boat swung around with the current or the wind. Then my clever system had the opposite effect of what I had intended. In addition, this created great difficulty in getting my anchors back on board.

One day Susi asked me," why do you pay such extraordinary attention to the anchoring system? I know it's important, but..."

"That's because cruising consists of ten percent sailing and ninety percent lying at anchor, and it is most desirable to be as safe as possible when the weather turns unfavorable. You see, I am fully aware that neither my boat nor I is a match for the weather and the ocean. If the elements are bent on my destruction, they can and will do so, no matter what the quality of my boat and equipment or what skill I might have." I explained it further, "it's different on a racing boat or a weekender. Boats like that don't stay for weeks or months in some faraway cove or anchorage, as I intend to do."

In the spring of 1989, I gave up my slip at Lippincott's and moved back on board permanently. I was impatiently looking forward to sailing south again, and this time it would be all the way to the Caribbean.

The six months of summer and fall went by at a leisurely pace. No hurricanes affected the Chesapeake Bay area, but there were some stormy and exciting days and nights.

On 16 July, a Sunday, I was in Annapolis when thunderstorms and heavy rainsqualls swept through the harbor with gusts of over twenty-five knots. There were two-foot waves with white caps in the anchorage. The harbor was crowded with boats. I did not have enough room to pay out sufficient line to achieve a minimum scope of 1:5, meaning five feet of anchor rode for every foot of depth. I was anchored in a depth of twelve feet and the boat should have been at a rode of at least sixty feet, half of that preferably consisting of chain. In a storm, a scope of 1:8 or better is recommended. I was seriously at risk. By noon my Danforth began to drag; even the piglead had not kept the anchor down. Other boats had also begun to drag anchors before their skippers could turn on the engines and prevent collisions.

With my engine in slow forward, I was working on the foredeck to bring my anchor and the piglead on deck, while at the same time trying to stay clear of other boats. Running back and forth between the cockpit and the bow, doing the work of two people, I managed to reach with the boat hook for a mooring ball and attach a line to it. I was safe. The storm continued into the evening.

Exhaustion mingled with satisfaction for having endured and prevailed. A good feeling. I deserved a treat. Late at night I inflated my dinghy, put the outboard on the transom and went ashore for some drinks and dinner. The storm was of course the topic of the rambunctious crowd gathered in the tavern. Everyone had some experience and told about it with much bragging and exaggeration.

I set my departure for the Caribbean for mid-October. Preparations were in full swing. *TRITON 3* had a new coat of bottom paint and two new deep cycle batteries. I converted the portside of the forward cabin into storage compartments and enlarged the chain locker in the bow for the steadily growing anchor equipment. A mechanic repaired the failing refrigerator/freezer. I bought the charts and chart kits I would need as well as the cruising guides, almanacs and nautical tables necessary to calculate positions from observations taken with the sextant. I had never ventured so far from land that I had to rely on celestial navigation, and even for the upcoming voyage that would only become necessary in the event that my SatNav, the Satellite Navigation System, failed.

On my leisurely sailing trips on the bay, I practiced my skills with the sextant, spending hours figuring out where I was with the help of books and tables and charts. In October, I pinned notices on bulletin boards at the harbormaster's office, in boating supply stores and Laundromats:

Crew Wanted! Male or Female!
Well Equipped Bristol 27.7
Leaving for Caribbean Mid-October
Contact Peter on TRITON 3
or phone (Julia's number) and leave message

Jon Reeve responded by placing a note with his phone number next to mine at the harbormaster's office in Annapolis. He was staying at the time at a hostel in Baltimore. I could not reach him on the telephone and had to sail from Annapolis to Grasonville where I had my car, in order to drive to Baltimore. He was not at the hostel when I got there, but I left a note and someone promised to give him my message. The next day, back in the anchorage of Annapolis, as I was coming to the dock in my dinghy, a tall, blond young man asked, "Are you Peter, by any chance?"

I liked him right from the start. I had the feeling that he would be right for a long, offshore voyage. He was Australian, like Paul Weir who had sailed with me from Miami to New York in the summer of '87 and had not disappointed me. Unlike Paul Weir though, Jon was a sailor. A native from Tasmania, he had participated in races out of Hobart where, according to him, "forty knots of wind made for good sailing."

He was impressed with *TRITON 3*, her general condition and the fact that she was a Bristol. "I am surprised how roomy she is," he said. "I'm six feet tall and I can stand straight up. That's amazing for a boat this size." He was enthusiastic with the idea of a major open ocean cruise. As we talked I became confident he would be a good shipmate; he must have felt the same way about me.

"Don't you think she might be a little too small for such a voyage?" I asked his opinion. "After all, this boat was designed for coastal cruising, weekend sailing."

"Not the way you have equipped this boat," he said. "Besides, smaller boats are more fun."

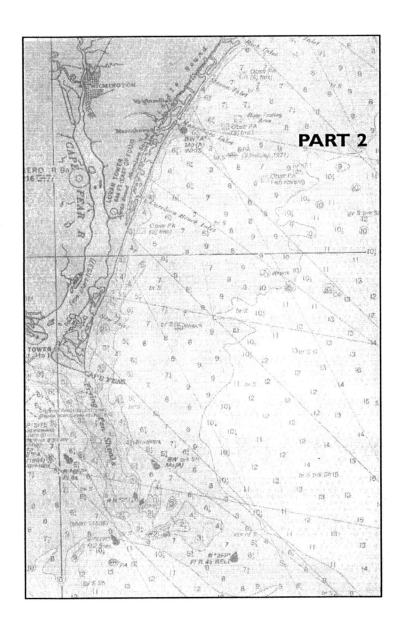

PART 2

OFFSHORE TO THE CARIBBEAN

Jon Reeve was an electrical engineer, an educated young man and, like Paul Weir, he traveled around the world on an open Qantas ticket. He spoke with only a slight "down under" accent and he had a fine sense of humor. At times he showed a certain arrogance, but not in an unpleasant way. It is more important, especially on a small boat, to have good company than a knowledgeable experienced crew. In Jon I had both.

We agreed on 19 October for our departure. That morning the wind blew at fifteen knots out of the northwest and it was raining. We had a fast sail down to Solomon's Island, the first stop on our voyage to the Caribbean. The next day the weather turned colder with intermittent rain and drizzle. By nightfall, the wind shifted against us and it became one of the nastiest nights ever on the Chesapeake. Wet and cold, often only with the storm jib, we fought hard against the elements and got into Norfolk by noon the following day. Even Jon, who liked forty-knot winds, said, "This was a bit much."

I became very sick with a cold. My throat was on fire and I had a painful cough. We docked at the Tidewater Marina in Portsmouth for the night. I didn't want to risk a confrontation with the marina operators for coming in by dinghy. I needed to buy something for my cough and to soothe my throat; fearing my condition might turn into bronchitis or worse.

We left the next morning for Beaufort, North Carolina. For Jon the Intracoastal Waterway was an interesting part of the trip; for me, boring—I had done it too many times already and wanted to get it over with. First night anchored at Currituck, second night at Deep Point, third night at Gale Point past Hobucken. Same old, same old. The Albermarle, the Pamlico, the Neuse River. All right, we had some good sailing now and then; the weather was cool but sunny. So it wasn't too bad. If only my throat didn't hurt so much.

I was glad to have Jon on board. He was tireless in switching from the jib to the Genoa to the drifter and back again, as conditions warranted. I felt too miserable to have any interest in how he worked the boat. Speaking and swallowing was painful, so I just followed our progress on the chart and made the entries in the logbook.

"Jon, make sure to keep strictly within the marked channel," I reminded him. "Outside the channel the water is in some spots only two or three feet deep." Jon was prudent and knowledgeable. I trusted him.

For sailboats it is too risky to travel by night, and so the trip from Norfolk to Beaufort is always a four-day event. The alternative would be to sail around notorious Cape Hatteras, and most sailors avoid that "Graveyard of the Atlantic."

We arrived at the anchorage in Beaufort by early afternoon of 25 October. Boy, was I glad that portion of the voyage was behind us! On the docks and in the bars of Beaufort people were talking about "that night" on the Chesapeake. "What, you were out on the Chesapeake that night?"

Jon had a few suggestions. He wanted a second reef point in the mainsail and insisted on a reef point in the small storm jib. We delivered both sails to a sailmaker and when we picked them up the next day, he charged me only for the work he had done on the mainsail. "Your jib is so small, I don't know what to charge for the few stitches and grommets it needed. Why do you want to reef such a small rag, anyway?"

I had asked myself that question. "I know, my point exactly," I said, "but Jon insisted."

Jon started, "Where I am from..." He began many comments with that where I am from.

"Yeah, yeah, yeah... Tasmania, the Bass Straight, the Hobart races," I said. "I know all that, but here, when it blows that hard, you take the damn sail down, go below, have a stiff drink and wait until it's over. But you wanted a reef point, so you got one."

I thanked the sailmaker and we took our bags back to the boat. Jon bought hacksaw blades to cut loose the shrouds, in case we should become dismasted in a storm. This made some sense; ragged ends of a broken mast have sunk boats by poking holes in the hull. I couldn't see, however, how we could saw through stainless steel shrouds with a hacksaw blade. Jon said, the wire cutter was too expensive.

I shrugged my shoulders. "Okay," and I asked him, mockingly, "What else do we need?"

"I need something to keep me from falling out of my bunk," he said and the next day he came on board with six-foot long strips of wood and a spool of thin rope, called small stuff on a boat. I allowed him to build a contraption that, when it was finished, and he was in it, looked like a cage or a dog kennel. I teased him a lot with this invention of his and he took no offense. He used his "kennel" once or twice during the entire voyage.

On 31 October, 1989, six days after our arrival in Beaufort we were ready for the open ocean part of our voyage. We had a good weather forecast and the tide was to start running out by midnight. With the dinghy deflated and stowed away in the cockpit locker, we tied up at the fuel dock for diesel and water and then had a fine last dinner on shore

"Here's to a successful, safe and fun passage," we toasted each other and one hour before midnight we cast off our lines.

The first three days the wind was moderate at ten to fifteen knots from the northeast. The weather was warm and sunny and we sailed a comfortable course of 150 degrees, roughly southeast. We had crossed the Gulf Stream in less than twenty-four hours and made over 140 nautical miles each day. Jon and I were pleased with our progress and the performance of the boat. We had agreed on three-hour night watches, starting at nine p m. The flip of a coin decided who had the first watch.

I have often been asked, "What do you do all day long on a sail boat. Isn't it boring?" It can be, if you don't like to be in a boat. For Jon and me, this was living! We shared the same interest, were compatible even in our humor. Examples:

What's the course?
One thirty eight.
Haul in on the main sheet, quarter of an inch.
A quarter of an inch?
Yeah.

Hey, what's that? Is that a ship out there?
No, just looks like it.
What looks like it?

It's a whitecap.
Then get that whitecap on the radio.

What's for supper?
Noodles with ketchup.
We had that yesterday; can't you make me a steak with a baked potato?
Sure, only it's your turn to cook today!

The camaraderie was great between us. We also had serious topics. One evening I asked him, "What's your goal in life, Jon? You've just finished engineering school, got your degree. What now?"

"I want to do research. I signed up for a stint at the research station in Antarctica. Six months, starting when I get back from my world tour, graduation gift from my parents."

"That's great, Jon. You have another adventure to look forward to." The sun, a big red fireball, sank into the ocean. Red sky at night, sailor's delight.

"You have any plans for the future?" he asked me.

"Right now I'm sailing to paradise. To live there and take it easy, to do whatever comes naturally, that's my plan. I've had plenty of excitement in my life. Growing up during the war and all that. The postwar years and then Ecuador. Marriage, kids, divorce. New York."

"Tell me about the war. Did you ever see Hitler? What was it like when the cities were bombed?"

"The war was bad, but the first years after the war were bad, too. No food, no clothes, no shoes, no heat—nothing. Hitler? Yeah, I saw him twice. No big deal. Once standing up in his Mercedes as the motorcade drove through a crowd, he with that stupid Nazi salute. My brother was so close, he jumped on the running board of his car. The second time was at the railroad station of our town. He looked out the window as the train slowly rolled past us, the crowd screaming "Heil Hitler."

"And the air raids? Your city was bombed, too, right?"

"Oh, and how!" I didn't really want to get into that. "Lost our house. We were in it. I'll never forget the sound of the splintering wood, the last big cord of the piano on the upper

44

floor, then the silence before the bomb went off. The house settled in an angle. We breathed mortar and cement dust, but weren't hurt." I gave him the short version of it. I didn't tell him about the clinic next door on fire, the strafing from the planes on the civilians, the smell of fire for days...

We were silent for a moment. "There's a boat! I wonder if that's the BANDU. Give me the binos!" Jon had spotted a white sail a couple of miles distant.

I called on the handheld VHF. "Bandu, Bandu, Bandu. Triton 3. Over." A voice came back. It was *BANDU*. We had made friends with the crew of that yacht in Beaufort. They had left the day after us and were also underway to the Virgin Islands. Sailing a bigger and faster boat, they were soon lost in the distance under the darkening sky.

"Good bye and bon voyage!" came over the radio. Then we were alone again, but how exciting it was to see another yacht in this vastness. I made the appropriate notation in the logbook.

During that night we experienced a heavy thunderstorm with strong gusts. For the first time we tried out our double reef in the mainsail and the reef in the jib. "What a ridiculous sight that tiny thing is," I mocked Jon. "I'll call it Jon's handkerchief!"

"You'll be damned glad to have it when it really starts to blow," he shot back at me.

The next night the container ship *STELLA MAERSK*, underway from New Orleans to Rotterdam, overtook us. We spoke on the VHF and got a fine weather report. The radio operator was glad to have someone to talk to. An hour later, when the ship's lights had already sunk below the horizon, he called us back just to wish us a good voyage.

Fine weather report aside, in the morning heavy rain squalls came at us with a vengeance, as a front passed from west to east, packing gusts up to forty knots. As the first raindrops hit us like bullets, Jon went forward to the mast to take down the mainsail and tie it down on the boom as best he could in the storm.

"You want the Genoa down, too?" He screamed at me over the wind howling through the rigging.

"Leave it. I think we can handle it." I thought it was too dangerous for him on the foredeck to take down that big sail in the conditions that had developed so suddenly.

He came back into the cockpit. "Want me to take over?" Jon saw me struggling with the wheel.

"I can handle it, you've done enough with that main. Take a rest for awhile." I eased up on the big headsail by bearing away from the wind a few degrees. "We're doing eight point three knots! Man, is this safe? It's downright scary!"

Jon was exhilarated. "This is great sailing, like the race round Tasmania!"

We took turns at the helm. Blue sky returned, but the wind remained strong all day into the evening. By nightfall conditions calmed considerably. The logbook entry for Monday, 6 November, reads:

"Great sailing, E-NE 10-12, sun/clouds/hot. Speed 6 to 7 kn. Course 135. Pos 27.55 N. 67 58 W.

On the way to Paradise

That put us approximately 350 miles southwest of Bermuda, 700 miles east of the Florida coast and 600 miles north of the Virgin Islands—the farthest point from any land on our voyage. To commemorate the moment, we took photos of each other at the helm, holding a can of Budweiser."

From here on, the course was almost due south, also known as the milk run on route 66, along west longitude 66, usually a fast and easy sail in the steady easterly trade winds.

Except for some showers now and then, we had great weather and gorgeous sailing, making excellent progress. My cough and the sore throat had gradually improved and I enjoyed our cruise fully.

Jon's arrogance mildly annoyed me sometimes, but he was good-natured enough to accept laughingly when I told him "You have a superiority complex."

"I've been told that before," he admitted.

One of our batteries had gone flat. "You should know what went wrong," I said, "you're an electrical engineer." But he didn't know, and another day I asked him to fix the knotmeter. I taunted him, "Isn't that what electrical engineers do?"

Indignantly he answered, "I am a scientist. A scientist does research. A scientist works in a lab, at a desk. A scientist doesn't fix things." But then he fixed it anyway.

We had a good time, made fun of each other, drank beer, took turns in cooking and had no trouble maintaining our three-hour watches. When it came to changing sails in heavy weather, or any other job for that matter, we both showed the same ability and willingness and he respected me for doing the same difficult and potentially dangerous tasks as he did, being three times his age. We did make a good team.

On Saturday, 11 November, at four a m, Jon called me up. "Land ho!" He yelled. I scrambled on deck. All the islands came into view in the moonlight, except Anegada, a flat island, which was still under the horizon. At ten o'clock, ten days and eleven hours out of Beaufort, we anchored in Great Harbour, Jost Van Dyke, the British Virgin Islands. What a glorious voyage it has been! What a feeling of accomplishment, to have arrived in the Virgin

Islands in my own boat! I was proud of *TRITON 3* and of myself, and Jon and I congratulated each other.

We inflated the dinghy, attached the outboard motor to its transom and in no time we landed on the beach. After checking in at Customs and Immigration, we toasted our success at Foxy's with a piña colada or two.

Foxy plays the guitar, when he's in the mood, and tells dirty jokes. When pirates first came to this tiny island, the captain sent a couple of men ashore in a boat. As they rowed back to the ship the captain yelled down to them, "Are there any women there?" They answered, "Just one dyke!" And that's how the island got its name, according to Foxy.

I was so elated, I wanted to share my success with family and friends. I asked Fat Albert, the man at Customs and Immigration, to let me use the telephone, the only one on the island with a population of fifty-one. First I called Julia, "I made it! I am here!"

She said, "Did you hear about the Berlin Wall? They tore down the Wall!"

I didn't know what she was talking about. How could I? I just crossed an ocean, and now she is going to steal my thunder? At that moment I couldn't understand her emotion and enthusiasm, and she couldn't understand mine.

Then I called The Cat. "Hey, The Cat, guess where I am!" I wanted to show off my success.

"You tell me. How should I know, you hardly ever tell me anything anymore."

"I'm on the phone!" The old joke between us whenever she asked me where I was. "No, really, I am in the Virgin Islands. Just got here."

"You don't know about the wall, then?"

There it was again. What is it about this wall? "No. Didn't you hear me? I just got here."

It was hours later, maybe a whole day, that I became aware of the significance of what Julia and The Cat had said. What had happened while I was on the high seas was the beginning of monumental changes affecting the whole world.

We were far away from that world—we were in paradise! Tropical beaches, clear water right down to the bottom, palm trees, summer heat and blue skies, a steady breeze and delicious concoctions of rum and fruit juices at the two watering holes on this island, Foxy's and Rudi's. For us, the world stood still, or moved at a considerable slower pace.

Jon Reeve was in no hurry to end his time in paradise and we stayed a full day on Jost Van Dyke, walking around and slowly getting our land legs back. We swam in the clear water, talked to the locals and sailors from other boats in the anchorage, ate roast pork or chicken with rice and plantains and drank the special island drinks at Rudi's. What had happened in the world so far away had no effect on us.

Then we cruised leisurely for a whole week in the British and US Virgin Islands. Sailing through the Cut at Great Thatch and Little Thatch, rounding West End, we went into Roadtown, Tortola and anchored for two days. We had to change the oil and fuel filters and did some routine maintenance on the boat. Roadtown is an excellent harbor and the largest town in the British Virgin Islands, but does not have the charm of some of the smaller settlements in these islands.

We tacked across Sir Francis Drake Channel into the Salt Island Passage and had our lunch anchored off Ginger Island. A boat with British Customs officials came alongside to inspect our papers, which were, of course, in order. Then we sailed hard on the wind to the eastern end of Tortola into Maya Cove. We half expected to find the crew of *BANDU*, but they weren't there. In the morning we tacked toward the Baths of Virgin Gorda. Anchored close in, we swam ashore to explore the huge boulders the size of houses with their large cavities filled with ocean water heated by the sun. Later we motored into the Yacht Haven at Spanish Town, Virgin Gorda, for a good meal and a quiet night at the dock.

We had a few last wonderful sailing days, blowing downwind from Virgin Gorda with the strong trade winds in Sir Francis Drake Channel using the big balloon sail, nicknamed the Dolly Parton by my daughter. *TRITON 3* flew along the south side of St. John, US Virgin Islands, and into the anchorage of Cruz Bay where we cleared quickly through Customs and

Immigration and then enjoyed Jon's last night in the slow, rhythmic island life in Paradise.

On Thanksgiving Day, Jon Reeve, my crewmember, shipmate and friend left for New York from Charlotte Amalie. Jon visited Julia in New York, but he missed Susi and Carlos who were away on a ski trip. I received his Christmas card with the photo of me, a can of Budweiser in hand, taken the day we were the farthest from any land, on 6 November. He had returned to his home in Hobart, Tasmania, Australia.

I put this fantastic voyage away in the memory file of my brain and spent several days at anchor near the Yacht Harbor in Charlotte Amalie, before returning to Cruz Bay on St. John. This small and crowded anchorage was to become my permanent home in paradise. I day-sailed, or took overnight trips, to explore the little nooks and coves, the smaller cays and passages and the protected bays and hurricane holes of St. John and the surrounding islands. I acquainted myself with the easterly trade winds, which blow constantly at fifteen to twenty-five knots or more, and with the currents, quite strong in some of the narrow passages.

IN PARADISE–THE VIRGIN ISLANDS

I sailed to Charlotte Amalie a week before Susi and her fiancé JP were to arrive for a five-day vacation in the islands on TRITON 3. I had done this three-hour sail from Cruz Bay through the Pillsbury Sound, past Christmas Cove, Dog Island and Little St. James on Thanksgiving Day with Jon Reeve, but this was my first time doing it alone.

On 26 December, 1989 a taxi dropped Susi and JP off in front of the Yacht Haven. After the dinghy ride out to the boat, I greeted them formally with a bottle of Champagne.

"Welcome on board TRITON 3," and we toasted to a successful, fun filled cruise in paradise.

Early in the morning we sailed out of the harbor and tacked toward Virgin Gorda, heeling sharply, with reefed main and jib. "We have a tough course ahead of us," I warned them. "There's a twenty-knot wind today and it's straight out of the east."

Under full sail, gunnel awash, i.e., heeled with the lee rail under water, it was sailing at its best. "Is it always like this, Dad? I have never sailed like this."

"This is one of the best days I have had," I said, "but we won't make it to Virgin Gorda in one shot. We will have to anchor overnight."

In the afternoon we passed Lamshure Bay at the eastern end of St. John. "Can't we get as far as Norman Island?" asked JP. He was looking at the chart. "Can we anchor in The Bight?"

"Yeah, Dad, let's try that. Then we get so much earlier to Virgin Gorda tomorrow."

"There is Flanagan, this little US Island. Norman is British and we haven't cleared in."

"Who's gonna know? They don't come around in the night to check us out!"

Probably not, I thought, and so with the last of daylight we dropped the hook in the crowded anchorage of The Bight. That was against my better judgment. I wanted to anchor in the lee of Flanagan, but I listened to Susi and JP who did not want to stop as long as there was daylight. I was nervous the whole night, but luckily we were not inspected. Lesson learned: never listen to the crew.

The following morning we left The Bight early and headed toward Virgin Gorda. Heeling sharply, we tacked half a dozen times as we sped under full sail through Sir Francis Drake Channel. This was real sailing! Only in paradise! As we closed in on the easternmost of the British islands, we saw in the distance the ocean swells breaking over the rocks marked on the chart as Sunken Jerusalem.

I insisted on checking in properly at Customs and Immigration in Spanish Town before heading for the Baths on the southern end of Virgin Gorda. The sight of the enormous boulders, gray like gigantic elephants, piled up on the beach, amazes everyone who sees them for the first time. From the boat, at anchor a hundred yards away, we looked at this phenomenon and asked ourselves: who put those rocks there, and why? We swam to the beach, climbed to the top of the boulders, explored between them and splashed in the sun-heated water in their cavities. We played Frisbee, sunbathed and then cooled off swimming back to the boat.

At night, with *TRITON 3* docked at the Yacht Harbor, we had a wonderful fish dinner at the restaurant on the premises—I remember I had Wahoo—and then we enjoyed some cocktails sitting in the cockpit, talking until well past midnight. My young guests had the time of their lives in this so different world, far from their big cities.

The Crew at Virgin Gorda

We left Virgin Gorda in the morning for the terrific downwind run past Roadtown, Tortola and continued through Thatch Island Cut to Great Harbour, Jost Van Dyke. There were several boats and we had to anchor inconveniently far from shore in nineteen feet of water. Limited space allowed for a scope of only 1:3, meaning three feet of anchor rode for each foot of depth. A scope of 1:5 is considered safe in normal conditions, but a much larger ratio is recommended in stormy weather.

Great Harbour was calm that day. I could risk leaving *TRITON 3* on a rode of sixty feet, chain and line. We launched the dinghy and motored to the little dock in front of the Customs house.

Great Harbour, Jost Van Dyke

For Susi and JP, Jost Van Dyke was the highlight of our cruise. They enjoyed the laid-back island attitude where time seems to pass so much slower, as if in slow motion. With plenty of piña coladas or margaritas in them, they behaved like a couple of drunken sailors. My daughter's free-spirited personality infected even her fiancé's stiff Parisian manner, as she took pleasure in her temporary freedom. Acting out in crazy antics, yelling "O-wahoooo" at the perplexed island folks, JP and I encouraged her. "Do your island cry, Susi!" and she belted out another "O-wahoooo". Sailors and tourists from some charter boats joined in the fun and we just about turned the whole island upside down. "Give her another rum punch!" There was joking and laughter and barefoot dancing. We were having a great time.

Susanne at Jost Van Dyke

I have no idea what the inhabitants of this island could be doing all day long. Some might sell T-shirts—or drugs—to cruising sailors, others work at Rudi's or Foxy's restaurants, and Fat Albert has one or two helpers at Customs and Immigration. The rest of them just hang out, sitting or lying on the sandy ground under some thatched roof with a lazy dog, a couple of chickens and a pig. There were a few automobiles—how did they get here?—and some mopeds, but nowhere to go with them. There is one dusty dirt road along the waterfront, which connects Rudi's on one end with Foxy's on the other, the Customs house in the middle, and then disappears up the steep mountain. Coming from New York, or in JP's case Paris, they marveled at this totally different way of life, these opposing extremes. Where and what is our purpose on earth: here and this, or there and that?

Well, I thought, I can stay here, but JP and Susi have to go back to their worlds. Reflecting in the evening back onboard, I philosophized, "Maybe you'll take back with you a little bit of this paradise, as you have brought here something with you. Your schedules, your airline tickets, things that don't belong here."

After a day of total abandonment and exuberance, we had to leave Jost Van Dyke. We sailed the short distance to Cruz

Bay, St. John, and checked in with the US authorities. Here Susi and JP had a chance to get to know my new homeport. We had chicken and beer and rum drinks at my favorite little corner shack, strolled through the quaint village and looked in at all the shops and eating places. Then, back on the boat, we sat under the awning in the cockpit and talked about all that had happened in the few days they had stayed with me on *TRITON 3*, how great it was to sail in the strong but steady trade winds in these islands, how different my life was becoming "at island speed" and how easy it was to get used to paradise.

Cruz Bay, St. John

At the Chicken Hut

Their visit came to an end on 31 December. We sailed back to Charlotte Amalie, St. Thomas. That morning it was raining, a rare occasion. In the afternoon, under the umbrellas by the pool at the Yacht Haven, we said goodbye and they took a taxi to the airport. New York greeted them with a blizzard.

For one week I stayed in Charlotte Amalie, feeling lonely. I had taken the Genoa to a sail maker on Water Island for repairs. On 6 January I picked the sail up and returned to Cruz Bay. It was a new decade, and I had no idea what to do with it. Should I stay in these islands, sail down the chain of the Windwards or back again to mainland USA?

I loved Cruz Bay and decided to make it my home, established a mailing address and opened a bank account in the local branch of Chase Manhattan.

The anchorage in the bay in front of the town dock was crowded with sailboats, most of them anchored permanently, or at least for long periods of time. The holding ground was not very good and I felt safe only on three anchors, with the boat in the center, like a spider in its web. Through this anchorage a narrow channel is kept open for the ferryboats that come in at breakneck speed on their way to and from Charlotte Amalie or Red Hook, St. Thomas.

My logbook indicates some day trips or overnighters during the first month of the New Year; I didn't want to sit idly on the boat all the time, letting the barnacles grow below the waterline. I sailed to Charlotte Amalie and registered with Capt. & Crew, a crew referral agency. At the fuel dock of the Yacht Haven I filled my tanks with diesel and fresh water and then motored over to Frenchtown in Krum Bay. The station where Propane gas used to be available was closed down and I found myself almost out of gas for my galley stove.

On my return trip to St. John, I encountered harsh weather conditions. The wind blew at thirty knots straight out of the east, seas mounting to ten feet. I sailed hard on the wind with double reefed mainsail and storm jib. The dinghy, which I trailed, turned over twice as I struggled to pull it up onto the transom. In order to make any headway at all I started the engine. In the shelter of Christmas Cove, I managed to take down all sail and then continued under Diesel power alone. Late in the evening, beaten and bruised from fighting with Mother Nature for eight hours, I came into Cruz Bay harbor.

Before leaving for other sailing trips, I devised a system, by which I left my anchors in place and tied their chains to my mooring ball. This way, on my return, it was easy to retrieve the chains by picking up the floating ball, which had TRITON 3 written on it.

There were only a few worthless inquiries through Capt. & Crew, the referral agency. Besides, I had no real plan what to do or where to go. Island hopping? In reality, I wanted to stay in the Virgin Islands, at least for the time being, and Cruz Bay, bigger and more lively than Jost Van Dyke, was ideal.

At Marcelino's bakery, there was a tiny sign, "Help wanted".

I asked, "What kind of help? I'm not a baker."

Marcelino said something like, "You could help me with the trays, algo asi." He had a thick accent, his speech mingled with Spanish. "Las horas are from five en la mañana to about noon. You want to try?"

"Sure," I said. I got up the next morning at four, had a quick breakfast and then rowed to the dinghy dock for the five-minute walk to Mongoose Junction where the bakery was. And that's what I did for the next ten weeks, Monday through Saturday. The hours often stretched to two or three in the afternoon.

I rowed my dinghy in the early morning; people living on the other boats in the anchorage would have complained strongly—and rightfully so—if I had used my noisy outboard motor. However, I did wake my friends Carole and Ingo with the light splashing sound the oars made when pulled through the water as I passed closely by their boat *SEPTEMBER SONG*. They also had to be at work early, at Ellington's Hotel. Carole worked in the garden and Ingo in maintenance.

Marcelino was easy to work for. He talked little and I learned mostly by following what he did. Marcelino was from Mexico and he didn't speak much English; so we talked mostly in Spanish. At the sales counter he had a nice, pleasant, fat Island Mama who liked to laugh a lot. His wife Dolores, a very efficient younger woman, came in every day and worked in the bakery, or wherever help was needed.

I promptly learned the recipes for all the different kinds of bread, buns and pastries, how to handle the dough, weigh and shape it into portions, shove it in the oven. After a few hours each day at the shop in Mongoose Junction, Marcelino sent me to his house on the hill, where he had another, much larger bakery, but no shop. The dough for the French bread was made there. After a week I handled this job alone: ninety one-pound loafs every day. Kept overnight refrigerated in their trays ready for baking, Marcelino brought them early in the morning in his old Jeep truck down to the shop. Baked in the large, modern upright electric oven, the first customers bought fresh, warm French bread as early as six o'clock.

I also drove that old truck between his house and the bakery on the hill, and the shop in the Junction. Sometimes I had to drive to the dock to pick up supplies that came by ship from Puerto Rico. Marcelino filled large orders for different kinds of bread, hamburger buns and hot dog rolls from the resorts and hotels on the island. Sometimes I went on deliveries with him. On these islands, although US territory, traffic is on the "wrong" side of the road, and it was downright scary when Marcelino drove. He was a calm, benign man, except behind the wheel, where he turned into a savage maniac.

I kept exact track of the hours I worked, but on Saturdays, when he paid me, Marcelino never cared to see my sheet. He just took a huge roll of bills from his pocket and counted out what he thought was right, usually a good ten or twenty dollars more than what I had calculated. "You went to the locksmith for me el otro dia," or "I sent you al banco."

I said, "me pidió un favor. When you pay me, it's no longer a favor!" He didn't want to hear of it.

Others told me that he had said I was the best worker he ever had. "Peter never stops working, even for a drink or a bite to eat," he had told his nephew, who helped out sometimes.

I earned about 240 dollars per week, much more than I needed for food and drink. I had practically no expenses. Sometimes after work, I took the ferry across to Red Hook, St. Thomas and then the Safari bus into town to buy different foods not readily available on St. John, or I looked around in the hardware stores and ship chandlers for gadgets I could use on the boat. I bought additional charts, books, courtesy flags and rope to replace worn anchor lines. Liquor was duty-free in these islands and ridiculously cheap. I bought excellent rum for under two dollars a bottle and had an assortment of different liquors on board that I could never have afforded elsewhere. Spending money more freely than at any other time, I still saved more than half of my salary and never touched the income from my pension. I felt as if slowly becoming rich! I didn't mind getting up so early in the morning. On the contrary, the routine gave my life meaning. Marcelino was good to me and good for me.

He and his wife had two kids, a teenage boy and a younger daughter. The boy was his mother's idol; she loved him as if he were her lover. "Mi amor," she called him. The father had no use for the boy. "El no trabaja, solo listens to rock music," he told me. He adored the girl, called her "Mi amor." Dolores didn't care for her daughter. It was weird to observe these demonstrations of love and indifference. Marcelino and his wife didn't have much in common. Dolores, quite a few years younger, was modern, paid attention to her appearance and took aerobics classes. She spoke better English and had a sense of humor. He completely lacked all of that.

One day I stuck my right hand into one of the smaller mixing machines to test the dough and the "hook" almost broke my hand. I could do that in the large machine without a problem, but didn't realize the hook left little room for a hand in the smaller bowls. Had my hand been a little bigger, I would have had a few broken bones; I was lucky to get away with a very painful bruise. Marcelino told me of a baker back in Mexico who had been pulled by his sleeve into a machine. "Estaba borracho, drunk, and he was killed."

Then came the day, toward the end of March, when Susi called at the bakery from New York, something I had allowed only in case of emergency. I was not there at the time and got the message to call her back.

I phoned her from the public booth at the plaza in front of the town dock. "What's up, Susi? What's so important that you call me at the bakery?"

"Dad, JP asked me to marry him and I have said yes. Can you come and help me? There's so much to do."

"Well, Susi, sure, but that'll take some time. When are you planning to get married?" I totally forgot to say congratulation.

"It's not going to be until November, but I'll be moving to Paris and there's so much I have to take care of. Can you come, please?"

How do I say no to my daughter? "Yes, of course, Susi, but I don't know how soon. I mean, it's not that easy. It's hard to find anybody to help me sail the boat home from here."

"I know, I know. It doesn't have to be right away."

"What about your job, and what about your apartment?"

"I have to quit, but not yet. And the apartment, I'll have to sell it. That's why I need you, to help me with that."

"Okay, Susi," and now I remembered to say, "Congratulations! I'll see what I can do."

"Oh, thank you, thank you, Dad." She hung up.

I called her mother. "Julia, Susi just called me with the news. What am I to do? I mean, I live here now."

"It's up to you, of course. But it would also be good for Carlos, if you came back. He has finished school, has no real job yet. He's trying to get into publishing."

"Okay. I have to think this whole thing through. See how things work out. I'll let you know."

"It's your decision. Don't tell me later, I..."

"I know, when it's difficult, it's always my decision." My daughter, my son... I really have no choice.

Wow, I need a drink! Susi had bought her apartment on East 80th Street in Manhattan just two years ago. How difficult would it be to sell it at present real estate market conditions? She has a nice position in a Public Relations firm. Maybe she can take her job to Paris.

Carlos had come home from college in upstate New York and then finished his education at the Fashion Institute of Technology. He had just left a temporary job and was looking for a permanent position as a graphic designer.

It had taken me over three years to get here. I had bought *TRITON 3* to fulfill this dream. Finally accomplished, it should

60

last no longer than six months? Well, there are priorities, which cannot be ignored. I need another drink.

I had friends who had come to paradise for the same reasons: to live a leisurely, trouble free life. I had retired early from my company, which made this possible. Others had sold a business or a home, bought a boat and came to live their dream. Now I was called back, apparently needed. Oh, it feels good to be needed, but back to New York again?

I began looking for crew and posted notes on bulletin boards in the town's shops and bars.

Crew wanted. Leaving for U.S.
Inquire at Marcelino's Bakery
or see me on TRITON 3 in the anchorage.

When I told Marcelino that Chris Nielsen, a young rock musician, showed strong interest in sailing with me, he told me, "el no vale para esto, no good for this," and he repeated, "no good, este músico. Oígame, he no sailor!" Of course, Marcelino had an ulterior motive: he didn't want to let me go.

Chris was about twenty, seemed in good health and of an agreeable nature. Sure, he was no sailor and had no idea what such a voyage would be like. I warned him to consider carefully. "This is not a piece of cake. It's not a playground out there."

"I know, but I really want to do this. I feel good about it," he pleaded.

When I had just settled on St. John, I sent a postcard to The Cat in New York. It had a picture of a bearded man in ragged clothes sitting on the running board of an old wreck of a car, hood open and tools lying around, a door missing, overgrown with tropical vegetation. Two half-naked island beauties were by his side. The caption read: *Even if I get it started, I ain't gonna leave!*

The situation had changed and I made up my mind. Chris seemed slightly better suited for the long haul back to the States than any of the three or four other candidates who were interested. I had imagined people would line up to hitch a ride, but I guessed they were all too happy in paradise.

LEAVING PARADISE

Chris came on board with his backpack and a bass guitar. I showed him how to stow his gear properly in the forward cabin, gave him a quick run down of the main functions of the boat and the safety equipment, and familiarized him with the workings of the propane stove. His first job was to remove the barnacles, which had plenty of time to glue themselves to hull, keel, rudder and propeller. I sent him over the side with a mask and a scraper; he broke one scraper and dropped another, but other than that he did a fairly good job.

I advised Chris of the no-drug policy on board and he admitted that he had used marijuana in the past. I hoped I wouldn't find a box full of weed someday, as I had found the condoms in Michael's baggage. Chris was friendly, well mannered and pleasant to have around. He was interested in learning everything from the engine to the sails and anchors, from the charts to the instruments.

"How do you feel about this? Ready to go?" He gave me a thumbs up. "Okay" I said, "then let's go!"

I did not want to leave the Caribbean by the shortest route, without seeing some of the other islands. There was a good inventory of charts and cruising guides on board.

"I worked out a route that would take us along the southern coast of Puerto Rico to the Dominican Republic," I showed him on the chart. "From there through the Bahamas to Florida."

"How long will it take us?" That same question all landlubbers ask.

"Look, Chris, this is a sailboat. We depend on Mother Nature. No wind, no go. Too much wind, another problem. Things can break down. You want to know how long it will take? I have no idea."

"Oh, I have the time, that's not it. I'm just curious."

"I understand. I only want you to understand. Okay with you?"

Chris nodded. He said he was looking forward to this adventure. "I've never been on a sailboat, but I love the water."

I showed him that our route would provide us with some of the best downwind sailing, that we would stop at ports and places frequented by cruising sailors, without getting too far from a direct course. "The itinerary, where to anchor or to dock, is flexible. Let's say a week or ten days to Samaná." I pointed to the northeastern corner of the Dominican Republic. "The second stage, through the Bahamas, is longer. Those details we'll work out later."

Chris and I fixed the departure for 4 April. I contemplated the long haul back with mixed feelings. On the one hand, I wanted to stay where I was, where I had found the leisurely life I wanted, but the prospect of sailing in the unfamiliar waters of the Caribbean and the Bahamas, exploring along the coasts of islands I had not yet seen, intrigued me. Once I had met my family obligations and accomplished my mission, I would return to my dream islands.

The last evening in Cruz Bay I spent at the home of Marcelino and Dolores, watching TV, drinking beer and eating popcorn. In the morning I said goodbye to my good friends, Carole and Ingo Wagner, on *SEPTEMBER SONG*. Then Chris had his first dose of ugly work on the boat when we began to pull up the anchors, one after the other. The chains and lines were encrusted with barnacles and for an hour and a half we scraped and washed them down, then left them on deck to dry. The last anchor to come on board was the plow, or CQR, which had its place on the bow roller. The two Danforths were stored one on the bow pulpit, the other on the stern rail.

By eight thirty we were underway and in three hours, running downwind under the Dolly Parton, we sailed into St. Thomas. We filled fuel and water tanks at the fuel dock and did some last minute provisioning. For the night we anchored and at this time I sank the cement block in the harbor of Charlotte Amalie. That thing had bothered me by now long enough. It had taken up too much room in the cockpit locker. I needed the space badly to store spare docking and anchor lines as well as other accessories.

Fully provisioned, we took off the following morning for the short run to Culebra, the small island between St. Thomas and Puerto Rico. The winter season with the stronger trade winds came to an end and from now on we experienced more often lighter winds, perfect weather for sailing down wind. We would get plenty of use out of the big balloon sail, which my daughter had so aptly named after Dolly Parton.

Before entering Dewey, Culebra, I noticed big rocks under our keel in the clear blue water. I had mistaken one marker for another. A quick course change to the south got us back into deeper water before entering the harbor. We remained anchored at Dewey until noon the next day.

We found the immigration office. "We need a sailing permit to leave US territory," I explained to the elderly official.

He didn't know what that was, but he gave us some paper with a date, a stamp and a signature on it. "Is that what you want? Then you can consider yourselves cleared out."

At night we heard the practice bombing and saw flashes of explosions on the island of Vieques about eight miles due south of Culebra. It surprised us to feel the boat trembling, that the vibrations traveled so far through the water into this quiet anchorage.

Actually, our voyage began in Culebra. I was in unfamiliar waters. The logbook states:

"... closed in on the southeastern corner of Puerto Rico, sailed past Roosevelt Roads, the US Naval Station, and entered Vieques Sound. Average 6 knots on broad reach under main and Genoa. Rounded Punta Tuna at 20:30. Weather gentle."

By two in the morning we were off Jobos, and at four o'clock we hove to outside Cayos de Ratones. "We wait for daylight, Chris. Don't want to enter the shallow cut in the dark."

Chris looked tired. We both had not slept for twenty-four hours.

Anchored at Playa de Salinas we took a nap before going ashore for something to eat. It had been an easy trip for me, but Chris showed signs of weariness after his first night sail. Is he beginning to see what I meant by "it's not a piece of cake?" We have just barely begun!

The same day in the afternoon we left in strong southeasterly conditions and got into open water after passing Caja de Muertos. Again from the logbook:

"Rough 6 to 8' seas. Storm jib only, making 5 knots or better."

We stayed within two to four miles of the south coast of Puerto Rico. The lights of Ponce, the second largest town on the island, were in sight from seven to eight thirty. By midnight we were off Punta Brea at the southwestern corner of Puerto Rico and we turned north. The seas moderated in the lee of the island and we set the Genoa.

I too felt tired after sailing through the second night, but I did not dare leave Chris alone on deck. I didn't know him well enough yet. What if he should fall asleep? There are often small fishing boats, most without lights, and big shrimpers to watch out for.

At eight o'clock in the morning of Sunday, 9 April, we dropped the anchor deep inside the Bay of Boquerón. While I get a lot of satisfaction out of making port after a successful passage, which makes up for the lack of sleep, Chris did not look all that happy. He used to be talkative, but now he was pretty quiet. Is he just tired, or is something wrong?

I made breakfast, pancakes á la Triton 3, thin crêpe-like pancakes, eaten with syrup or jam. Chris enjoyed the treat, made a few appreciative remarks, but then again remained gloomy and quiet.

"I'm going to take a nap for a couple of hours," I said after cleaning up the breakfast dishes. "You want to go ashore? You can take the dinghy, be back by noon."

"No, I'll just lie down, I guess. I really don't feel that good."

"Yeah, maybe you should get some sleep. You'll feel better afterwards."

Oh boy, something's not right with the guy. I felt bad about him feeling bad and I really hoped he would come around after a good rest, but something told me he was unhappy and that sleep wouldn't fix it.

When I woke up an hour or two later, Chris was sitting at the table reading a book. "Would you make us some chicken soup, Chris, or whatever you like?" I asked him, more to see if he would snap out of his mood, than wanting to eat.

"I'm really not hungry, but I open a can of Campbell's for you, if you like." He seemed a little more animated.

"Thanks, but I think I want to go ashore now. Find some local food. Empanadas or something. You want to come?"

"Yeah, all right." He put the book away and got up.

I didn't want to press him too hard, so I pumped up the dinghy with the foot pump and launched it. He handed the motor down to me and I fastened it to the transom.

Together we motored over to the concrete harbor wall where we found steps and an iron ring to tie up the dinghy. There was a plaza from which streets led into the neat little town of Boquerón. I suggested we split up; I needed some time by myself and I also wanted to give Chris freedom to do what he wanted. "Let's meet at that place over there at, say six o'clock, for dinner, okay?" I said casually. "If you're not there, find something else to do, that's fine with me, too." I tried to make him feel as comfortable as possible.

In the evening we met at the rustic restaurant at the corner of the plaza and had a lobster dinner. I had mine broiled, which was a mistake. To me, there is no better way to prepare a lobster than boiling or steaming.

After a good night's sleep, we weighed anchor and motored out of the bay into the Mona Passage that separates Puerto Rico from Hispaniola. The sea was flat and the wind calm. We were in the lee of the island. The sun was burning down on us already early in the morning.

Two hours into the Mona Passage and still under power, we met two fishermen in a skiff with an outboard. They were diving for lobsters. I stopped the boat and asked, "Tiene langostas?" and we struck a deal, two tails for fifteen dollars.

One of the guys came up with two lobsters, but now they wanted twenty. Typical, I thought. It seems to be in the Latin nature always to try for a better deal, even after reaching an agreement. I said: "Muy bien, veinte, but for three tails, and you can keep the rest of the lobsters."

So, he dove for one more of the critters and we boiled the three tails right then and there. They were delicious, making up for the broiled one I had the night before. These langostas are warm water lobsters and instead of claws, they have only

66

antennae. The loss for rejecting the body of this delicacy is therefore not so great.

Although we had initially agreed on alternating kitchen duty, I usually ended up doing the cooking. So far we had not done much more than heating a can of soup or stew and making coffee. My pancakes had been a special treat on the occasion of our arrival in Boquerón.

It was not before noon that we finally came out from the lee of Puerto Rico and the wind came back at fifteen to eighteen knots out of the northeast. We broad-reached under full sail on starboard bow, making seven knots and at two thirty I spotted a ship of the US Coast Guard on our stern. I raised her on the VHF.

"Coast Guard Vessel, this is TRITON 3. Do you have any instructions for us? Over."

"This is the US Coast Guard cutter One Five Three. Identify your vessel, POB (persons on board), last port and destination. Over"

"TRITON 3. US documented sailing vessel No. 636505. Two POB. Last port Boquerón, bound for Samaná, D. R. Over."

"We need you to give us names and passport numbers of all POB."

"Will comply. Stand by," and to Chris, "Get your passport. You heard them." I went to my strong box to get my papers, then I got back on the radio and gave the requested information.

"Stay on your course and keep watch on channel sixteen." The cutter fell back, almost out of sight, but within an hour came up to our starboard quarter and announced, "We have decided to board your vessel. Keep your course and speed."

"Acknowledged." We observed them lowering their Zodiac inflatable. I hoped Chris wasn't carrying any dope. If they found anything suspicious, they would confiscate my boat, arrest us and who knows what else.

At that time we had close to ten-foot seas—not unusual for the Mona Passage. We put out fenders, as they tried to bring their inflatable alongside, first on port, then on starboard. I thought it would be the best policy, to show a lot of cooperation. The four or five young fellows in their boat, in full uniform, boots and guns, were starting to get green around the gills, as they were one moment high above my gunnel, and then way below it. They tried several times. Chris switched fenders from port to starboard and back again, until I received the message from their mother ship, "We abandon the attempt to board." The Zodiac went back to the cutter, and I asked if anything else was required of me.

"No. Thank you for your cooperation. Have a good trip!" We broke radio contact. The cutter steamed away in a northerly direction and was soon lost from sight. Of course, I was relieved. It would have been an interesting experience, but what might they have done to my boat? I have heard horror stories of how they ripped the entire insides of boats apart.

Chris had shown eagerness in handling the fenders, but he had few comments after the whole thing was over. He did not appear to be seasick, only sluggish, unresponsive, dissatisfied. I left him alone.

The wind continued strong, the seas with long, gentle swells at eight to ten feet. Our progress was very good at six knots all through the rest of the day and the night. Since one in the morning we had land in sight and by four o'clock we closed in on the east coast of Hispaniola, the Dominican Republic and sailed north toward Balandra Point.

At ten o'clock, the D.R. gunboat #106 approached and contacted us by radio. "Request to clarify your intentions. You are in territorial waters of the Dominican Republic."

We were already flying our Q flag, the solid yellow Quarantine flag, required when entering foreign waters.

"This is TRITON 3, US registered sailing vessel, bound for Samaná."

Given clearance to proceed, we anchored a few hours later near the town dock at Samaná. Promptly four men came aboard, three of them uniformed and armed. They were a lieutenant of the police, a Customs guard and an Immigration official. The civilian had an English accent. His name was Alan Tooley.

SAMANÁ, DOMINICAN REPUBLIC

They inspected the vessel's papers as well as our passports and the sailing permit we had secured in Culebra, although it seemed they didn't really know the procedure. We were all sitting in the cockpit. The Englishman, Alan Tooley, had brought them in his dinghy and he would have been the interpreter, had it been necessary. Apparently, the authorities did not have a dinghy and Tooley, for all intents and purposes, was harbormaster, water taxi driver and a whole lot more in this port. They charged me twenty dollars, US currency, which I paid, although they had no legal right to ask for payment in US money. Anyway, I didn't have much of a choice.

Alan Tooley was the confidant of the cruisers and link to the authorities, advisor in matters of getting around in and out of town, where to buy supplies and, most importantly, where to get the best rate to change dollars into pesos. His Spanish was minimal, just good enough to be of some help to those cruisers who didn't speak a word of it.

Most boats anchored on the other side in the bay, half a mile away from the town dock. Tooley, too, lived there on his boat. My little outboard motor was slow and I liked to be closer to the dock, although my spot in eight to ten feet depth was less protected. It didn't bother me if it got a little bumpy at times; after all, we were going to stay only for a few days. Little did I know.

After the authorities had left, I discovered that the antenna of my SatNav on the stern rail was broken; not totally, but bent enough to have cracked the plastic insulating cover. Also, one of my vent cowls was missing, probably kicked overboard by one of these clumsy people, who came on board wearing boots and carrying weapons.

As soon as I had my second anchor in place and I felt securely hooked, Chris and I went ashore. There was a wooden town dock at the head of which the gunboat had her berth. The rest was for local commercial shipping and a passenger ferry. Next to the town dock, down a rickety ladder, was a small floating dinghy dock. The water here was very dirty with debris and garbage floating on the surface and I didn't feel good about tying up my dinghy. We set foot on the dock and were immediately surrounded by a bunch of people, offering all kinds of services and children selling peanut brittle and banana chips. Trying to be friendly and not to offend them while not accepting any of their offers, we headed for the customs office. I lodged a complaint for the loss of the cowl and the damage to my SatNav antenna, which they acknowledged and apologized for, but did nothing about. Instead, I had to buy their poorly made courtesy flag for ten bucks.

Chris, obviously unhappy and discontent, announced to me right there in the Customs office that he could not continue the voyage with me. He complained about not being able to eat or sleep; he felt sick and weak and unable to spend another day or night on the boat. After he bought a plane ticket at the travel agency next door, papers were drawn up that released me from being responsible for him. He got his stuff from the boat and left me a note, thanking me for understanding and for all that he had learned from me, and he apologized for leaving me without crew in a foreign port.

What could I do? I can't and don't want to have anybody on board, who doesn't want to be there. Of course, I felt abandoned and I had no idea what to do next. It is quite impossible to take on crew in this country. Many locals would love to leave with anybody willing to take them to the United States, but they were not even allowed to visit yachts in port without a permit from the police. Besides, I would be in deep trouble for bringing a Dominican national to the US without proper papers.

Until I could sort things out, get a clear picture of my predicament, I was stuck in Samaná, Dominican Republic. Marcelino had been right. "No me gusta ese músico," he said. I had clearly warned Chris that this would not be as easy as it might seem to him, but he thought he could do it. He just didn't know what to expect.

By telephone I explained to Susi in New York the situation I found myself in. The following days she tried but failed to find someone willing to fly to Samaná to help me sail the boat back to the States. I did not see a solution to my problem. Besides, Samaná was to me the worst place on earth; the poverty, the dirt, the corruption drove me to desperation.

Then, to make things worse, the discharge hose of the head clogged up. No means of unclogging worked. I had to take the hose off. Repeated pumping had built up pressure and the loosening of the hose caused an incredible, unavoidable mess of toilet contents spreading throughout the head, the hanging closet and the bilge.

Oh, shit! The only really fitting expression. Efforts to clean and eliminate the smell were only marginally successful, as all water and cleaning liquids, chemicals and disinfectants ended up under the sole and in the bilge. The obstruction in the hose had calcified and become rock hard, I could not remove it. My only choice was to switch discharge into the holding tank instead of overboard. By regulation, holding tanks are to be in use on all boats, but are impractical as there are only very few pump-out stations in US ports, and consequently the regulations are hardly enforceable. In this port, in this county, there are no pump-out stations at all and nobody cares.

I tried every day again and again with different methods to clean all the unreachable places, under the cabin sole, between the hoses in the closet, in the bilge, with detergents and sprays and deodorizers and anything recommended to me and what I could find in this godforsaken place. Finally, with a mixture of numerous different scents, from ammonia to Lysol, bleach to Drano and lemon, and a constant airflow through the cabin, I obtained a less nauseous, almost tolerable living condition. I continued to pour water with disinfectants in crevices and below the sole, then pumped out the bilge on an hourly basis. My hands were raw from the chemicals and the many cuts and scrapes they had received in the process of dealing with this nightmare.

Gradually, the frustration left me. I seemed to be getting used to the conditions on my boat and in this town. People surrounded me as soon as I stepped out of my dinghy on to the town dock and offered me anything I didn't want or need. When I did need or want something, they promised but never delivered. I once asked for a block of ice, for which I had to pay in advance. When

I found the guy days later and asked for the ice or my money back, he finally handed me a plastic bag with water and tiny pieces of ice floating in it. "Su culpa," he said to me. "You were not here when I came to deliver the ice, so it melted."

A little girl came to the restaurant where I was drinking my beer. "Meester, I am taking care of dinghy," she said, a subtle way of asking for money. Really, she had no idea where my dinghy was. The men on the gunboat had allowed me to tie it up near their berth at the head of the pier, in cleaner water and harder to steal.

Tooley's wife, Nilda, came to me with a friend, a rather nice looking female in her mid-forties, and she asked me if I would want her to take care of my laundry and cooking on my boat and "anything else I would like." She would get the permit from the police and could stay with me on the boat. Yeah right, anything else I would like? Tempting as it might have been, it was also dangerous. The next thing could easily be that her brother, cousin or father paid me a visit with his revolver forcing me to marry her. I told her I was about to leave for the States.

Little girls were running after me, calling out, "Penis, penis, meester! Penis!" What do they want from me? I mean, they are eight or ten, for god's sake! Then I got it, they were selling peanuts. "Peanuts, mister!"

So, I was getting used to Samaná and the people, and after a couple of weeks it did not seem quite as dismal any more. I spent more time in the town and less on my boat. I was able to find most of the needed supplies, took long walks in the exotic surroundings of this town, climbed to high points with spectacular views over the bay and I discovered the beauty of this corner of the world for which at the beginning I had no eyes.

In Samaná they have a unique form of transportation, a kind of taxi. It consists of a guy on a motorcycle pulling a two-wheeled trailer with a seat for two. They call this contraption motoconcho. Some have a bigger trailer, with two benches facing each other, for four. There are varying grades of comfort or sophistication in these motoconchos with upholstered seats and colorful awnings, handrails, ornaments or advertisements. For a few pesos they carry you at breakneck speed anywhere in or around town. I used them a lot to transport my purchases at the open market or when I had to carry anything heavy, especially during the hot hours of the day.

Much of my time I was sitting in the shade outdoors of Don Domingo's restaurant where all the sailors were hanging out. Often I started my day there as early as nine o'clock with the excellent local beer, Presidente, which I could drink all day long without getting drunk. Tooley was usually there and old-timers as well as newcomers gathered around. Don Domingo was also the source for black market money at a better exchange rate than the official course. Such transactions took place behind the counter, under the table. My great advantage was, of course, that I spoke Spanish and often I served as interpreter. I took most of my meals at Don Domingo's. The food was first class, and there was a menu with a wide variety of local and international meat and fish dishes. One day the waiter brought the chef out to meet me. I must have been an important guest! At the exchange rate, life was rather cheap for me. I lived on savings from my days as a baker.

Alan Tooley had married Nilda, a very pretty, very vivacious local girl. He was much too dull for her, quite a bit older, and she looked elsewhere for fun and excitement. Tooley never learned more than the most marginal Spanish. He complained to me about her behavior; he was jealous, couldn't control her. She lived in a house with a daughter of hers and the baby she had with Tooley. He stayed mostly on his boat. Rarely, or never, did she stay on the boat and rarely did he sleep over at her house. I had become good friends with both of them. Nilda used to call me Peter Pan. I found most of the girls and younger women of Samaná, very beautiful in an exotic way. It was especially their large, black, almond-shaped eyes that called my attention and their evenly light brown skin color. The men, however, were generally ugly.

I began to like my life in Samaná. I had plenty of friends among the locals and there were always new people coming through on boats, mostly Americans, but also British, Germans, Spaniards and South Africans. I did not think too much about leaving, except that I had made the promise to return to New York, and sooner or later, I had to come up with a solution how to make that possible. It became clear to me that I had no other choice than to make it a single-handed, long cruise through the Bahamas. I dreaded the thought of a solo voyage, which would probably take a month. Would I even be able to do that? I already felt the loneliness I would be experiencing. But I knew that eventually exactly that would have to happen and I had to get used to the idea.

Fuel and water were available at the town dock when the old man in charge showed up. I ran the engine two or three times a week for an hour to keep the batteries charged. Then, one morning about ten days into my stay in Samaná, the Diesel started but shut down abruptly and did not start again. What the fuck happened? My reliable engine! How could this happen? The surprise, the shock, was so great that it actually kept me from panicking, from realizing what this meant. Major engine repair in this place was unthinkable. Was I condemned to remain here forever? My money would run out, and what would I do then?

All this did not sink in right away. I had to find Tooley before the panic started. I rowed to the dock; my outboard motor had quit a few days earlier. I ordered a Presidente at Don Domingo's and waited for Tooley, but this day he appeared uncharacteristically late and panic was on the verge of setting in. Tooley was a calm, typical Englishman. The only thing that excited him was Nilda's indifference toward him, her wandering off with other men. When at last he showed up, he listened to my engine problem as if it were no big deal. I explained to him what happened, and he already had an idea what could be the cause.

"That might not be possible to fix here," was the first thing he said.

"That's unacceptable," I said. "There is always something that can be done," and I asked him to come on board and take a look. He was not a mechanic, but he knew a lot about engines and he just had to come up with a solution.

"The only thing that could have caused such a breakdown is water in the cylinders," he explained. "Diesel explodes when under great pressure and makes the engine run. Water does not. That means the engine has to be taken apart."

"Shit! Could it be anything else?" I asked, hoping for something less serious.

"Possible, but not likely," he said in his English way, hardly unclenching his teeth.

"This engine needs a new head gasket."

"How can I get a new gasket, and who would do the job? Here in fucking Samaná? Is there anything you can think of?"

Alan thought for a moment. "I'll try to have a gasket made in the capital. With a new gasket I can do the job."

I had little confidence in this approach, but I didn't know what else to do. I also thought of how mechanics in undeveloped countries often come up with primitive ways and means to fix things. I had nothing to lose. Tooley, if anyone, was the only person I could trust in this situation and I saw that he was right in his diagnosis when the fuel he drained from the engine contained water.

"Okay," and with a shrug of resignation, "go ahead. Take the damn engine apart."

The following day, Alan removed the cylinder head. "See the pitted gasket?" He showed me where the water had found its way into the engine.

We settled on a price for his labor and he sent the damaged gasket by special courier to Santo Domingo where a new one was to be made, using the old one as a template. My logbook shows the price of 175 US dollars, but I don't remember whether that was for the gasket, Tooley's labor, or both. Anyway, in the States a job like this one would cost me over a thousand, no doubt.

Still I felt very uneasy about the whole thing. "You think they'll be able to make such a precise gasket, where a fraction of a millimeter counts? Would they have the right type, size and thickness of the copper material? And would it be better than the damaged one?"

"We'll see," was all Alan had to say.

He dismantled the engine. I could not recharge the batteries and therefore I did not use any electricity for the refrigerator, lights or the fan. I spent my days on shore. There was always a crowd at Don Domingo's until late at night. There were dance festivals with live music and blaring speakers on the Malecón, the waterfront, and proclamations and rallies for the upcoming presidential elections. The very old Señor Balaguer, blind, deaf and in his eighties was again the front-runner.

Once, Naval officers had come from the capital and they organized a clambake on board the gunboat. Nilda and her absolutely beautiful sister Victoria had invited me and I met some of the higher officers of the Dominican Navy, all elegantly dressed in white uniforms. It was a splendid evening, one of the highlights of my time in Samaná.

Don Domingo's was not the only eating-place and watering hole frequented by the sailors, but it was the most popular one. Located on the Malecón close to the town dock, the open patio afforded a fine view over the bay and the anchored boats. At lunchtime, tourists from the capital and other big cities of the Dominican Republic mingled with the usual crowd and the waiters were busy among the eight or ten outdoors tables. Even in the morning and between lunch and dinner the place was never empty. If one wanted to meet someone of the "floating community," a prominent or popular individual of the town or an official of the port, Don Domingo's would be the most likely place to find him.

I rarely ventured into the saloons or taverns of Samaná that were remote from the waterfront; those were strictly for the locals and any stranger would not feel welcome or comfortable. Only on a couple of occasions, and then as one of a larger group of heavily drinking people, did I set foot in the bar of some whorehouse, where the girls joined us and used their art of persuasion to lure the guys "upstairs." They might have been successful with some of the guys—I didn't keep track.

El Naútico was a restaurant of a more elegant or formal setting. At least that's what the owners, Javier and Leticia, wanted it to become. Located on a cliff a few hundred yards from Don Domingo's farther along the Malecón, some twelve or fifteen steep and rustic steps led up to the entrance. The main hall was a huge, empty space with a window front overlooking the bay. The entire opposite wall was a mirror with a long bar in front of it, and only a few stools covered in dark leather. There were hardly any bottles on the shelves, no lighting and there was no bartender. The room was forlorn, abandoned.

A glass door led out to the patio, which was almost entirely covered with a green and yellow striped awning. There were several intimate settings of comfortable chairs and sofas around cocktail tables in a garden-like atmosphere with tropical plants and palm trees, but here, too, seldom guests were to be found. In the middle, incongruent with the rest of the decor, was a long trestle table and folding chairs for dinner guests.

Javier and Leticia were struggling to keep the place alive and gain a reputation for fine and elegant dining. It was their dream to make it the tourist attraction of Samaná and the whole República Dominicana, and possibly beyond. They were Spaniards and undoubtedly of aristocratic background: Javier a former diplomat, a degenerate and a drunk; Leticia an attractive lady in her forties.

To have dinner at El Naútico, it was necessary to let them know at least in the morning that a group of so and so many would show up at such and such a time. It was best to order Paella, their only specialty, in advance and plenty of sangria. Javier and Leticia always joined their dinner guests and such evenings were great fun in a relaxed, friendly and familiar ambiance. They tried to teach Phipps, their only waiter, the correct way to serve the meal and the beverages. I don't think there was a chef. On the other hand, I cannot imagine Leticia in the kitchen preparing the meals herself.

In the course of the evening, Javier tended to get boisterous and his voice then roared across the table, drowning out everybody else. On leaving, when I kissed Leticia's hand, Javier's laughter boomed throughout the patio, "Are you trying to seduce my wife? Ha, ha, ha!" Not a bad idea, but... naw. Possible? Absolutely.

My time in Samaná rolled along pleasantly at island speed, mostly between Don Domingo's and El Naútico. We contemplated the big job of putting my engine back together with some trepidation.

When the new gasket arrived in about ten day's time, we saw that they had done a remarkable job. We compared the new gasket with the old one, which they had returned.

"Every corner and opening seems to be exact," said Alan. "The thickness is correct and the quality of the copper as good as the original one."

"Yeah, I see. So, what's the prospect then that my engine might actually be running again? Can we get to it, like tomorrow morning?"

Alan still seemed to be procrastinating. He had never done a major overhaul on a Diesel engine. "Let's see."

He showed up in the morning and once he started working on the engine, he became more confident. The job was tedious in the small engine compartment, especially with the jerky movements the boat made when the easterly wind beat the bay into choppy seas or in the wake of passing motorboat. Sweat pouring down his face and back, Alan worked quietly, except for a grunt, "shit" or "fuck" now and then. I was there to hold something for him, hand him a wrench, a nut or a bolt.

In a couple of days, working only a few hours in the morning before the heat of the day became unbearable, the moment of truth had arrived. On 3 May, more than three weeks after my arrival in Samaná, Alan Tooley hooked up the last wires, connected the fuel line and tightened a few hose clamps.

"Turn the key and hope for the best," he said and I turned the key. The engine came to life immediately and ran smoothly. The relief was enormous! I let out a big sigh and Alan had a smile on his face I had never seen before.

"I promote you, Alan Tooley, to Master Mechanic of Samaná, no, la entera República Dominicana! Wait, of the Western Hemisphere!" We shook our greasy, sweat-drenched hands. I realized how little faith I had had in the whole thing. My relief was as big as my surprise. Later we met at Don Domingo's for some cool Presidentes.

After ten days, running the engine daily for an hour, Alan readjusted the torque of the bolts on the cylinder head and I was essentially ready to continue my voyage back to the States. Only, I was no longer so eager to leave.

78

I liked my life in Samaná. Nevertheless, I started working on my charts, trying to find a possibility to accomplish the inevitable task before me.

I considered how to break up the voyage into manageable portions, finding suitable places to anchor. I plotted my course with eight to ten rest stops, depending on weather conditions, but mostly with my strength and endurance in mind. No portion should exceed a stretch of thirty-six hours. I was aware of the importance of sleep to remain alert and agile. With the general north to northwest direction of travel, and the prevailing winds out of the east, the islands of the Bahamas give protection, but the cays and reefs can present dangers.

The more I calculated, measured, estimated and developed a plan, the more I became aware that I could do it and my enthusiasm grew for the adventure of a single-handed voyage. I was not sure, though, how I would be able to handle the loneliness. With an occasional full day at anchor to relax, for some repair or unfavorable weather, the passage to Palm Beach should take at least three weeks.

I consulted with other sailors and copied from their cruising guides, if I did not have them in my own library. One experienced British cruiser gave me pages from a volume of sailing directions for commercial shipping. He also told me how to repair the damaged SatNav antenna with bee's wax, which I happened to have in my sail sewing kit. I sat for hours on my boat or at Don Domingo's with the skippers of two South African yachts discussing how best to accomplish the voyage to Florida. They were planning the same trip, but they had crew, their wives or girlfriends.

Provisioning was a major challenge. Durable foods and canned goods were in limited supply in this part of the world. Soft drinks, juices and beer were no problem. Fuel and water were available at the dock only when the guy in charge of pump and faucet could be found. He, and only he, had the keys. When he was sick, out of town or drunk—usually the latter—nobody could get gas, diesel or water, and that happened often.

Word spread that I was about to leave for the States. Locals, wishing to get to the USA tried to persuade me to take them as crew. Yes, they had the papers, "tengo permiso," or they would get them. "Mi pasaporte ya viene." They lied and promised, but there was of course no way for me to take any of them.

I contemplated 18 May as the date of my departure. There were farewell parties. I went to a pig roast in the saloon of an American sailor who years ago had jumped ship in Samaná. He named his establishment Morgan's, after the daughter he had with a local girl. Other raucous gatherings took place at local bars of varying degrees of disrepute and parties on boats. Three guys invited Alan, Nilda and me for a lobster dinner on their boat. They were diving for the lobsters but didn't find any, so we had noodles and ketchup with the wine we had brought. It was not quite clear to us who the owner of that yacht was. At any rate, it seemed to us far too big and luxurious for any of those three penniless fellows, ranging in age from the mid-twenties to about forty.

My Spanish friends, owners of the elegant but failing restaurant El Naútico, invited me and a group of people to a fine dinner of several courses with sangria, but the invitation was not free. We ended up paying a hefty sum.

I paid Alan, and I gave him a hundred dollars and my Cruise 'n Carry outboard motor, which was in need of repair, in exchange for his good Yamaha. By the time I was mentally and physically ready to leave, I had only a few pesos left, which I invested in some small bottles of Bermuda rum, a good local brand. Low on cash, I could not afford to exchange any more dollars for pesos. It was time for me to get underway.

Four days after my Diesel had passed the final test, I finalized my preparations. I had spent thirty-eight days in this town I hated so much at first, but liked more and more as the days turned into weeks.

Cruz Bay, St. John, and now Samaná—places I had grown fond of and had to leave behind. Sailor's fate. Forever restless. The ocean, not the harbor, is your home.

ONE THOUSAND SOLITARY MILES

I arranged for two guys to get permits and come to scrape the bottom of *TRITON 3*. Over five weeks barnacles had a good chance to settle on the bottom and they did just that in a thick layer. For twenty dollars, a good amount of money for the two fellows, they did a mediocre job, but it would have to do.

I must admit, I did have butterflies in my belly. Doubts kept creeping up in my mind, questions whether I had overlooked some important factor in my calculations, about the courses and the distances. Again I asked myself: will I have the stamina, will I be able to endure the physical and mental stress, the solitude? Am I equipped for bad weather? How about places to replenish water, food and fuel, or get parts if something breaks down? And, the biggest concern of all: would the Diesel make it all the way to Florida?

My last guests on board were Alan Tooley and Nilda whom I had asked to come and have a farewell Bloody Mary with me. Then, by noon my first chain and anchor came on board, very dirty and encrusted with barnacles. It took at least an hour to clean the gear enough for stowage below decks. I pulled up the rode of the second anchor until only eight or ten feet of chain with the lightweight Danforth held the boat in place. I had reached the point of no return.

The two most exiting moments in long distance sailing were for me the departure and the arrival. On the one hand, there is the anticipation of adventure when the last anchor breaks loose from the bottom and the boat is free; and on the other, the great feeling of accomplishment when the anchor goes down at destination.

At two in the afternoon of Friday, 18 May, I started the engine. The Danforth came on deck and I steered out of the anchorage. I am not superstitious, but some mariners will not sail on a Friday. The sky was overcast, the wind at ten to twelve knots from the east, seas one to two feet. It was hot and humid. I saw Samaná and the boats at anchor blend into the afternoon haze. As soon as I had a straight course ahead of me, I set the autohelm and stowed the Danforth and chain, then washed down the deck with buckets of water. Settled in the cockpit with the left over Bloody Mary, the butterflies disappeared gradually and I began to enjoy the scenery of the coastline, a steep slope with rich vegetation and a forest of palm trees on the top. The northeastern corner of Hispaniola is said to be very much like Bora Bora in the South Pacific.

During the next two hours, I passed Las Flechas and Balandra Head. Then, with Cabo Samaná behind me and Cabo Cabrón in sight I turned north, hoisted the mainsail and finally shut off the engine. By nightfall I had rounded Cabo Cabrón. The upwind part behind me, I set the Genoa and was on my way downwind along the north coast of the Dominican Republic, less than four miles offshore.

After the typical morning, calm a good breeze set in, which took me past Cabo Macorís and Sosua at a speed of seven knots.

The port of Puerto Plata was a spacious commercial harbor. The water was extremely filthy with trash, debris and flotsam. I saw no place where to anchor a yacht and did not waste time in Puerto Plata where I had planned to spend the first night. The next possibility was Luperón and I had to reach it before nightfall.

The chart showed Luperón as the only well protected inlet before the border with Haiti and just before dark I entered through the breaking seas into the calm waters of the lagoon. I wanted to hide away in the darkness of the eastern cove, but two uniformed men in a boat approached and told me to come in closer to the village. Then the two guys came on board and said I couldn't stay there. "No se puede quedar aquí" one of them gestured with a sweeping move of his arm. "No es puerto de entrada. No port of entry."

I knew that. "I am too exhausted, muy cansado, I have to stay overnight!" I said and added that I would not go ashore and leave early in the morning.

Then they wanted money. I told them, I didn't have any, but I could offer them—if it would not offend them—each a small bottle of rum. "Es todo lo que tengo." It helped me again that I spoke their language and knew how to deal with them.

They were reluctant at first, but then accepted the gift and let me stay.

The following morning I motored out of the cove for the first real open ocean part of the voyage. Soon I could broad reach under jib and main, steering a course of 330 degrees, about north-northwest, and I enjoyed cutting through the waves at a good speed. Before noon, the coast of Haiti and the Dominican Republic was out of sight. The wind picked up considerably in the afternoon. I had to double-reef the mainsail and finally take it down. Seas built to six to eight feet with some breakers. These conditions continued through the night.

My course was directly to West Caicos where I intended to anchor. During the night a cruise ship passed me en route to Turks and Caicos. Good to know I'm not alone. It was still blowing hard when West Caicos rose above the horizon in the early morning light. An hour and a half later I anchored. Although in the lee of West Caicos, it was still quite windy, but the sea was flat. It had been a rough twenty-six hours from Luperón. I felt good about my first solo experience and my confidence was at a high level. Before starting out on my second leg, from West Caicos to Plana Cay, I treated myself to a full day of rest. I slept and ate and went for a swim. The water was so clear, the bottom white sand; I could see the chain all the way to the anchor.

In the morning, refreshed after a wholesome sleep, I raised the anchor. There was only a light breeze from the south, perfect for the Dolly Parton and mainsail. Later the sea was like a mirror and the wind died. I looked for ripples on the water indicating puffs of air and tried not to miss even the lightest stirring.

Late that day the autohelm broke down, a major inconvenience. I had to leave the boat to its own devices when I went below for a bathroom break or to make a cup of coffee. Otto, the autohelm, had jumped ship. All right, no problem in calm weather. But what about when it get's rough?

In the night I heard a ship's engine, but didn't see anything. Later, as I came up to Devils Point, Mayaguana, I saw two fishing boats. My progress was slow in the calm conditions and I did not get to Plana Cay until noon the following day.

I was able to fix the autohelm. It was only a temporary repair. The connection was corroded and there was nothing I could do about that.

My next destination was Rum Cay. The wind was at ten knots from the east and I wrote in the log:

"Great sailing, making up for yesterday. Main and Genoa, 4.5 knots, course 318. Sun, hot. Autohelm working."

Acklins Island showed far on port. I headed for Samana Cay where four years ago the voyage of the *CHANDELLE* ended on the reef. Acklins fell behind and Samana Cay rose from the mist on starboard. I came close enough to see the rusted hulk of a freighter on the beach and the seas breaking over the reef.

That night was clear in my memory. Dennis O'Reilly, confused and not trusting his SatNav, steered his boat straight for the rocks. It was midnight. I came up the companionway and saw the reef, but it was too late. "Diesel on!" Dennis screamed and he turned the wheel sharp to port. The keel struck... I shuddered as I relived the moment, heard the crunching, the scraping on the hard coral, felt the boat coming to rest in an unnatural angle.

I went back on course for Port Nelson, Rum Cay. In the evening the autohelm quit working again. The plug was all but falling apart and I did not carry a spare. The wind came around to the northeast and I had to reef the mainsail. I called out for Otto, but there was no answer. By midnight I reduced the main to the second reef point. Without the autohelm the boat was out of control. Hanging on to the forestay on the plunging and rising bow, I managed to take down the jib and stow it in the sail bag. Wet, cold and exhausted I crawled back to the safety of the cockpit and brought the boat back on course. The thought occurred to me whether I had any business to be out there, alone.

Making three knots under double-reefed mainsail, by six o'clock Port Nelson, on the south coast of Rum Cay, was five nautical miles away. I switched on the engine and took down the sail for my approach. The wind was blowing hard and the seas were choppy. I could not clearly identify landmarks, although "conspicuous" according to the cruising guide. As I closed in on the anchorage near the town dock, the keel hit a rock or coral head in the lumpy sea; not hard, but hard enough, like a warning, to tell me it's too risky to anchor under the circumstances and to give up on Rum Cay.

Conception Island was only three or four hours away. I had hoped for a calm anchorage, but found choppy and breaking seas. My afternoon and night turned out to be quite uncomfortable. On the morning of the following day, someone in a skiff came alongside. "It's much calmer around the corner in West Bay," he told me.

"This is not West Bay?" I asked.

"No, it's around the headland," he shouted over the noise of his outboard motor and pointed me in the right direction.

I waved, "thanks." I had been sure I was in West Bay, but picked up my anchor and went around the headland where I found two other yachts lying at anchor in fairly calm water.

Logbook entry on 26 May, Saturday:

"I am between a Tropical depression over Cuba and low pressure system over NW Bahamas. Forecast for weekend: unsettled weather and T-storms with strong gusts, small craft warning. Stormy weather overnight."

I listened to the weather station on my radio, and reports indicated that a storm, or at least bad weather, was approaching. I did not consider West Bay of Conception Island a well enough protected anchorage to ride out a storm. This was a shallow bay, the flat land would not shelter me from the easterlies and to the west, there were miles of open sea.

An elderly couple from one of the boats anchored nearby came over in their dinghy to say "hello."

"What do you think of the weather that might be coming this way?" I asked.

"We don't worry much about the weather, hardly ever listen to the forecasts. Most of the time they are wrong, anyway," the gentleman said in a Boston accent. He seemed to be an experienced sailor, but I found his response either arrogant or naive.

I did not share their wait-and-see attitude. "I'm getting out of here. No protection here at all, like an open roadstead." I told them.

Consulting my charts and books, I decided to sail for Cat Island, which with higher elevations would provide better shelter, at least for weather from the east. The distance to cover was only about fifty miles, or ten hours. To ensure my arrival at the Bight of Cat Island in daylight, and ahead of the storm, I left Conception at midnight.

It was totally dark when I easily broke out my anchor from the sandy bottom and sailed out of West Bay. The wind was still light from the south-southwest. Once again I had been able to fix the autohelm, bypassing the outlet, but again it did not last. The wire between the control panel and the plug was also corroded. That most valuable accessory, especially for a singlehander, was out of commission for the rest of the voyage.

At three in the morning I encountered a rainsquall and at four-thirty I saw Devil's Point light. I had made good time and at Hawks Nest, staying far out to avoid the narrow sand spit at the point, I was one hour ahead of schedule. As I headed due north for The Bight, the wind had already increased noticeably and I reefed the mainsail. In these strong but favorable conditions, with the wind still mostly from the south, I gained another hour and I set my first anchor by ten o'clock.

The Bight was a much better place in a storm than West Bay of Conception Island; however, as the wind turned more toward the southwest, I was not so sure how safe I would be here in a real blow. None of the islands within my reach could give protection in strong westerly conditions. I had chosen a spot close to the shore under the high land with a castle-like building on top, marked on the chart as The Hermitage. This place provided good protection, but only for weather from the east.

Soon it began to rain, the wind came around more and more to the west at fifteen to twenty knots. I inflated the dinghy, lowered it into the water and carried a second anchor almost a hundred feet out. With two strategically placed anchors the boat was secure for the time being and I rowed ashore before the weather further deteriorated. The dock was too high for me to reach, so I had to pull the dinghy up on the narrow beach.

So far, I had not legitimized my presence in the Bahamas with the authorities and nobody knew my whereabouts.

There is no port of entry on this island, but I found a police station, nothing more than a shed, in the small settlement. The lone policeman did appreciate my good intentions, but he did not know what to do with me. However, he had a pencil and a piece of paper on which I wrote down for him my name, passport number, name and number of my boat and the date. Then I signed it and he said, still baffled over what this all meant, "Okay, mon, no problem."

In the little grocery store farther down the sandy road, I bought some canned goods, a six-pack of beer and a Coconut bread, and then I was in a hurry to get back to my boat. The wind had turned rapidly and was already blowing steadily from the west, generating surf with breaking waves pounding the beach. The rain slanted almost horizontally over the sea and I saw *TRITON 3* bouncing precariously with only eight feet of water under her keel.

I pushed the dinghy into the surf and before I could get in to start rowing, it flipped over, spilling my groceries, which I didn't care for at this moment. The surf drove me back to the beach. I managed to get hold of my oars and turned the dinghy right side up. I salvaged the beer and some of the cans, then tried again, forcing the dinghy farther out through the crashing waves. This time I was able to climb in and I started rowing like hell to get through the breakers. I reached the pitching boat, prepared a third anchor with chain and line and took it out in the dinghy as far as the rode reached and dropped it. Back on board, I hauled in the slack and was satisfied that all three anchors were holding.

At last I could change into dry clothes and make myself something to eat. I had been wet and cold for hours. While heating up a can of beef stew, I took a few swigs from a bottle of the good Dominican rum I had bought with my last pesos in Samaná. The boat was behaving like a mechanical bull and I worried that my anchors might break out. The lines were stretched to the limit, like guitar strings. The heaving seas churned up the sandy bottom, which made the water murky so that I could see only a few feet down. I thought of the huge boulders I had seen earlier as I rowed to the beach in the dinghy. They had not seemed dangerous to me then, but, as wind and waves had picked up considerably, they began to worry me. Everything depended on my three anchors.

Attached to my harness, I frequently crawled to the foredeck to inspect the lines and to replace chafing gear—rags, old T-shirts, tape, anything to protect the anchor lines from wearing thin where they came through the chocks.

The weather did not improve for the rest of the day, the night and the next day. On deck, cumbersome in my foul weather suit and lifeline, I was pelted by rain and salt spray. Below, tossed about in the cabin, I felt safest in my bunk, cushioned with sail bags.

Toward evening of the third day at Cat Island, the storm relented and there were some breaks in the clouds. The sun came out briefly before sinking into the sea. Anxious about bringing this ordeal to an end and to continue my voyage, I brought the anchors up, one after the other. From the logbook:

"18:30 last anchor on deck. Course 255 degrees. 20:00 jib and reefed main, wind 5 to 10 kn., seas 2 ft."

I was on my way to Eleuthera. The night air was mild and the wind not more than a light but steady breeze. Soon the previous forty-eight hours were nothing but a memory. My boat was unharmed and instead of being exhausted or discouraged, I felt invigorated and strong. Bring it on, I can handle anything!

I passed Little San Salvador and in the early morning hours, I saw Point Eleuthera, but the light on its tower was not working. It was shortly after noon when I rounded Powell Point and ten minutes later, I ran aground. I had not been able to find the marker, a mere stake, indicating Davis Channel. With the engine running at full throttle, I was slowly cutting a new channel through the sandy bottom—the width of my keel. It took an hour and a half to reach the deeper water of Davis Channel.

A fierce thunderstorm and strong counter current further hampered my progress. Governor's Harbor on Eleuthera was in sight by five thirty, but I didn't reach it until after eight o'clock. It was dark when I anchored in a cove of Levy Island. The next morning I moved *TRITON 3* into Governor's Harbor.

I had not expected to find moorings in the ample anchorage and, what's more, they were free of charge. Only two or three boats were in the harbor. What a luxury it is to tie up to a mooring ball. No worry about dragging anchor, no hard and dirty work when it is time to leave—just untie the line and get underway.

At last I checked in properly with the authorities of the Bahamas. The couple on a French boat, anchored close to me the night before at Levy Island told me about the trouble they had run into at the Customs office. The official did not grant them entry and cruising permit because they had been in Bahamian waters for ten days without clearing in. I don't know what the consequences of their failure to do so were; perhaps a fine or expulsion. Bahamians are proud of their island nation and they want foreigners to respect their country, and they are right, of course.

I was sure the lone policeman on Cat Island had not reported my presence in the islands and, with the lesson learned from the Frenchmen, I did not say anything about that to the officials who treated me with courtesy and granted me a thirty-day cruising permit for the Bahamas. "Okay, mon, no problem."

In the pleasant settlement of Governor's Harbor, I allowed myself a longer rest. I had made good time and deserved it. Everything, except for the autohelm, had gone well throughout the voyage I had contemplated with so much trepidation. I had some great sailing, lived through a storm at Cat Island, was in some nice anchorages and in a few rough ones. I hit a rock or a coral head at Port Nelson and ran aground at Powell Point, but the boat suffered no damage. With two thirds from Samaná to Palm Beach already behind me, I intended to enjoy some leisure time on the island of Eleutera. I did not need to worry about the boat, which I had tied securely to a mooring.

I obtained a one-day visitor's ticket at Club Med, located on the ocean side of the island, a twenty-minute walk over the hill. I thought of the vacation my daughter and I had spent so many years before in Tahiti, where my dream of cruising in my own boat began. Susi worked at the time at the New York headquarters of Club Med. She had the benefit of free vacations at any of their resorts and could bring one close relative.

After exchanging some money for beads, the Club Med currency, I had a drink and a snack at the Tiki bar and relaxed for a few hours at the beach and by the pool.

"You need a ride back to the other side?" the driver of the courtesy van asked me. I had just started walking up the hill to get back to my dinghy.

"Thanks, I'd like that. This is quite a hill." I got into the car with a group of tourists. The driver dropped me off at the place where I had beached my dinghy.

"Is that your boat out there?" Someone asked. "So small, and with that you sail on the ocean? You must be crazy."

"Small boats float just the same as larger ones," I said. I always had fun telling landlubbers something like that.

My fresh water tanks on board were nearly empty. After a restful day at Club Med, I had the energy necessary for the tedious and wearisome job of replenishing my water supply. For this purpose, I used a dozen one-gallon plastic bottles. Water was available at the gas station, about a mile from where I landed my dinghy. When filled, I carried four bottles at a time, two in each hand, from the gas station to the dinghy and returned for the next four bottles. When all twelve bottles were in the dinghy, I ferried them out to the boat and filled the tanks through the spout on deck. I made three trips that day, amounting to thirty-six gallons. The fresh water capacity on *TRITON 3* was forty gallons. On long trips, I started out with my twelve plastic bottles full, thus carrying over fifty gallons.

On this occasion, I went back to the gas station one more time with my two five-gallon Jerry cans for diesel fuel. My eleven horsepower Universal was an economic little engine, and the total capacity for fuel, thirty gallons, lasted a long, long time.

That evening, after this backbreaking job I sat in my cockpit, sipping a cool sundowner, a cocktail of fruit juice and rum, when the couple from the boat next to mine came over and offered me one of their numerous cats. I declined.

After three full days of work and rest, I left Governor's Harbor. A light breeze was blowing from the southeast. With the Dolly Parton and main sail, I came off my mooring without the use of the Diesel, a stunt I sometimes like to show off.

As I swung around my neighbors and waved farewell, they called out, "are you sure you don't want a cat?"

I was sure I didn't want one.

I headed for Fleming via the Six Shilling Cay. Feeling weary of the length of this voyage, I had reached the point where I wanted to end it as soon as possible. No more sight seeing. Get it over with. Instead of sailing via Nassau, I decided on the more direct route by way of the North Berry Islands.

Although an open roadstead, it was completely calm at Six Shilling and in the morning, with a mild breeze, I sailed leisurely past Fleming and entered the open waters of the North East Providence Channel. Between some light puffs of wind, the big drifter hung like a wet rag from the forestay. From time to time throughout the day and the following night, I put the engine to use in order to make some headway.

The heat during the day was relentless and the night brought almost no relief. Crossing the North East Providence Channel by night was a thrilling affair. There was heavy traffic in this main route for freighters and cruise ships to and from Nassau. Running lights and range lights on the big vessels are easily distinguished with a watchful eye, but the Bahamian island freighters not always carry all of the required navigation lights. In addition to my own running lights, I frequently turned on spotlights to illuminate my white sails in order to be more conspicuous. In this busy thoroughfare it sometimes seemed to me just luck that I was not run down by one of the recklessly operated Bahamian freighters.

My aim was to get into Great Harbor, North Berry Islands, my last rest stop before Palm Beach. It was still dark after crossing the shipping lane, and I approached Great Stirrup Cay, which I mistook for Great Harbor. As it became lighter, I recognized my error and motored into the adjacent Bertram's Cove. I had been underway for twenty-four hours, keenly vigilant all the time, and without the use of the autohelm. I was drained, mentally and physically. All I wanted now was to end this voyage.

I was too exhausted to be able to sleep. By midday, I inflated the dinghy and rowed ashore. There were a couple of Tiki huts, nothing else. Two men were working on one of the huts, installing a bar. They ignored me as I walked around on the beach like a zombie. I found the grave of a British Naval officer.

The name on the tombstone was Bertram. I couldn't make out the date on the weathered slab.

Back on the boat, I ate something, drank something, and still I could not sleep. I stowed the dinghy and tried to relax.

Late in the afternoon a cruise ship anchored outside the cove and a tender brought some of the tourists ashore. A woman had set up a table to sell T-shirts. An umbrella shielded her from the burning sun. There was no cloud in the sky and the air was perfectly calm.

By evening, still without sleep, I decided to leave Bertram's Cove for Isaac Light, a serious challenge for my powers of endurance. I did not know whether it was possible to anchor at Isaac, a rock with a lighthouse on top of it, a lone sentinel to guide ships from the North American continent to the islands of the Bahamas. I also did not know how long it would take me to get there.

Weary from lack of sleep, hungry but without appetite, fatigued from the heat, I set the Dolly Parton and a light breath of air coaxed me out of the cove and past the anchored cruise ship. The gentle breeze soon died. I took down the sail and continued under power through the night. At last, in the early morning hours, the temperature dropped a little, only to climb again as soon as the sun rose over the horizon.

The light tower on Isaac did not come into sight until noon. My exhaustion at that point was such that I no longer cared about the safety of my boat or myself. I saw the tower, still miles away, and steered directly for it. Working against a strong current, the approach seemed endless and my fatigue made me impatient. I neglected common sense and prudence, but looking down into the clear blue water, I saw the rocks on the bottom. I remembered there was a reef extending from Isaac. I had seen it on the chart. My reaction was slow; I awoke as if coming out of a trance, but heading away to the north and steering clear of the reef, I approached the small rocky islet safely from the east.

Finding the conditions for anchoring unfavorable, I summoned the remnants of my physical and mental power, motored around to the west side, and dropped the plow anchor. It was five thirty in the afternoon of 6 June.

My body felt numb, a humming ran through my limbs, like a mild electrical current. There was a trembling in the nerves of my arms and legs. My hand was shaking when I lifted a bottle of fruit juice to my lips. As I stood at the stove, preparing a bowl of larmen, Japanese noodle soup, my knees did not stop twitching. I sat down to fill in a page in my logbook, but I could not control the pen. Sitting in the cockpit with the logbook in my lap, I figured out how long it has been since I last slept. That was at Six Shilling Cay. I woke up at eight that morning, 4 June; now it was the 6th, seven o'clock in the evening. That's fifty-nine hours. Fifty-nine hours without sleep!

While I was still sitting in the cockpit, a man, a woman and two children in a small motorboat approached. "Por donde queda Bimini?" the man called out to me. He wanted to know where Bimini was.

What the hell are they doing out here in a twelve-foot boat? Are they for real or am I imagining things? I showed them due south. "Tiene brújula? Have you got a compass?"

"Si señor. A que distancia? How far?"

I didn't know exactly. "Como diez millas, ten miles, mas o menos."

"Gracias!" They took off to find Bimini. But what are they running from—or to? I wondered. Well, stranger things have happened. I've got to get some sleep.

I had anchored in exposed, open water, Isaac Rock with the lighthouse on one side, the Gulf Stream separating me from Florida on the other, but regardless of the bouncing and pitching, I was asleep the moment I was in my bunk.

It was amazing how ten hours of sleep could restore me to a fresh, functioning human being. I awoke ravenous. First a cup of coffee; instant, because it's faster. Then my famous pancakes á la Triton 3, using the last three eggs bought at Governor's Harbor. Did I really see those people in that little boat last night? Wasn't that odd, out here, asking me how to get to Bimini? And in Spanish? Was I perhaps hallucinating?

I remained at anchor for the rest of the day, wanting to cross the Gulf Stream at night for an arrival at Palm Beach in the morning. Well rested and nourished, I got my anchor on deck as the sun was setting and sailed into the night with a fine southeasterly wind of twelve to fifteen knots.

At nine o'clock in the morning I phoned Customs from Singer Island, where I had tied up briefly for that purpose, and then docked at Florida Diesel and Marine in Riviera Beach. I intended to have my engine checked out thoroughly. Alan Tooley had done a remarkable job, yet I thought it might be time for a complete overhaul.

I wrote in my logbook:

"Distance sailed 905 naut. mls. in 21 days. Actual hours sailed (not counting rest stops) 212 hrs."

I called New York to let Julia, Susi and Carlos know I had safely arrived in Palm Beach. My announcement did not cause a great deal of excitement or even a surprise. Well, they hadn't been there.

RIVIERA BEACH, FLORIDA

Where a sailboat is involved, questions like "How long will it take" or "When will we get there" should not be asked, because they cannot be answered. The concept of sailing is timeless and unpredictable. Unforeseeable events—a storm, a calm, a mishap or a breakdown—determine the length of a daysail or long voyage.

In the early days, when I still sailed on the Hudson in my Cape Dory, Susi might have asked, "Dad, can we be back by six? I want to meet my friends"; or Carlos might have said something like, "I want to go, but only for two hours."

My answer to that was usually, "If you don't have the time, let's not go."

So, when I left Cruz Bay, St. John, with Chris Nielsen, on 4 April, I thought I would arrive in Florida three weeks later and could be in New York by the middle of May. What was to be a three-week cruise through the Bahamas, turned out to take two months, and I still had to go north to the Chesapeake. That could take ten days, two weeks or a month.

I decided to have my engine thoroughly examined at Florida Diesel and Marine Services before embarking on that last stretch of the journey. Mario, the Diesel mechanic, came on board and we discussed what ought to be done. I explained what had happened in Samaná and the consensus was to take a good look at the inside of my Universal engine, which, after all, was ten years old.

Mario suggested, "Water in the block may have caused damage to the pistons and rings and what not. That ought to be checked out."

"Okay," I said. "Let's go ahead with it." I still considered Alan Tooley's job provisional. He had replaced only the head gasket and that was all he could do. "Let's take the whole thing apart and rebuild it." I had made my decision.

Mario said, it would take several days. "The engine has to be removed from the boat and taken apart in the shop. The cylinder head needs to be machined and the pistons replaced with new ones. See the little pockmarks? Water does that," he pointed out.

He ordered the parts and the estimate came to about twelve hundred dollars. "And don't worry, the yard here don't charge you nothin' for dockage while we work on your boat."

Some of the parts were hard to find. They had to be flown in from California or Michigan. The cylinder head was sent out to a machine shop and days became weeks. I was not in a hurry. " No problem, mon." I was still on island speed.

Another boat, a Pearson 32, arrived with engine trouble and occupied the slip next to mine. *LINT* was her name and on board were Heinz Gebhard and Inga. He was from Berlin, she was Dutch. We became friends and many parties took place on both *LINT* and *TRITON 3*.

One evening a young woman friend of Heinz and Inga's came to a party on their boat and she brought with her one of the South African couples I had known in Samaná, Brian and Elaine.

"Small world! How did you get here?" I had last seen them at Don Domingo's, where we discussed the details of the trip, bent over charts and drinking Presidentes.

"Same way you did. We followed exactly the route we had worked out together. We left Samaná a few days after you."

"Great. Let's hear about it. Where were you during the storm of May 27, 28?" I asked.

"We were in Nassau. It was rough, but nothing happened."

I told them about my experience at Cat Island and that I had to do most of the trip without my autohelm. They had made fewer stops and sailed according to plan via Nassau and Bimini, while I took the northerly route, stopping at Bertram's Cove and Isaac Light. "Did you take one of the cats at Governor's Harbor? How many did they have?"

Brian laughed. "They had a bunch of them, but no, we didn't take a cat. I guess nobody wants to take on a feline crew!" Elaine made a sour face, as if the remark about feline crew was aimed at her. Maybe it was.

A good party developed that night on board *LINT*. We all had a lot of booze. Heinz got naked, Inga made obscene gestures at him and Elaine ended up with her face in my lap, drunk.

Time passed pleasantly enough, but my impatience grew. Riviera Beach is not exactly paradise, nothing like Cruz Bay or Samaná. I wanted to get going and Susi in New York also became increasingly anxious. At last, four weeks after my arrival at Florida Diesel, Mario installed my rebuilt engine. When I turned the key in the ignition for the first time and the engine started to run, I was shocked. The whole boat shook.

"What's wrong, Mario?" I shut off the engine. "What happened?"

"Don't panic. Don't get crazy! It's the alignment. I have to make a few adjustments, that's all." It was late in the day. "I come tomorrow morning and take care of it."

"How long is that gonna take? I want get out of here."

"Give or take a couple of days. Don't make no difference to you. You've been here a month, what's a day or two?" He laughed at his own joke.

Yeah, he's right, I thought. I hope he is right about the vibrations too. And, I'd like to find somebody to go with me, so I can swoop up the coast nonstop as far as Beaufort.

In the morning, Mario didn't show up. Great. Now what? A day later he came back.

"Had an urgent job to do. Sorry." So, my job isn't urgent, it's only that my daughter wants to get married.

Mario finally, after three more days, got the engine running without all that shaking and shattering. "It'll still get better, you'll see. It's all new parts, they've got to be broken in. Oil change after twenty five hours and she's gonna be all right."

That evening, two characters drove into the yard in a station wagon. They looked familiar.

"Hey, you guys, what are you doing here?"

"Peter! We heard you were here. How's it going, man?" They got out of the car. The older one was smartly dressed, like a used car salesman, the other in cutoff jeans, T-shirt and barefoot. I didn't remember their names, but they were the guys who had promised us a lobster dinner on their boat in Samaná, but there were no lobsters.

"Noodles and Ketchup," I said, as if those were their names. We laughed and shook hands. "What are you up to?"

"Dan's girlfriend showed up in Samaná and moved on board, so we left with this couple from Boston on their boat and got into Palm Beach last Tuesday."

"Come on board," I said. "Where are you staying?" We walked down the pier to my boat, then sat down in the cockpit.

"I have an apartment here and got a job at this dealership. Rolls Royce, Jaguars and Mercedes, you know?" the one in the cheap suit and loud tie said and went on, "Chris needs a ride up to Rhode Island. Aren't you about to go up north?"

Chris, that's right, Chris DeBoer, fisherman from Rhode Island, I remembered. "Yeah, I'm almost ready to leave for the Chesapeake," I said. "Maybe we can work something out."

I take Chris rather than that fast talking car salesman. Rolls Royce? He must be kidding me. More like used Toyotas and Chevy trucks.

Chris hadn't said much so far. The salesman did all the talking. "Hey, Chris, you see? You got your berth. Get your stuff from the car." To me he said, "Peter, great seeing you, man. Have a good trip." He got up and off the boat and walked back to his station wagon. Chris followed him to get his stuff.

Hmm, a little too sudden for me. That guy's a real deal maker, I wonder if he sells many Rolls Royces that way. The guy in the suit—I could never remember his name—drove off and Chris walked back to the boat with a bundle under his arm, a pillowcase with not much in it. He was practically broke, had only ten dollars his friend had given him. There was no agreement between us. The suit had dropped him off and left. Chris had no place to go, except *TRITON 3*.

"Gee, Peter, I'm glad we ran into you. I couldn't stay with him in that little place he has in West Palm. Women in and out all the time, stuff like that. Anyway, I've got to get back to Rhode Island, find a job on a trawler or something."

"You got only ten bucks, Chris; how do you think you can get by on ten bucks for two or three weeks? I don't have that kind of dough that I can feed you. Usually crew share in the expenses; that's the arrangement. Now, I am willing to take you, but it's not going to be a luxury cruise."

"Hey, I'll get a job wherever we stop, don't worry. I wash boats, scrape barnacles, paint or varnish. I start on your boat tomorrow morning. I go over the side and take care of the bottom."

"Good, that's a start." We had noodles and ketchup that evening, something he relished.

Heinz and Inga had found jobs somewhere and I didn't see much of them the last two days before my departure on Sunday, 15 July. I paid my bill at Florida Diesel and Marine Services, almost fifteen hundred dollars, with my credit card, and at three in the afternoon we backed out of the slip. There was nobody aboard *LINT*; we had said good-bye the previous evening. Five weeks in Riviera Beach—it wasn't hard to leave. It had never become home to me, like St. John or Samaná.

Even before reaching the deep water channel at Peanut Island, we set the main and Genoa, but kept the engine running until we were through the inlet and on the open ocean. The vibrations did not seem to be as bad as during the trial sail two days earlier. I hoped Mario was right and the new parts would work themselves in.

NORTHWARD

The wind was at ten knots from the east. We settled in on a course for Hetzel Shoal and began to enjoy a leisurely sail as the coast gradually disappeared under the setting sun. I had replaced the corroded wire and plug of the autohelm and Otto took over while we ate our evening meal, canned beef stew. We both had a beer. "Whose boat was that you were on in Samaná," I asked.

"I don't know. Dan was hired to deliver the boat from Tortola to Puerto Rico. That's where I met him. His girl friend was with him, but she got off in San Juan. Then Ferd flew in from Palm Beach. He's Dan's cousin. I don't know why Dan decided to sail to Samaná." Chris stopped there. "I tell you about that..." He paused. "Some other time."

"Ferd's the Rolls Royce salesman, who brought you to me?"

"Yeah. But I don't know what he sells." Again he didn't want to say more. There was something he was holding back, but I didn't want to press him. He seemed sensitive.

Late in the evening, off Fort Pierce, we encountered a heavy thunderstorm. Chris had a strong aversion to thunderstorms. "I once had an experience..." He didn't say more—he often left things hanging in mid-sentence—and went below until the storm had passed.

Next day we passed the security zone off Cape Canaveral, headed for St. Augustine and closed in on the shore. In the afternoon we made landfall off Daytona Beach and spotted the St. Augustine seabuoy at midnight. Because of constantly shifting sandbars, channel markers are not shown on the nautical chart. With the help of the depth sounder and with a vigilant eye we motored into the St. Augustine inlet and by three in the morning we came to anchor just before the Bridge of Lions.

Two days we spent in St. Augustine, a town I never get tired of visiting, but I wouldn't want to live there. The historic part of this oldest town in the US is lively in the daytime, but at night it is dead. Most of the restaurants cater to the tourist trade.

There are some bars frequented by locals, mostly fishermen and those involved in the marine services and industry.

Late afternoon I found Chris DeBoer in one of those watering holes as I stopped in for a beer. He must have had already more than he could pay for with his ten dollars. I bought him another beer and stayed for a while, surrounded by his new friends. As I was leaving, he asked me for five dollars, which I gave him. "I get a job in Beaufort and pay you back."

"Yeah, okay." I waved my hand. "You've got to find your own way back to the boat, but," I told him seriously, "don't come on board drunk. Do what ever you want, but don't show up drunk on my boat."

"Don't worry, I'll get a ride on somebody's dinghy and I won't be too drunk."

By three in the morning I heard a dinghy come alongside and Chris climbed on board, quiet and respectfully. I did not find out how drunk he was. Separately we spent the day in town. I walked all the way out to Camachee Cove to see the yacht harbor where I spent the first winter on *TRITON 3*, after Lynn had sailed off with 'Mr. Westsail'. It looked almost the same, except for the condominiums next to the marina. Still under construction in 1987, they were now finished and occupied.

I had an early dinner at the Chinese restaurant and then met Chris at the City Marina, where the dinghy was tied up. We had a shower at the marina facilities before going back to the boat. Chris was still barefoot and certainly broke, but he was clever to get by without any money. He was an honest guy with good intentions, and I knew he wanted to pay me the moment he had some money, but I also knew that wouldn't happen. I liked him and I didn't expect money from him.

We sailed out of St. Augustine just before dark and caught the Gulf Stream, which together with a light breeze carried us toward our next port of call, Beaufort, North Carolina. At times we were becalmed, and then again we faced unsettled weather with rainsqualls and choppy seas.

Chris carried a big photo album, his most precious possession, in his bundle and one calm afternoon he showed it to me as we sat in the cockpit. Otto was in charge. There were mostly pictures of him and other seamen on fishing boats. On one page in the middle of the album, he had fastened a huge hook.

"That hook almost killed me." He seemed sentimental about that monster hook. "It caught me in the ankle as the line ran out. I was yanked off the deck and would have been in the water the next second, hadn't the winchman seen what happened and stopped the motor." There were pictures of him with his foot all bandaged up. I had seen the ugly scar on his heel.

Then there was a photo of a beautiful young woman. "My wife," he said.

"What? You're married?"

"I was, until I found her in bed with my father." He lingered over the picture next to his wife's. "The little girl, my daughter. She's almost two."

I was shocked. "When did this happen?" I felt he was willing to talk. "Where is she now, and where is your father?"

"My father, the old bastard, is somewhere in New England. She's in Puerto Rico. Her old man is very rich, some politician in San Juan. When they heard of the scandal, they threw me out. That's when I met Dan and I went on board his boat. His girlfriend left and Ferd came and joined us. This album is all I have. They threw me out on my bare ass."

Unbelievable, yet Chris seemed completely sincere. For a moment I thought he had a tear in his eye. He got up to put his album away and stayed below for a while.

In the third night out of St. Augustine, one hundred twenty five miles off the coast of Georgia and South Carolina, we were caught in winds of up to thirty knots. All sails were down, the engine running in slow forward to keep steerage. Thunderstorms developed after midnight and lasted into the morning hours. Lightning struck all around the boat and thunderclaps rolled incessantly. Chris went below and refused to come out. I stood at the wheel the entire night, rain and salt spray hitting me like darts. I was beyond fear, waiting for lightning to strike the boat, while I saw the lights of several freighters to the east in the shipping lane, apparently unencumbered by the storm. How safe they are, and I so vulnerable! I felt alone and abandoned. Rain and salt water had entered at the sleeves and the neck of my foul weather jacket. I was cold and exhausted.

A gray morning crept over the turbulent sea. The storm had lasted six hours. Chris had disappointed me. Through the night and the terrifying storm, I had been alone out there. He was embarrassed when I went below to make a cup of coffee. I didn't say anything and he too was quiet for a long time.

"I saw a man struck by lightning. On a fishing boat, north of here. Years ago. He was killed instantly." Then he fell silent again.

I wanted to believe him, but I wasn't sure, so I didn't say anything. He, too, remained quiet.

Half an hour later, the engine stalled. Chris discovered that the fuel line between the two injectors had ruptured. I found a replacement hose among the spare parts and while Chris worked on the engine, a tug and barge headed straight for us. I called the tugboat captain on channel 06 of my VHF radio. "TRITON 3 unable to maneuver due to engine trouble. Please acknowledge. Over."

"Okay, TRITON 3, I saw nobody on board and was going to check if the boat was abandoned. Do you need assistance? Over."

"Thanks, but we are okay. Will be underway shortly." I switched the radio off and said to Chris, "He thought he had an easy salvage prize on his hands."

Chris finished installing the new, thin four-inch long fuel line and I bled the engine, which started, but stalled again. After bleeding a second time, removing all air from the system, the engine ran smoothly.

In the meantime I had forgotten that I was angry with Chris for leaving me alone out in the storm. We arrived in Beaufort at eight o'clock that evening and anchored. In the morning we changed oil and filters. The engine had run more than the twenty-five hours Mario had recommended.

I saw Chris sitting at a table with a bunch of rugged sailors outside the harbormaster's office, telling his yarn for a beer. I joined the group for a while, enjoying a cool Budweiser myself. We had been out of beer for the last couple of days.

When I got up to leave, Chris came after me. "Can you let me have another five? I think, I might find a job here."

"Listen, Chris, we have a long way to go. I can't even afford to buy the provisions we'll need. I really can't do this anymore."

"I know. I know you would give it to me, if you had it. Thanks anyway. I'll get by. I'll pay you back when I have it."

"Forget about it."

Next morning he found me at the greasy spoon across the street from the marina, where I had my breakfast and wrote some postcards. "Peter, I got another boat. They're going all the way up to Newport. And they'll pay me! It's an elderly couple, they need some help."

"That's great, Chris! You're in business. When are they leaving?"

"I don't know yet, but I can move on board right away. Are you gonna be all right?"

"Don't worry about me. I know the Intracoastal by heart. I'm happy for you."

Chris, still barefoot, picked up his bundle at my boat and then I met him outside the harbormaster's office. He was talking with his new skipper whose wife was there, too. I listened to him as he told them about our trip up the coast from Palm Beach, embellishing considerably in his favor some of the incidents. I wondered how much or how little of what he had told me was true. I saw the fishhook, and the scar in his foot; the photos in his album did not lie, but the stories that went with them might have been somewhat altered or enhanced. Well, I thought, everybody is entitled to tell a story. No harm in that. His is a vagabond's life and will always be so. I liked Chris, and I was glad that he had been taken on board another boat, where he would get paid. I said some nice things about Chris to his new patrons and wished them smooth sailing.

Chris and I patted each other on the back. "Nice folks," I whispered into his ear as we parted.

"Thanks for everything," he called back to me, as they walked away on the boardwalk.

I left Beaufort in the morning of 25 July for Annapolis and shortly after noon I anchored in Adam's Creek. The Neuse River was too choppy, and the wind came out of the north at up to twenty knots. I waited in Adam's Creek until the following morning. The conditions were still rough, but I did not want to sit in that creek for another day. So, I started out, with main and jib, both reefed, and the engine running. I made four knots, beating into the wind and seas. Logbook entry:

"Neuse R. at its worst! 3 ft breaking waves."

After nearly five hours I reached Bay River. It took two more hours to Hobucken Bridge and Goose Creek. That night I anchored at Durants Point in the Pungo River, where it was relatively calm.

The following day the weather turned cooler; there was a light drizzle until the sun came through the clouds and the wind moderated. At three in the afternoon I anchored at Deep Point in the same spot where I had been five times before. As always, there were two or three boats there.

When I awoke in the morning, the other boats were already gone. I had to make it through the Alligator River and the Albermarle Sound to the next anchorage, at least ten hours, so I left Deep Point without a lengthy breakfast. The weather report upgraded tropical storm Bertha to a hurricane. The center was east of the coast of Florida, and no immediate threat for me. It was sunny, with dark clouds in the south. In the Alligator River, I had the wind against me and progress was slow. I decided to take Route 2 of the Intracoastal via Dismal Swamp and Elizabeth City. I could steer a much better course in relation to the wind and I had actually a very nice sail until entering the Pasquotank River. Low, dark clouds had gathered and strong gusts forced me to reef the main sail. At Elizabeth City the wind was on the nose. I took in my sails and proceeded under power to Lambs Corner in the Pasquotank River, where I anchored. I had covered sixty-three statute miles in twelve hours.

On Sunday, 29 July 1990, at six in the morning, Hurricane Bertha was reported at 375 miles southeast of Cape Hatteras, heading out to sea.

I left Lamb's Corner early. There was a delay of nearly two hours at South Mills Lock and the Swing Bridge, before I could enter the Dismal Swamp Canal. Dismal, indeed! I was locked through the Deep Creek Lock quickly in the afternoon and then joined Route 1 of the ICW. I arrived at Hospital Point near the unfriendly Tidewater Marina in Portsmouth shortly before six in the evening.

The Diesel was now well broken in. The vibrations had disappeared. I had put a total of eighty-three hours on the rebuilt engine and made another oil change before starting out on the last leg of this journey.

All that was left to end the round trip was the Chesapeake Bay to Annapolis where I had begun my voyage nearly ten months ago: offshore to the Virgin Islands with Jon Reeve; Puerto Rico and the Dominican Republic with Chris Nielsen; Samaná; the Bahamas by myself—even Otto had jumped ship; then up the coast with Chris DeBoer, and now little more to go than a hop and a skip. Quite an accomplishment for little *TRITON 3*.

I took it easy, almost as if not wanting to end this long voyage, as I sailed into Chesapeake Bay. There was much activity aboard the aircraft carriers and other warships as I passed their piers. I saw a submarine being pulled out of its slip by two tugs. Helicopters seemed to be practicing search and rescue operations over the open water, outside Hampton Roads. I set the Dolly Parton near bell buoy "1" and sailed leisurely in light wind from the southwest.

The weather on the Chesapeake was stifling and by the time the Wolf Trap was in sight at two thirty, the wind died. I got as far as Windmill Point and anchored in Indian Creek, Fleets Bay, just before nightfall.

A strong northwest wind and four foot seas greeted me on 1 August. I fought hard against the weather and my progress was poor. That day I made it only as far as Point Lookout, Maryland, and I anchored in Cornfield Harbor, where I had to fight a pest of flies, reminding me of the trip along the ICW with Julia, two years earlier.

One day later than anticipated, I reached Solomon's Island, another of my favorite maritime places. The wind still came from a northerly direction and I had to make several tacks. I wrote in the logbook:

"11:30 rounding Point No Point, N 5-10, great sailing, reward for yesterday."

By six o'clock I anchored and went ashore for a nice dinner. Sitting at the bar in one of the better restaurants, I had a steak tartar, served with a raw egg on top, chopped onions and only the tiniest slice of rye bread. I felt good after several drinks, celebrating already the end of my long voyage. Only one more day! Some young people, happy with a good deal of liquor in them, were having fun at the beach. One of the girls got into my dinghy. She wanted to sail with me to Annapolis, but the others didn't let her. "I tend bar at the Charthouse. Come and see me. I get you a free drink!" she called after me, as I rowed back to my boat. What did the others call her? I can't remember.

The next day was another hot one. There wasn't much wind. The Chesapeake can be very rough, but in the summer, there is often no wind at all. This was one of those days. Motor-sailing all the way, I arrived in Annapolis at six in the afternoon.

A week later, after many visits to the Charthouse, I sailed to Grasonville and rented a slip at Lippincott's Marina. I called Susi. " Can you come and pick me up this weekend?"

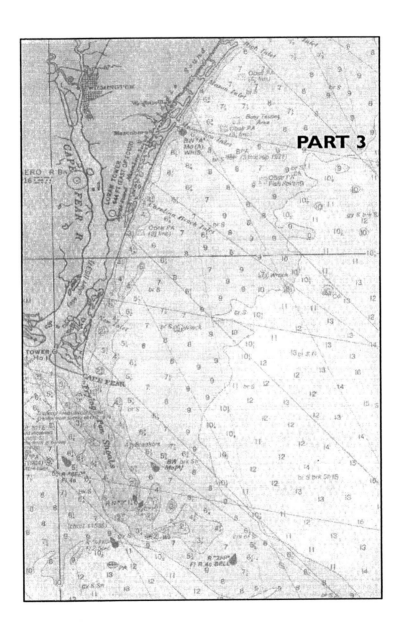

PART 3

1990/1991 — AND SOUTH AGAIN

Amidst a series of beautiful, sunny days in November of 1990, was one rainy, stormy Saturday. That day, Susanne got married in a little church on Manhattan's upper Eastside to JP, successful architect from Paris. The reception was held at the Beekman Tower.

Even though my arrival in New York was delayed by a few months, I was able to give the required assistance and all obstacles, preceding most weddings, were overcome in good time, nor did the rain hamper the ceremony or the reception. The young couple went off to Arizona and Colorado for a week and then took up their residence in Paris, France.

Carlos was doing very well in his new job in the design department of a major science publishing house in New York City. He gave up his apartment in Brooklyn and moved to Manhattan. We all liked his girlfriend, Linda, an editor in the same publishing company.

My mission in New York accomplished, I began preparations for my next voyage south. *TRITON 3* was hauled out for the winter and jacked up in the yard at Lippincott's Marina. The first job I attended to was the head. I installed a new discharge hose and replaced all working parts. Marine heads are a major pain in the butt on most boats, and mine was no exception.

Back in the water in early spring, with a fresh coat of bottom paint, *TRITON 3* underwent a rigorous overhaul, from the refrigerator/freezer to the automatic bilge pump and the hand bilge pump; from the chain locker for my secondary anchor to a new battery for the EPIRB (emergency position indicating radio beacon); to the rigging and replacement of worn sheets and halyards. Then I sanded, cleaned and oiled all exterior teak and varnished the woodwork below.

While all that and much more was going on, I sailed extensively on the Chesapeake Bay, a wonderful, almost year-round playground for boaters. I felt at home in Annapolis, explored the eastern shore and remained for days at Solomon's

Island or St. Michaels. Much of the above listed work I did while anchored in remote coves or quaint harbors.

In the summer the Bay waters provided me with the famous blue crabs, which I loved to catch along the seawall or on the pilings in the marina. Sometimes I drove to New York in my trusty, old Honda Accord with a bucketful of live crabs, a delicacy we all enjoyed.

In mid-August, I drove back to New York for the last time before sailing south. I had a vague plan, which consisted basically of not more than that: going south. How far? I would figure that out along the way. I had become a lot mellower in making plans in my "floating existence."

At Julia's I recovered all the personal items I had left at her house and equipment that accumulated in her basement: a new awning for my cockpit, two enormous boat batteries and coils of rope. Carlos drove me back to Grasonville and in a two-hour trial sail we tested all the functional parts on the boat. *TRITON 3* was in top condition.

I wanted to be in Florida by the end of the hurricane season and again impatience took hold of me. A young man and his father came to me at Lippincott's Marina, as I sat in my cockpit splicing an eye into a new halyard. "I want to go with you to Florida, or wherever you're going," said the eighteen-year old. "My name is Aaron Lester. I saw your note at the harbormaster's office in Annapolis. *Well-equipped Bristol 27.7*, I like that."

"Come on board," I said and handsome Aaron and his overweight father stepped on deck, the boat healing under the load. "Coke? Water?"

"Water is fine. Nice boat, a little small, but looks seaworthy." The father looked all around, then went down into the cabin, uninvited, and looked around some more. "Have you done a lot of sailing in her?"

I didn't much like his attitude, but, what the hell, let's see what this amounts to. I told them of my experiences in other boats and in my own.

"Sounds good to me. Aaron, what do you think?" He asked his son as if the decision were up to them, and not to me. "Aaron's a sailing instructor," he nodded in my direction.

Aaron said, "I like it. I want to go with him," and then to me, "when are we leaving? You won't get other applicants, I took care of that. Ripped your note from the bulletin board. 'This one's for me,' I said to myself." He seemed so proud of his cleverness, had no inkling that what he did was conniving, dishonest and just wrong.

At the moment I was amused by the way this kid had resorted to such stratagems, and I said, "I want to leave next week, before the end of the month, at the latest." It was already the middle of September. There was a number of things wrong with this father and son team: Aaron's unethical action of removing my notice from the bulletin board, his father's pompous behavior and his unrestrained use of my paper towels to wipe the sweat from his face, neck and arms, and their collective decision making without considering my view on the matter. Then they proceeded to make suggestions here and there on the boat, asking to install additional safety equipment, talking about what food and drink we should be stocking and how the money problem should be handled.

Five days after Carlos dropped me off at the marina in Grasonville, I sailed to Annapolis and anchored in Spa Creek just past the drawbridge. Spa Creek is a narrow inlet extending from the harbor. The hospital, where I had stayed for five days with a knee infection in 1986 before my first trip south, was right there near the water's edge.

Aaron had been in touch with me and knew where to find me. Departure was fixed for 24 September. On the morning of that day, the Lester's station wagon backed down to the dinghy landing at the foot of a quiet lane and I rowed over to pick up Aaron. His father, his mother and his grandmother came out of the car, which was piled high with boxes, bags, bundles, carton, a briefcase, a knapsack, loose gear and a case containing cooking utensils. After a short greeting, father and son started unloading the car, while I was involved in conversation with mom and granny.

"Excuse me for a minute," I disengaged myself from the women. "That can't all go on the boat! Where am I going to put it?" Did they think this was a moving van?

"That's his gear, he'll need it. He's going to take up his career as a chef in the Virgin Islands. You know, Aaron went to culinary school. The rest is his personal stuff, clothes, his outfits, his sailing gear and some food and drinks he likes. He has a lot of his paperwork, too, his certificates, his records, his books. He can't be without all that!" His father rattled that off; I expected him to finish, 'what, are you nuts to think he could go without his stuff?' He didn't say it, but it was implied.

"Okay," I said, "We will mount the man-over-board pole on the stern railing, we will take his sailing gear, maybe his utensils and outfits, the backpack with his clothes and some of this bag with his dried noodles. That's it. I can't take more."

As it turned out, even that was too much, and they managed to sneak in a few more items here and there. I had to make two trips with the dinghy and the fo'c'sle was so packed with Aaron's personal junk, it was impossible to get to the forepeak when anchor chains and lines had to be tended to. This was a bad situation, and I was angry with myself that I didn't say No, with a capital N, to this abuse. I'm just too soft, a real pushover, letting these people walk all over me. Part, of course, is also that I am too eager to get going. My impatience...

I grumbled my goodbye to the Lesters, took Aaron on board and started without a word to work the anchor. I was in a hell of a mood; the kid must have had second thoughts about this whole adventure.

Slowly we motored down the creek, waited for the drawbridge to open and then sailed with very little wind out of Annapolis harbor into the Chesapeake Bay. Sailing instructor, huh? I don't think so. He's been on boats before, I can see that, but... We'll see.

I had been led to believe that Aaron would come on board with just his backpack. Instead, they conned me into transporting him free of charge to some destination in the Caribbean where he would seek his fortune in the restaurant business. I was very unhappy with the whole thing, to say the least.

"The situation with all that junk of yours in the forward cabin is impossible and unsafe. We can't get to the chain locker in a hurry, if we have to. Your stuff's in the way. When we get to

114

Solomon's Island, you call your father. He has to come and pick up half of it. We can't continue like this. It's insane!" I should throw him out with all his shit.

He called his father the evening we arrived at the fuel dock at Solomon's Island. In the morning I personally removed boxes and bundles through the forward hatch and had Aaron put it on the dock. His father came in the afternoon and they carried everything we had accumulated on the dock back to his station wagon. I didn't say much to the man, and he didn't argue with me. Maybe my resolute, albeit belated, way of dealing with this mess took him by surprise. He hugged his son, but spared me from shaking his sweaty hand before he drove off. We had lost a full day.

Aaron still had his case with the cutlery and utensils, his cook's outfits, some of his clothes and the foul weather gear, but whatever else he had brought was gone.

"You see," I said to Aaron as we sat at a Tiki bar sharing a bucket of steamers, "we could have avoided all of that, if you had been reasonable from the start. This boat isn't a moving van. One duffel bag would have been all right, but, I think, we're okay with what you've got now." I wanted to create a friendlier atmosphere. After all, we were in it for the long haul. "See if you can keep it all on the port side, leave starboard free for access into the bow and to the anchor gear."

"It'll be fine. I take care of everything. You don't have to do a thing." Aaron wasn't a bad guy. It seemed to me he had been brought up to think of himself that he could do no wrong. Pampered by his mother, imbued with overconfidence by his father, he naturally had developed a cocky attitude. He needed a bit of cutting down to size.

"I don't have to do a thing? Just remember, on my boat I set the rules."

"Aye aye, sir." He made a funny face and mocked me with a military salute. He's a good kid, just a little misguided. If he keeps up his good humor, we'll be okay.

"Sailing instructor, huh? Haven't done much instructing, though, right?"

"I learned on my father's Catalina 22', and taught some of my friends. So I guess, I'm an instructor." He was convinced of that and I let it go.

The next morning we pulled out of Solomon's Island and had a great day, sailing in the best of conditions. In the evening we passed Smith Point and Windmill Point and by midnight, at the Wolftrap, we had to reef the mainsail and switch to the smaller jib. Aaron had a touch of seasickness, but he got over it. We anchored at Hospital Point in Portsmouth at six in the morning, twenty-two hours from Solomon's Island. I had never done it so fast.

Aaron had friends in the Norfolk area. He wanted to spend the afternoon and evening with them. I warned him. "We want to make it an early start tomorrow. It's a long stretch to where we can anchor the first night along the ICW."

"I will be back in time, I promise."

"How can you promise that, if it depends on your friends to bring you back?" These kids, they want it all. Always combining one thing with another. No dedication to the purpose at hand, no sense of responsibility or timing, no discipline. "The dinghy can't be left at Tidewater Marina, so I have to take you ashore. I want you back here before twelve midnight, since I have to row in to get you." It had happened before that I, the captain, had to accommodate the crew. "You have to whistle from the dock. You come late, you're on your own. And don't come back drunk!"

"I don't drink, you know that."

His friends picked him up in the afternoon and I was glad to have the boat to myself. Midnight came and went. No whistle. Aaron didn't show up. I went to bed. Six in the morning. No Aaron. I wanted to leave no later than eight. I had my breakfast and was just going to deflate the dinghy and stow it away, when Aaron came running out on the dock, whistled and waved his arms.

I really had it with this guy, but I got into the dinghy, rowed in and picked him up. "Get in and don't say a word. I don't want to hear anything from you. I am so mad, you should pack you bags and get off the boat."

He mumbled something like "worst night of my life" and "it's all their fault" and "I would have been here if it weren't for them," nonsense like that. I deflated the dinghy and packed it away. That's something I have to do; nobody else gets it right. I ordered Aaron to get the anchor up.

He was still in his shore clothes. "Can I change first?"

"No. We are an hour late as it is." I didn't say more to him until at least after we passed the Great Bridge Lock. We anchored at the usual spots, Currituck, Deep Point and Hobucken. When Aaron did not pay attention at the helm and sailed us briefly aground in Goose Creek, I gave him a good tongue-lashing about his irresponsible attitude and lack of interest in the navigation and the workings of the boat.

This time the Neuse River was at its best behavior and, after one more night at anchor in Adams Creek, we sailed into Beaufort, North Carolina in the morning of 2 October. The weather was warm but rainy. Thunderstorms rumbled from the time we arrived in this favorite port of mine.

TRITON 3 was at two anchors in the crowded anchorage. In the second night gusty winds forced me to move the boat to a safer but more remote place. A front passed through and the wind shifted to the northeast at twenty-five knots. Aaron proved helpful in the maneuvering and with the work at the anchors.

Much of the time I stayed on board, but in the evenings I usually went ashore for a few beers and chatting with other sailors at the harbormaster's office. On 6 October we continued our voyage. There were still lingering storms as we left from the fuel dock in the early afternoon. The cold northerly wind hurried us along. We hugged the shoreline to avoid being slowed down by the Gulf Stream. Except for the good progress we made, it was a miserable rainy day. We considered briefly interrupting the trip in Charleston, South Carolina, but by then the weather improved. In the second night out of Beaufort, the first time in a week, we saw a star-filled sky. We crossed the busy shipping lane to and from the port of Charleston and continued on our way south to St. Augustine, Florida.

Forty miles off the coast of Georgia the sea became rough in strong gusts. Aaron was at the helm. I double-reefed the main, then took it down. The upper two batten pockets had ripped in the night, one batten was missing. As I furled the sail, I slipped on the wet deck and came down hard on the handrails on the cabin roof. I was in great pain and feared I might have cracked a rib. Damn it, not again. I once fell off the cradle on which I stored my first boat. At that occasion I had fractured two ribs, so I knew what a broken rib felt like. From here on Aaron had to do most of the hard work.

We had seventy miles to go to St. Augustine. In the morning we tried in vain to set the mainsail, but the halyard was fouled at the head of the mast. The wind continued strong from the northeast and we were doing just fine with the Genoa. By mid-morning we had land in sight, passed Jacksonville and the St. John's River inlet. We closed in on the shore and reached the St. Augustine seabuoy in a rainsquall. In the turbulent sea it was difficult to find the channel markers; nevertheless, we braved the inlet and set our first anchor in late afternoon at the Bridge of Lions.

We allowed ourselves three days of rest in St. Augustine. The boat had performed very well, but there were two jobs that had to be taken care of. The main halyard had come off the block at the masthead. Since I could not winch Aaron up in the bo'sun chair, because of my injured rib, I had to go up. First of all, I had to overcome my fear of height and secondly ignore the pain. Fighting fear and pain, forty-two feet high, it was quiet an ordeal for me to dislodge the fouled halyard and replace it on the sheave. Once down again, the deck of the boat never felt so good under my feet.

I had a little spare rubber dinghy, really just a plaything, in the cockpit locker, which I had used only once to see if it was serviceable in a pinch. To be independent from Aaron, and give him independence at the same time, I let him use the toy dinghy to go ashore. While Aaron was in town, I started on job number two. There was quite a lot of sewing to be done on the mainsail. Sitting on the cabin roof, I replaced the first batten pocket with new material and repaired the second one. The leach, the after edge of the sail, was badly torn. I stitched it back together as best I could and reinforced the upper five or six feet right into the head of the sail. Handling the tough sailcloth and pushing the curved needle through two or three layers of material, is time consuming and requires some strength. Time I had, but the effort caused me pain on my left side. I avoided coughing, sneezing, laughing, moving as much as possible, but this job had to be done. I worked a couple of hours at a time and spread the work out over the three days we remained in St. Augustine.

There was a dinghy dock at the Municipal Marina on the other side of the bridge where, for a nominal fee, shower and laundry room were available. I could not mount the motor on the dinghy, but it was just as painful to row to the dock. Every day, after a couple of hours sewing, I went into the quaint, old town. Aaron made good use of his toy dinghy and, besides one lunch or dinner together, I did not see him very often. Once I ran into him in the park, where he tried to impress a group of teenage girls. I don't know whether he told them of his exploits as a sailor or his expertise in the kitchen, but the giggling girls did not seem very interested.

The financial arrangement I had with Aaron was simple. As on the boats, on which I had crewed, food and drink expenses were shared equally. Liquor, however, was on the captain. Aaron did not drink alcohol, not even beer, and so he thought that beer should not be entered into the food bill. This caused an argument.

"I don't drink your mass quantities of coke and Sprite, so I shouldn't pay for that," I told him. "Is that what you want? Well, it doesn't go that way. We don't divide item by item what we do or don't eat or drink." He didn't agree with it, but too bad. "That's just how it is on my boat," I added. "Besides, who eats more, you or I?"

Diesel fuel was also divided between the two of us, but other expenses for the boat, oil, filters, repairs etc, were the captain's responsibility. Docking fees could become more complicated. If I wanted to, or had to, take a slip in a marina, the expense would be mine. If I acceded to crew's wishes to dock, crew would have to pay. In most cases, however, marina expenses were for my account. Whatever we spent on land was the individual's business.

Galley duty on board was evenly divided. In spite of all the cooking classes Aaron might have attended, I still thought of myself as the better cook. Aaron became an arrogant bastard, when he started to chop up vegetables, seasoned meat or fish and splattered cooking oil all over the place.

"Where is your vegetable peeler?" he asked, as if it were mandatory to have one.

"What, no saffron?" He barked orders around as if he were the head chef at the Four Seasons. "I only use Extra Virgin olive oil. I can't cook with this stuff," he complained.

"Then you can't cook at all," I countered. "A good cook makes something out of nothing. That's the real proof of the pudding!"

I ate and criticized what he concocted; he ate and criticized what I put on the table. I laughed at his antics at the stove and let him have his field day.

Sunday, 13 October Aaron got our anchors on deck and we motored into Camachee Cove Yacht Haven. There is no entry in the logbook as to the purpose of that, but it was probably to take on fuel. That, of course, I could have done at the municipal dock; so, perhaps it was because I wanted to take a look around the marina where I had spent my first winter on board *TRITON 3*, a nostalgia trip. The logbook shows we spent three hours at Camachee Cove, perhaps had lunch, before leaving and powering through the inlet against the incoming tide.

The wind was still mostly from the north and east, and we stayed within three miles from the coast as far as Cape Canaveral. The restricted area east of the cape for the recovery of whatever rockets and space shuttles jettison or drop makes it necessary for boats to go far out into the Gulf Stream. This nuisance slowed us down considerably, especially in the light breeze. At six in the morning we were treated to the fascinating sight of a rocket lifting off and soaring into the dawning sky.

After Bethel Shoal we closed in on the shore again and, out of the clutches of the Gulf Stream, we again made good progress. Forty-eight hours after our departure from Camachee Cove, we anchored at Peanut Island near the Port of Palm Beach. I had much less pain in my left side, which suggested to me that I had probably only bruised a rib or two. I knew that a broken, or cracked, rib would take six weeks to heal.

Again Aaron disagreed with me over a grocery bill. I finally put it to him this way: "If you don't accept the conditions under which you crew on my boat, you'll have to get off." I considered my options, continue to the Caribbean, with or without Aaron, or stay in Florida, perhaps sail to the Keys or the Gulf coast.

I don't have to decide anything right now. I don't have to do anything. That's the beauty of living afloat. Go where the current takes you, decide 'mañana'. No problem, mon.

Aaron went to visit his grandmother in Pompano Beach. I had given him a set of written rules to think over or discuss with his family. Those rules included:

1) Your gear is limited to two pieces of soft luggage (duffel bag, backpack.)

2) Orderliness on board. Things are always put, not thrown, in their proper place.

3) Expenses are shared equally, incl. food, beer, sodas, bottled water, excl. wine and liquor, fuel, maintenance, dockage.

4) 3-hour night watches. Crew is called 15 minutes early to allow time to prepare, pass on information, discuss course and change sails if necessary. Off-duty crew may be called on deck at any time. No compensation for off time lost.

5) Opinions or suggestions are welcome, but decisions remain mine alone.

I knew that he might not accept some of the stipulations. So be it. It's his decision. I phoned him at his grandmother's and told him that *TRITON 3* would be in Stuart, anchored at the Roosevelt Bridge.

In the Intracoastal Waterway, on my way from Palm Beach to Stuart, the Florida Marine Patrol stopped me for not displaying a Florida registration decal on the boat. I was not aware that in this State even documented vessels had to be registered, like a car.

Regulations like this severely curtailed my feeling of freedom. The officer gave me a written warning and in Stuart I had to go to the registration office and pay a fee, but I was not required to put those ugly letters and numbers on the bow of my boat.

121

I anchored near the old town dock, and I happened to be on board when Aaron hailed me a few days later. His mother and grandmother were with him. There was no resentment or unfriendliness when I met them on the dock.

"I came to pick up my things I left on the boat," Aaron announced. I took him aboard and he started immediately dismantling the man-over-board pole from the stern rail and then gathered his stuff from the forward storage area. Back on the dock, I helped him carry his belongings to the car. After a short goodbye and good luck, they drove off. I had the boat to myself again, the way I like it.

I made the following entry in my logbook for 27 to 29 October, 1991:

"Hurricane Grace S of Bermuda, heading N, being absorbed by N Atlantic storm. Heavy swells Georgia to Florida."

This storm became known as the Halloween Storm, subject of Sebastian Junger's book *The Perfect Storm*.

A series of unusually strong cold fronts passed through South Florida during November and December. Boats in this anchorage at the Roosevelt Bridge—and there were regularly more than two dozen of them—were exposed to weather from the west. In those conditions good anchoring equipment and technique are essential. I endured several sleepless nights during these months when boats dragged their anchors in winds of twenty-five knots or more.

The winter of 1991-92 was active with thunderstorms, tornadoes and some very cold nights. I suffered the consequences of being against a heater on board. Some cruising boats are outfitted with kerosene or propane heaters, which I considered a nuisance and even dangerous. Besides, *TRITON 3* was crammed enough with gear and accessories. I preferred an occasional uncomfortable night to having any more gadgets to deal with.

On 15 February, I left Stuart to meet my friend Frank in Miami. He had taken a slip for *CIN CIN* at the City Marina in Key West. Separated from Frieda, who now lived in San Diego, he had once again become the vagabond he has always been in his heart.

Frank was a professional soldier, retired from the army with the rank of staff sergeant. Of Mexican descent, he was fluent in three languages, which included German. When not traveling, usually as standby on military transports, he lived on *CIN CIN*. He was well familiar with the Florida Keys and it seemed a good idea to invite him for a cruise from Miami to Key West in *TRITON 3*. He readily agreed to come to Miami.

I started out to meet him in Coconut Grove, but stormy weather kept me for two days anchored at Peanut Island. I had tried once to get through the inlet but breaking seas made progress difficult, and I returned to Peanut Island. Two days later the sea was flat and the wind variable and light. I reached Miami days before Frank was to arrive for our cruise along the Florida Keys.

The anchorage at Dinner Key was as crowded as ever. I searched for a spot where I could safely lie on two anchors, yet be conveniently close to the shore. I had to settle for a spot between a derelict wreck and a houseboat with cats, dogs, chickens, a parrot and a hippie on board. Frank will be extremely happy here; it's just his milieu.

THE FLORIDA KEYS

I was early for my rendezvous with Frank Gallardo. We had convened to meet at Dinner Key on or about 25 February. Frank arrived on the 28th.

"About time you show up. I've been here a week!" I said jokingly. I could never be mad at him. He was so laid back, a typical Californian. He grew up in Los Angeles.

Frank just smiled his almost embarrassed, disarming smile. "Still impatient, huh? You ought to learn how to relax. What's your hurry, anyway?"

"Get in the damn dinghy." I told him. We were good friends and totally at ease in each other's company. Frank carried only a small backpack; he never traveled with anything more than that.

I had plenty of time to provision us before Frank arrived and we sailed on the morning of 29 February. "Hey, a leap year, you gained a day!" Frank said. "That makes up for my being late. See, it all works out." He was so pleased with himself.

"As soon as we are underway, I'm no longer impatient. I get restless when I'm sitting too long at anchor anywhere, especially among those boat bums you're so familiar with."

With a light breeze we sailed leisurely through Biscayne Bay. It was a cool but sunny day. Soon after the Featherbed Bank, sails had to come down and we continued under power. This southern-most part of the Intracoastal becomes very narrow in some places and, though well marked, leads over shallow banks. The depth sounder often read under five feet, something that always made me nervous. In Card Sound we turned off the engine and actually sailed for an hour. "Drifter or Genoa?" I asked to get him involved.

"I don't care, it's your boat!"

"Should we turn off the engine and set the mainsail? What do you think? And don't give me that it's your boat again."

"I don't care, it's your boat," he said again, accompanied by a big smile.

"Hey, give me a little more than that. I could have taken the trip alone, you know."

"Peter, it is your boat! I'm the crew, I do what you tell me."

I gave up. After Jewfish Creek Bridge we anchored in Blackwater Sound, Key Largo and got underway early next morning. I wanted to get to Marathon that day. With a nice northeasterly wind, the Dolly Parton pushed us along at a good speed. By two o'clock we passed under the high bridge through Channel Five into Hawks Channel on the ocean side. Unfortunately the wind died and we had to resort to the Diesel again. The sun was burning down on us with no mercy. Come on, wind. We have to make it to Marathon. East Washerwoman Shoal by six, entrance to Boot Key by seven and, at last, just before eight o'clock, we anchored in crowded Boot Key Harbor. Frank carried a second anchor out in the dinghy, and then we went to the Dockside bar and restaurant for dinner and a few beers.

Frank in Marathon

Marathon, located on Vaca Key, was one of Frank's favorite hangouts. The scenario in the anchorage was about the same as at Dinner Key. Among seaworthy yachts of all sizes and degrees of luxury, there are wrecks, derelicts and boat bums. Frank easily blends in with all of them, while I am generally seen as a gentleman sailor. Years earlier, as I sailed into Sheepshead Bay in Brooklyn in my Cape Dory, some roughnecks called out to me, "Go back to Wallstreet!" In T-shirt and cutoff jeans, or oil- and rust-stained pants, they still did not recognize me as one of them. Along the waterfront and the docks of Marathon Frank and I must have looked like an incongruous pair, a vagabond and a gentleman.

We stayed a day and two nights at Marathon, then set sail for Boca Chica. We had a fine wind that took us quickly past Bahia Honda Key and Nine Foot Shoal. At Boca Chica, a short distance from Key West, was the Naval Air Station. There were a few moorings in the harbor and Frank, a veteran of US Special Forces, obtained a permit for *TRITON 3* to tie up on one of them.

That night both of us got pretty drunk on Rum & Coke in the bar of the veteran's post, where we were the only patrons. There was no bartender. Booze was available on an honor system. A sign read, "Leave money in the box on the counter, or replace what you have consumed." We stuffed some cash into the box.

Frank and I got into an argument about something to do with the Nazi era, the holocaust and the shameful period in German history. I said, I couldn't really be proud of being a German, or something to that effect, and Frank, who had spent years in post-war Berlin, thought that was nonsense. Back on board the debate got heated and became a bitter argument. Frank said he wanted to get off the boat. For a moment it seemed he was going to jump overboard, but at some point we either fell asleep or passed out.

We awoke in the morning and, to my surprise, I had no hangover. Frank was fine, too, and nothing was ever mentioned of the ugly, drunken fight we had that night in Boca Chica. We stayed at the base for a full day and I met a few of Frank's buddies, all veterans of post-World War II conflicts. Some were enthusiastic, others sarcastic or disillusioned, but all were distinctly military. I felt like such an oddball among that bunch of former soldiers.

From Boca Chica to Key West was a three-hour trip. The wind was steady out there, so far from any major land mass. We anchored among a wide variety of craft at Christmas Island, named Wisteria on the chart. The anchorage is wide open and unprotected to wind and ocean swells. It is far from the town of Key West and exposed to a great deal of traffic, from big sailing vessels to jet skis, speed boats to runabouts, Navy ships to police patrols.

All sailors know that Key West is notorious for theft. Any item, from outboard motors to dinghies to oars not secured by chain and lock, cannot be expected to ever be found again. I kept my outboard motor chained to the stern rail of *TRITON 3*. Although almost three quarters of a mile, I rowed in and locked the dinghy to an old pier. The oars I carried with me wherever I went.

Frank took his backpack and went to his *CIN CIN* at the City Marina. He got around town on his bicycle.

After a week at Key West, I took *TRITON 3* around the north point of Fleming Key to Steadman's Boat Yard for bottom paint and some minor adjustments. Two days later I was again at Christmas Island, in the same spot. That first night back at two anchors, strong gusty winds caused some boats to drag anchors. I was awake most of the night. On the next evening, Frank and I had a lot of drinks at one of the taverns. We were saying goodbye to each other. Long after midnight I managed to row across the harbor, found my boat in the darkness and went to bed. It was a stormy night and I awoke as two sailboats dragged into *TRITON 3*.

On one of the boats, a ketch from Australia, a naked guy was working furiously at his anchor. "Get the engine on, steer away from here! Get that stupid anchor later!" I yelled at him. He acted kind of confused, didn't know what to do first, but in the end got clear of my boat.

The other boat had her anchor fouled with the chain of my Danforth. While the ketch finally got away from me, I had to work with the crew of that other boat to free my anchor chain and line. That done, I repositioned the Danforth and then went below to resume sleeping off my hangover. During the entire procedure I had forgotten that I was actually still drunk, but the headache came back to remind me.

Frank told me much later that he fell from his bike that night, hit his forehead and lost his glasses.

I postponed my departure from Key West by one day. The weather report for the Gulf of Mexico was good. *"S-SE wind 5 to 10 kn. Hi pressure, cool, sunny."* I sailed at two in the afternoon of 16 March, destination Fort Myers.

FLORIDA'S GULF COAST AND LAKE OKEECHOBEE

The weather report was wrong. The wind was a lot stronger than predicted. I left Key West under Genoa and mainsail, and headed for Middleground, the eastern exit route from the anchorage at Christmas Island. In four-foot seas, putting the rail under, I sailed close-hauled on starboard bow. The boat was fast and, with the fresh bottom paint, a pleasure to sail.

At four o'clock I came through the jetties and turned toward the north. The wind came at me from the northeast at fifteen to twenty knots. I took down the Genoa, set the jib and reefed the mainsail. *TRITON 3* behaved like a young colt. Beating as close to the wind as I did on this course, put a lot of strain on the equipment, as well as on me. The constant smashing into the seas made the boat shiver and sent gushes of salt water from the bow back to the cockpit. Standing at the wheel on the bucking boat, heeled at a thirty-degree angle, I soon felt the stress in my back, arms and neck. Yet, to harness the forces of the elements to his advantage is for the sailor the most exhilarating feeling and the greatest joy.

Late at night, a full moon crept over the horizon and then promptly hid behind clouds. Without the direct moonlight, the night had an eerie transparency, never turning completely dark. The wind came around to the east at twenty knots and I could steer a more direct course for Ft. Myers. The seas continued rough. I took down the jib and sailed with only the reefed main, still making four knots. The night air had turned cold and I was wet from spray. Water always finds a way in at the neck and the sleeves of the foul weather suit. In the morning, as I came within sight of land, I set the Genoa and made an average of seven knots, almost scary in those rough conditions.

At four o'clock in the afternoon, I spotted the sea buoy for San Carlos Bay. The wind had become mild and backed to the west. The typical afternoon onshore breeze made my approach easy. The current, however, had turned against me. At Matanza Pass, I took in the sails and motored into San Carlos Bay. I anchored in the calm water at Estero Island, inside Fort Myers Beach.

It was an exhausting, but glorious, twenty-seven hour sail from Key West. Seldom have I had a more intensely satisfying experience in my years of sailing. Instead of feeling tired and worn out from the exertion, I was exuberant.

Strong winds came up from the northwest and lasted for several days. The weather turned colder. It was still March; winter was still raging in the north and the tail ends of cold fronts swept over southern Florida. The anchorage, however, was well protected and there was never more than a light chop on the water.

Ft. Myers Beach is a fun place with a beautiful beach, plenty of restaurants and bars, lots of entertainment and shopping. All that was within walking distance from a small wooden dock, on which dinghy landing was permitted, courtesy of Mr. Wallace, whose property came right down to the water's edge. He invited sailors to tie up their dinghies at his dock. *TRITON 3* rested at her anchors only yards away. What a friendly way to welcome a cruising sailor! Mr. Wallace enjoyed chatting with the sailors who passed through Ft. Myers Beach, and all he asked of them was to sign his guest book. He was no sailor, but he liked to listen to the stories about oceans and islands and boats. Most of the books he had on his shelf were about sailing. Mr. Wallace was a true armchair sailor.

I had to visit a dentist to replace a filling I had lost on the way from Key West. Perhaps I had clenched my teeth too tightly in the excitement of that terrific sail. The dentist was right next to the post office, only a short walk from Mr. Wallace's house.

I stayed in this convenient and friendly place until 26 March, a Thursday. The weather had been rather cool and breezy for a whole week. I started out late in the morning to investigate Point Ybel on Sanibel Island, but did not find it interesting enough to spend time there. A cold wind had come up and I decided not to linger. Instead, I headed for the Causeway Bridge, where the Gulf Coast portion of the Intracoastal and the Okeechobee waterways intersect. A strong northwest wind hurried me toward the city of Fort Myers. I entered the Caloosahatchee River and before the Cape Coral Bridge the sails had to come down. I followed the waterway, which swings around downtown Fort Myers and then passes under two parallel highway bridges. I found a nice place to anchor at Beautiful Island, just past the twin bridges, beyond the city's outskirts.

From here to Lake Okeechobee my mainsail remained under the cover and the jib in the bag. The navigable channel in the Caloosahatchee River and Caloosahatchee Canal is narrow. The sails were of no use. At the little town of Olga was the first of several locks. With only a foot or two difference in water level, there was hardly any delay in locking through. The bridges at Alva, Denaud and La Belle, all about one travel hour apart, were opened promptly for my passage. My first overnight stop after Beautiful Island was in La Belle at the little town dock. It was still early in the afternoon, but I did not know whether later on, before dark, I could find a place to tie up or to anchor.

The following day, still in the Caloosahatchee Canal, I had to negotiate the locks at Ortona and Moore Haven, as well as several bridges. Traffic was light in the waterway. I saw alligators sunbathing by the side of the canal, near a power plant. At Liberty Point I had my first glimpse of Lake Okeechobee, but did not reach it until the next morning; a dike separates the waterway from the lake. Since there was no room for me to anchor, I had to dock at Roland Martin's Marina in Clewiston.

On Sunday, 29 March, I entered Lake Okeechobee through the access channel. I was curious about this lake, which can become difficult to negotiate in bad weather. Outside the marked channel, the lake is shallow, with depths of only a few feet in the dry season. The wind was calm as I motored toward Rocky Reef. From this point I had a straight course for marker "6". A light northwest breeze came up and I set Mainsail and Genoa. I had to rely on the compass; the marker, a wooden stake, was too far to be visible from Rocky Reef. When I located it an hour later through my binoculars, I was right on course. By one o'clock I passed the marker, which is the halfway point across the lake to Port Mayaca. The wind had increased nicely and, at a speed over six knots, crossing Lake Okeechobe was a great experience.

From the midpoint of the lake, I reached Port Mayaca in little more than one hour. At three o'clock I was already through the lock that closes off the lake from the St. Lucie Canal. There was hardly any difference in water level. Under power, I entered the St. Lucie Canal. Only a few hours separated me from completing my circumnavigation of the southern half of the Florida peninsula. It was either that I didn't want to arrive in Stuart in the dark, or that I didn't want my voyage to end so quickly; anyway, I docked at the Indiantown Marina for the night.

In the morning, there was a lot of recreational traffic. Runabouts pulling water skiers, jet skis doing tricky maneuvers, people swimming and frolicking on inner tubes. At the St. Lucie Lock I encountered a seventeen-foot drop. The woman in the power boat ahead of me saw that I was alone on my boat and she sent me her teenage son to assist me with the dock lines. I was grateful to the mother and the young man, who was quite helpful. It had not been too hard for me at the previous locks, handling bow and stern lines by myself, but a drop of seventeen feet would have been difficult to manage alone.

It was orange blossom time. All along the St. Lucie Canal, I breathed the air filled with the sweet perfume that emanated from the groves on either side of the waterway. I reached the anchorage at the Roosevelt Bridge at one o'clock on Monday, 30 March, 1992. The spot I had previously occupied near the town dock was free, as if reserved for my arrival.

I was back in Stuart, which quite casually had become my homeport. The voyage, that began on 15 February and lasted no more than six weeks, was made up of three very different segments: first, the Florida Keys with Frank Gallardo, who knows his way around the islands and the towns. The drunken incident at Boca Chica had no effect on the friendship between us. Frank and I remain good friends to this day. The second stage was the Gulf of Mexico, where I enjoyed some of the best sailing in my memory. Ft. Myers Beach made the list of my favorite places, in part due to the hospitality of Mr. Wallace. And last but not least, the Okeechobee Waterway. I am glad that I chose this route through the middle of Florida. I got to know the Caloosahatchee, satisfied my curiosity about Lake Okeechobee, saw alligators in their natural habitat and inhaled the fragrance of the orange blossoms.

In the afternoon of my return to Stuart, I went to Mahony's Oyster Bar for a bowl of the delicious oyster stew and a couple of cool beers. Mahony's was my favorite restaurant in town. There was usually an interesting crowd at the bar. Michael Mahony sometimes came through the anchorage in his Kayak and I invited him on board. We became friends. Michael witnessed how I labored over a poem I was writing, the *Ballad of an Old Sailor*, and he helped me in its creation with some of his own ideas when I complained that I didn't know how to finish it.

At the time he was not aware that I intended to dedicate it to Sara.

BALLAD OF AN OLD SAILOR

A sailor came in from the sea,
Ended up in old Stuart town.
He wasn't a young man, over sixty
When he put his anchor down.

He thought he had seen a mermaid,
Though he knew this couldn't be.
So he stayed in Stuart, in Stuart he stayed
until he returned to the sea.

He saw dolphins and he saw flying fish
And sunsets and moonshine and ships;
But all he longed for, his only wish,
Was to see the mermaid and to kiss her lips.

He had no luck. He was in a storm.
Huge waves were crashing down.
A gale of wind had his mainsail torn
And he was certain that he would drown.

Under water, so peaceful and calm,
Near death he heard a sound --
A music, a voice -- then a pull on his arm
He opened his eyes and he looked around...

Oh no, oh no, this cannot be!
I want to see what I just saw!
Where did she go, in the deep blue sea?
...so beautiful, without a flaw.

He had dozed off in the summer heat,
Still anchored near the downtown dock.
His heart for certain did miss a beat,
But he recovered from his shock.

As so often before, he rowed to the pier.
A strong coffee had cleared his mind.
To his favorite bar he went for a beer,
Not knowing what he would find.

He settled down with his beer at the counter
And he almost fell from his stool
When he realized he had found her,
Live, and in person, and so cool.

With a friendly "Hello and how are you,"
She was as she'd always been here.
Confused and disturbed, "Who are you?"
He asked, but it seemed she didn't hear.

He stayed at the bar, had drink after drink
And tried to figure this out.
Finally he didn't know what to think
And what life was all about.

She was busy filling the glasses with ale
For the sailors around the bar,
careful not to show foot or tail
To Johnny, to Peter, or Jack Tar.

She looked at them -- what did this mean?
With a twinkle in her eyes.
Was she human, fish, or in between,

135

Or something in disguise?

He climbed from his stool, staggered out of the
place
And walked through the old part of town.
From a shop window now smiled the familiar face,
The dark eyes, red lips, black hair like a crown.

Next to the canvas was a mirror
And he saw his own portrait there.
He moved, with precision, a little closer,
Put his arms around her with loving care.

He swung around. He stared, couldn't quit.
"Come with me, I beg you! You must!"
She said, "I can't, he wouldn't like it!"
"But what about you? What you feel in your guts?"

She freed herself -- did she walk or swim? --
With a teardrop on her cheek.
Away, down the street, she moved from him
And disappeared at the creek.

Back at his boat, later that night,
He decided to return to the sea.
In the morning, sober, with the first new light
He sailed, and recovered his sanity.

It doesn't matter, girl or flounder;
He's far away from that all.
It is as if he'd never found her -
Yet, there's always that distant call.

When the days are long and the nights are still
And he looks at the stars above,
He sees old Stuart and his heart is ill

For living a life without love.

Should he return or find a new shore --
This burning question he ponders.
A new life, new love, new chances and more,
Or renew the old ones, he wonders.

Years had passed, or maybe less,
When he put the tiller down.
Firm resolve did his face express
As he sailed toward Stuart town.

At the bar, "You have come back!" she said,
And then, "I'll drink a glass with you!"
He felt happier than he ever had
And together they drank their brew.

"I decided to come back for you."
She said, "He didn't love me."
"Then let me show you that I do!"
"Oh yes, oh yes! I am free!"

But this is not the way it went.
It was just what he had dreamed
When the first night at anchor he spent
In his favorite port, it seemed.

What really happened was more like this:
At the bar she greeted him with a smile
And then went about her business
In her usual professional style.

She saved me, he thought, when I almost drowned.
She is who my dream was about.
Her beautiful shoulders I had my arms around --
She is the creature, no doubt.

He said, "I know you; you're not from here.
I met you in a different place."
Then he quickly had a sip of his beer,
But he saw a sad smile on her face.

When he looked up she wiped a tear from her eyes.
"I love you," he whispered, only for her to hear.
She said, "I know, but I have my family ties."
Yet what he'd said was music to her ear.

When he finally left, it was for good.
But forever he thought: Perhaps...
She waved as on the pier she stood,
And she, too, thought: Perhaps, perhaps...

ISLANDS IN THE STREAM

As I was actively preparing for my next adventure, I noticed one day a small sailboat at anchor near *TRITON 3*. It had just come in and, when a few gusts came out of the northwest, the boat began to drag anchor. An attractive redhead struggled in her dinghy, trying to reposition the anchor. I saw she was having trouble and I went over to her in my dinghy to lend a hand.

"That anchor you have here is nothing but a toy," I told her. "How can you expect it to hold the boat?"

"We just bought the boat and the anchor came with it," she said. "We are new at this, my husband and I. What should we do?"

"Buy yourselves a good anchor, a Danforth or a CQR. Preferably both. And some chain. What you have is good for your dinghy, maybe. In the meantime, I let you have one of my auxiliaries with 1/4-inch chain. I'll rig it for you."

"We don't know how to sail yet. Could you teach us, maybe on the weekend?"

"I think, I can help you out, to get you started. You know, I never learned to sail; I mean, I was never taught. We were twelve or thirteen, my friends and I, and we just got into the boats and sailed. Figured it out by ourselves. My name is Peter, by the way."

"I'm Debra. Hi! My husband's name is Brent. You'll meet him Saturday. Will the boat be all right for tonight?"

"I'll put her on one of my anchors. Don't worry."

She had to leave and entrusted the boat to my care. I rigged one of my Danforths with chain and nylon line and anchored the boat properly. As long as the wind would not pick up, it was going to be all right.

Debra's boat, a Morgan, twenty-four feet or so, was okay in the morning and for the next couple of days. On Saturday, Brent and Debra showed up with a brand new Danforth, some twenty feet of chain and a spool of nylon 3-strand.

"Now, that's more like it," I greeted them as they came over to show me their newly acquired treasures. "Want me to help you with it?"

"No, but thanks." Brent and I shook hands. "We can handle it from here on." He seemed a little cocky to me, the type that knows it all.

Twenty minutes later he sent his wife back in their dinghy with my anchor and gear.

"Thank you, again. I wouldn't have known what to do. Brent is a mechanic, he knows a lot, but he's also stubborn. Doesn't like to accept help or advice.

"I got that. I don't know if I can teach him anything. But, if you want to, I'll go out with both of you on your boat. Just let me know."

I didn't care much for going sailing with them, but that afternoon I did. Carefully, I pointed out a couple of things to them. Every time I hinted at something, he blamed his wife for doing this or that wrong. Now and then he called what she did dumb or stupid. Oh boy; I thought it best to stay away from them thereafter.

Brent and Debra both worked for the county; she as inspector of water quality, and Brent operated special x-ray equipment checking the pipes for cracks. Besides, as a hobby and for extra income, he bought wrecked cars, restored them in his garage and sold them.

I did not have much time for them. Susi and JP were coming to spend one week with me on *TRITON 3*. They wanted to sail to Bimini.

"Not before May," I told Susi on the phone. I used Julia's phone card number for long distance and overseas calls, and there were many of them. Of course, I got the bill later. This was costing me money, and the trip hadn't even begun. "Susi, the weather just isn't right. There are still cold fronts coming through." Winter did not seem wanting to quit this year, but I knew I wouldn't win the argument with my daughter.

"Dad, our free miles with Air France will run out by the end of this month. We can't let the miles expire. We must begin our trip before the end of April."

"I can't do anything about the weather, Susi. It's your call. No guarantees. Let's hope for the best, then." I couldn't let them lose their frequent flyer miles, but I wasn't sure about crossing the Gulf Stream for Bimini.

The three of them flew from Paris to New York and left little Julie with grandma. Yes, there was little Julie! She was born last November. Her first cross-Atlantic flight was for Christmas, when she was only three weeks old. Now, at five months, she was already a veteran flyer.

JP and Susi booked their flights from New York to Miami for 18 April. We were to meet at the Miamarina at Bay Shore Park. Never leaving things to the last minute, I prepared to leave Stuart on the 12th. But, to my surprise, Lynn Thordahl showed up in Stuart. Lynn had been in Orlando or Melbourne and she was on her way to Miami in a rental car.

"I have to sail to Miami tomorrow, Lynn. I wouldn't mind the company. Susi and JP are coming. They want to go to Bimini." Lynn was born and grew up in Norway. It would be good to have her on board, old Viking that she was.

Quickly she changed her plans, and she came on board. Our departure, however, was delayed by one day. She had to get rid of the rental car and in the evening she met Brent and Debra. We spent a few hours on my boat together. Later she asked me if I could get her a good used car through Brent. "I don't know," I said, "but you should meet Ferd, a used Rolls Royce dealer I know in Palm Beach." Then I told her the story how I met them in Samaná, my trip with Chris up the coast to Beaufort, his fear of thunderstorms and what happened between his father and his wife. "The characters you meet along the way…"

Lynn and I left Stuart on 13 April and we anchored for the night at Peanut Island, Palm Beach. The weather had turned nasty. A north wind blew at twenty-five knots and continued for forty-eight hours. We lost another day. On the 15th in the afternoon we ventured out through the inlet. If I had had the time, I would have turned back. There were five to eight-foot breaking seas in the inlet. Again and again the boat was knocked to a standstill as it slammed into the steep waves. The little eleven HP Diesel engine had a hard time getting us through. Finally we made it out to open water. The long ocean swells were a lot easier on us and on the boat.

"Sorry, Lynn, but I couldn't wait another day. They are coming on the 18th. That leaves me only two days." It was sunny although the wind was still strong from the north, and it was cold, but, I thought, they are used to rough weather, these Scandinavians.

"That's okay," she said, and we fortified ourselves with a couple of shots of Scotch. "Here, I take the wheel, you go and get the main and the jib up." She never went forward in rough weather; I remembered that from our voyage in the *VAMP* to Bermuda and the Virgin Islands back in '85, and our stormy experience in the Gulf Stream off North Carolina.

Lynn took over the helm, turned the boat into the wind and I hoisted first the reefed mainsail and then the storm jib. We practically surfed down the front of big waves. I thought we were overpowered and after a while I went forward again to tuck in a second reef. We were still making between five and six knots. It was a fantastic ride. "Another shot of Scotch, Lynn?"

"Sure, why not."

It always seemed to me that I could drink a lot more in rough weather without getting drunk. It only made me boisterous and fearless. After another couple of shots, Lynn and I were having a ball. Through the night the swells came rolling in from the east at eight to twelve feet. We were far off the beach in deep water where the seas were not breaking. From the crests we saw the lights along the shore and in the troughs between waves, we had a wall of water on either side. It never ceased to fascinate me.

At four in the morning we were at the entrance channel to the harbor of Miami. The intricate buoy system that leads to the Government Cut has confused me even in the daytime. I had taken the sails down and we motored at four knots, careful not to miss the channel. "Lynn, take the spot light, find me the markers. Read the numbers off to me."

"Okay. Here we go. You're okay. See that over there? Those are the apartment blocks on Fisher Island."

"What are you doing, sightseeing? Cut the nonsense! Look for buoys. Don't tell me I'm okay, I want to hear the numbers."

"Yeah, okay. '6 A' on starboard. You think Eddy Fisher lives on Fisher Island? Maybe they named it after him!" She thought that was so funny. "Fisher on Fisher, Fisher lives on Fisher," she rapped.

"Are you drunk or just crazy? Get me the next buoy. If it's '8' it better be on starboard." I was straining my eyes, following the beam of Lynn's spotlight. "Isn't Eddy Fisher dead?" I asked, surprising myself by picking up on her nonsense.

"Deady Eddy! Fishy Fisher! Ha, that's hilarious!" She was absolutely nuts. "You're doing fine," she said. "I think we are joining the other channel already. Gotta take a slight dogleg to starboard here."

"I see that. Hey, I think we made it. It's gonna get rough here between the jetties. But that's okay, the tide is with us. Stay in the cockpit, unless you're harnessed." I knew she wouldn't go on deck anyway. "Okay, we're in." I was sweating under my foul weather jacket, although there was a cold wind blowing.

We passed two huge cruise ships at their piers, ready to leave by daybreak for Nassau or Aruba, maybe the Panama Canal. Before six o'clock we docked at the Miamarina and immediately got into our bunks to sleep. The moment I lay down, I felt how tired I was. It was the fastest, but also the most strenuous trip I have ever made from Palm Beach to Miami and was glad to have had Lynn with me. She has a funny streak, but also helped me navigating into the port, in spite of all her joking and clowning.

At eight o'clock there was someone knocking at the hull. "Hey, somebody in there? You didn't check in."

"We came in at six a m. There was nobody here then." I slid the hatch open a couple of inches. "Give me a minute, I'll be right up. See you at the office."

This marina offered a special dockage at five dollars for three hours. The daily rate was seventy-five cents per foot. I didn't want to stay at the marina until JP and Susi arrived, so I paid five dollars and left at nine o'clock for Dinner Key. Lynn went to see her daughter who lived in Miami.

On 18 April in the morning I came back to Miamarina and waited for my guests to arrive. The weather continued blustery cold and the forecast was for more of the same for several days. I was afraid that this would happen, as I had told Susi on the telephone. They came all the way from Paris for a few days in the sun, sailing in mild, tropical breezes, playing on deserted beaches. I wanted them to have that, but I could not risk crossing the Gulf Stream in these conditions. One cold front with strong winds and showers followed another. How can I tell them, we can't go?

I went to the street corner to wait for them. There was Lynn! I should have known she'd show up. She had come with her daughter, a tall, blonde beauty. "I didn't want to miss Susanne and JP," Lynn explained enthusiastically. "Are they here yet? Peter, this is Krissy." Krissy was almost a head taller than I.

"Hi, pleased to meet you. No, they'll be here any moment now. I don't think, we can leave in this weather. What a disappointment for them."

"Does your daughter get seasick?" Krissy asked.

"No, usually not. But it's going to be ugly out there, and I'm not sure how it might affect JP. Here's a taxi now. Yes, it's them."

Lynn was right in the middle, the main character in the show. Susi and JP politely paid attention to her and to Krissy. Finally it was my turn to get a hug from my daughter and my son-in-law.

We stood for a few minutes by the curb, talking. Then I said, "Well, let's get your bags to the boat," and to Lynn, "Sorry. We want to be ready, in case the weather gets any better."

Susi and JP were surprised that it was so cold in Florida.

Now was the time to break it to them. "I don't know how to put it, but this is no weather to cross the Gulf Stream. You realize that, don't you?"

"What do you mean, we can't go?" Susi was incredulous.

"Well, you know how tricky it is to cross the Gulf Stream in northerly winds, and it's blowing like twenty, twenty-five knots. It would be pretty stupid; highly uncomfortable, to say the least. We still have a few hours to decide. See what happens."

JP, the optimist and always so positive, assured me, "Oh, no problem."

A rainsquall came down on us like a warning: do not do it! That helped me to be firm. I gave them my final decision. "We wait one day."

The singlehander in the slip next to *TRITON 3* was also headed for Bimini. I had talked with him earlier; he said, "No way!"

In the morning of 19 April, the weather was worse. Strong, gusty winds pushed heavy, iron blue clouds across the sky. "Only a lunatic would sail today," I said, and they knew that I was right.

The 20th looked dismal in the morning. By noon, there were some breaks in the clouds, but the wind continued from the northeast and the air was chilly.

"If we can't go today we might as well give up entirely," said Susi. "Our flight back to New York is on the 26th in the afternoon."

JP said something in French to Susi, and she translated for me, "he thinks we can go today. It's not so bad now, and there hasn't been a shower since last night."

TRITON 3 has proven to be a safe boat. I said, "Safety is not so much my concern. The question is, is it worth it? Bimini is only about fifty miles from Miami. We could find the same weather there. Think about it. If you want to go, we'll go, but be aware that it will be a very uncomfortable passage and that it might take us twenty hours to get there. I don't think we can sail, it will be all under power, most of it, anyway. The wind is almost east now." I can take it, the boat can take it, but can they?

JP talked with Susi for a moment and then declared, "let's go for it, if it's all right with you."

Susi nodded. "If safety is not a factor, let's go. By the time we get to Bimini the weather might be okay." It was settled.

At twelve noon we untied our lines from the dock and pulled out of the slip. We motored through Government Cut and the inlet. Susi took over the helm as I hoisted the reefed mainsail and the jib. I had expected worse conditions in the inlet. We turned south along the shore of Key Biscayne. As long as the wind was on our port quarter, we had a fairly easy sail.

"Time to put on our foul weather suits, the smooth ride is over," I told them as we turned east at Fowey Rocks and headed into the choppy seas. The wind was pretty much on the nose. I took down the jib and started the engine. The close-hauled main was still helping at first, but soon I had to take it down, too. In the Gulf Stream the waves were short and steep. During the night we had one brief shower. The rainwater was cold, but the salty spray that came over the bow back to the cockpit was warm Gulf water.

JP was seasick as soon as we began our eastward tack, and he was miserable. He went below to lie down. Susi went with him, but she came back up and asked me where she could find a blanket for him. "He's so cold, he's shivering. Throws up every few minutes. And he is embarrassed, too. He's so macho, you know."

I felt bad for him; there was nothing I could do. It was a horrendous night. By four-thirty I saw the lights of Bimini. An hour later we followed in the wake of a motor yacht, an easy way to find the channel into the harbor of Alicetown. It was just beginning to get light so that I could find the range markers, two thin stakes, one on the beach, the other farther inland among the shrubs. At seven-thirty we docked at Weech's. By eight o'clock I took our passports and entry forms to Customs and Immigration. Susi and JP went to take a shower. It was remarkable how fast JP got over the seasickness, once the bouncing and rolling of the boat had stopped.

"That's about as bad as it gets," I said to him. "All the way, the engine running, Diesel fumes coming back over the transom, no wonder you got sick." I wanted to give him a different reason for his seasickness, so he wouldn't feel so embarrassed about it.

"Yes, the fumes made me sick. That's it," and to Susi, "You see, Sooz, it's the fumes."

Susi told me that she wasn't feeling too well either on the way over. She had stayed in the cockpit with me most of the night, huddled in a corner and sheltered from wind and spray. "I didn't have to throw up, but I felt nauseous and I had a headache. But I am fine now."

146

"I thought you were sleeping, that's why I didn't talk to you. I was miserable, too. Cold, hungry, thirsty and tired." I have never been seasick.

We left *TRITON 3* at Weech's for the day and explored the little town of Alicetown. The weather was fine with a light wind, blue sky and much warmer than Miami. In the afternoon we went to the beach, swam and played Frisbee.

At Weech's dock, Alicetown, Bimini

The following morning I moved *TRITON 3* to the anchorage, while the young couple went somewhere for breakfast. The anchorage in this harbor is between the shallows on the town side and the landing area of Chalk's seaplanes that service Miami, Bimini and Nassau. Several times a day the planes come in and take off right next to the boats at their anchors. A strong tidal current requires boats to be on two anchors.

Two days in Alicetown was enough; there isn't that much to see or to do. We had dinner once at The Red Lion, and once at Opals; we had drinks at the Sport Fishing Club, at the End of the World saloon and at Hemingway's favorite bar. It was Ernest Hemingway who called Bimini the "Islands in the Stream". We had a good time both on the boat and in town and we were glad we made the effort.

In the morning of the 23rd we sailed south to Gun Cay and Cat Cay. After a leisurely afternoon at anchor, we rented a slip for one night at Cat Cay Club, where we had dinner among captains and crew of yachts belonging to the rich and super rich. Late at night the personnel, cooks and waiters of this private club played music in the pantry and JP and Susi danced, like I have never seen them dance before. They put on a show worth watching and people formed a circle around them. I didn't know my daughter could dance like that! It was like a choreographed performance.

The following morning we sailed farther south to South Riding Rock and spent the day at anchor. I had rigged a rope ladder, so we could swim off the boat and get back on board. We watched manta rays, barracudas and sand sharks. Susi had a hard time making it up the twisting rope ladder as a curious barracuda came after her. We laughed, but she didn't find it so funny.

We spent the afternoon, the night and the next morning at anchor near the beach of South Riding Rock, and then it was time for us to sail back to Miami. It was an easier course, as the prevailing winds were easterly and the Gulf Stream was now in our favor. As we came closer to the Florida coast, however, we hit choppy seas again. JP insisted on steering throughout the night. He wasn't seasick, as on the way over, and had to prove he didn't need to lie on his bunk all night. The weather had been perfect in Bimini, but as we approached Florida, it was almost as bad as when we left.

Back at Miamarina, I called Customs at once from a pay phone, a requirement that can cost dearly, if not complied with.

Too soon their visit came to an end. In spite of the weather, the delay, the rough crossing of the Gulf Stream, they had their vacation in the Islands in the Stream. The time came for them to take a cab back to the airport. They packed their bags and I accompanied them to the corner of the park, near Biscayne Boulevard. We flagged down a taxicab. A quick hug, "thank you" and "have a good flight," and the car pulled away from the curb. "I'll call you this evening!" I don't think they could still hear me.

The boat felt empty. The breakfast dishes were not cleared away, their blankets still rumpled on the bunks, a forgotten T-shirt here, a Milky Way wrapper in the corner. I sat down in the cockpit and lit one of the cigars JP had brought me, the kind we weren't allowed to have in this country. I opened the bottle of Pernod, also a gift from them, poured some in a tumbler and added water and ice. They knew I liked that licorice-flavored drink.

The slip where the singlehander had been was empty. I didn't know anybody in the marina and I didn't feel like talking. There was no one in the Laundromat on the premises when I went to wash my clothes and later, while they were in the dryer, I took a shower. In the evening I sat at the sushi bar where Susi, JP and I had had lunch the day before we sailed to Bimini. Now, it was a lonely place.

When I thought they must have arrived at Julia's home in Queens, I made a call from the phone booth at the harbormaster's office. Julia answered. "Haló?"

"Hi, are they there yet?" I was not very talkative.

"Si, aqui están. Here is Susi."

She came to the phone. "Dad, we are talking about the trip and everything. It was great, we already forgot all about the bad weather. We had a great time."

"Good, so did I. I'm lonely, now. How is Julie? Did she and Mom get along?"

"Oh, fine. No problem. We are flying back to Paris day after tomorrow."

"Okay, Susi, take care. Talk to you soon. Bye."

On 29 April I went back to Stuart. It was an easy sail offshore to Palm Beach although in the logbook I mentioned twice that it was a very cold night and that I wore gloves. The east wind was perfect. Under full sail, *TRITON 3* came through Lake Worth inlet. Without stopping, I continued north along the Intracoastal. This is a boring stretch of the waterway, especially the long Hobe Sound. That morning, however, I was able to sail and had to use the engine only to negotiate the several bridges. In the evening, thirty hours after I left Miamarina, I was back 'home' in Stuart. I found a good place to anchor near the town dock, south of the Roosevelt Bridge. That evening I did not go to Mahony's Oyster Bar. I was tired and did not yet feel like talking to people.

On the weekend I saw Brent and Debra. They were going sailing in their Morgan, which they had named *LAURENA*, after their daughter Lauren. They stopped briefly at my boat, asked how my trip was and whether I would like to go sailing with them, which I declined.

Lauren was five or six years old and Debra was expecting another child. They were buying a bigger house. Short on money for the closing, Brent struck a deal with me. He had just finished restoring a Chevrolet El Camino, a model I liked very much, and I agreed to buy it for a reasonable price. He had done an excellent job. The car was in top condition and looked brand new in shiny maroon color. Brent and Debra bought the house, and I was the proud owner of a much-admired El Camino Super Sport.

Shortly after they moved into the new house, Debra had another baby daughter. Then it happened that Brent had an accident on the job. I don't think he was seriously injured, but for a long time he was out of work. A half year later they suddenly came into a lot of money and I didn't see them quite so often any more. *LAURENA* was no longer anchored where I had kept an eye on her. I did not make an effort to keep in touch with them, but one day, after a long time, the whole family, including a Black Labrador, came by in their new motorboat, a thirty-six foot cabin cruiser. That was the last time I saw them.

THE BAHAMAS

In Bimini, Susi had said to me, "Dad, I'm having nightmares seeing you on the foredeck, hanking on the jib or taking down the Genoa, hanging on for dear life in all kinds of weather, day or night, alone on the boat. I want you to get roller-furling." Before we said goodbye in Miami, she asked me again, "Dad, please get roller-furling."

The idea of rolling up the headsail without having to leave the cockpit has seemed to me something a Sunday sailor might want. For a serious ocean cruiser, however, roller-furling is not just to make sailing easier, or more comfortable, it is a safety device. Balancing on the pounding and swaying foredeck, struggling with a big sail, is a perilous job, especially with no one else on board.

Susi was right. I knew she was right. Even wearing a harness, I could slip and go overboard. Without the help from a shipmate, how would I get back on the boat? It has sometimes scared the hell out of me, just thinking about it.

I went to Mack Sails, a renowned sail maker in Stuart, and consulted the experts about a roller-furling system for my boat. They recommended Harken, a well-known brand, and on 15 May, I had *TRITON 3* outfitted with roller-furling. I docked at the old town dock. A Mack Sails truck delivered the equipment, and two of their mechanics had come to install it. I also bought a new Genoa with it. The whole thing came to about two thousand dollars.

I sailed on the St. Lucie River, trying out my newly acquired equipment: furling, reefing, unfurling—it was a breeze! This was one of the best and most important addition to the boat and I was very happy with it. My next voyage would be so much easier and safer. I couldn't wait to be out there again and getting all the benefits from it.

I was eager to undertake a longer trip in the Bahamas. Two years earlier I had come through the Bahamas from the Virgin Islands and the Dominican Republic, without lingering anywhere, except on Eleuthera. Then I had been on a mission, had to get to New York for my daughter's wedding.

In the evening of 16 June, in preparation for my next voyage, I took up my anchors and moved *TRITON 3* to the town dock. I had always left my anchors hooked up to a mooring ball when I sailed away for a day or overnight. Undisturbed for six weeks since my return from Key West and Fort Myers, the chains and lines had gathered a lot of barnacles and slimy, green weeds. They needed a thorough cleaning. With a mild steel brush and a bucketful of chlorine solution I went to work on the hundred plus feet of chain and nylon rope, a messy and tiresome job, and then left them out to dry.

In the morning I was happy to stow the clean and fresh smelling gear in the chain locker in the bow. By eight a m I left the dock and headed for the Intracoastal Waterway to go south to Palm Beach. I took fuel at the Riviera Beach Municipal Marina in the afternoon and, as it was only three o'clock, I decided to go on to Miami. There was a brief shower as I came through the inlet to the open ocean, but from then on the weather was fine for the rest of the day and through the night. The wind had been light and I didn't get to the Miamarina before noon.

I allowed myself the luxury of twenty-four hours in the marina at Bay Shore, but then I sailed to Biscayne Bay and anchored in the lee of Key Biscayne. There were three other boats, far apart in this open anchorage, protected only toward the east. Across the wide expanse of the bay is Coconut Grove, the Rickenbacker Causeway to the north, and to the south the continuation of the Intracoastal Waterway to Key Largo and beyond.

I had a vague, flexible plan for my Bahama trip. At Bimini I would go through the entry formalities. On weekends, Bahamian Customs and Immigration charge a fee for clearing vessels and issuing cruising permits. It was 19 June, a Friday. I decided not to leave before Sunday night.

On Saturday morning I went for a swim to scrape barnacles off the hull and the propeller, as far as that was possible without putting my head under water. I tend to get claustrophobic, with or without a mask, and snorkeling is out of the question for me. I can just reach the propeller, my mouth and nose above water like a turtle.

I became impatient. I could not wait any longer. At one o'clock on Sunday I got my anchors up and motored along the shore of Key Biscayne through the well-marked channel. At Cape Florida, the southern tip of Key Biscayne, I followed the buoys across the reef to the open ocean. Steering southeast, to allow for the Gulf Steam, which ran at about three knots, I had perfect wind and moderate seas. Within an hour after passing the reef, I had crossed the busy shipping lane, making five and half to six knots. This is too fast! At a quarter to ten at night I saw the lights of Bimini. I was on a perfect approach, only too early.

By midnight I anchored near the entrance channel to Alicetown, about a mile off shore. As long as I was underway, I was hardly aware of the effect the little waves had on the boat, but stopped dead in the water, the wavelets of a foot or less, made me think I was in a hammock, on a swing, or on a see-saw. My daughter used to call these conditions rolley-polley—she had an expression for everything.

Six hours of rolley-polley, and I had enough of it. I lost my patience and proceeded into the harbor. At six thirty I tied up at Weech's and filled out the Customs form Jerry, the dock attendant, handed me. I walked the short distance to the Customs house. The clerk charged me fifteen dollars for having arrived before office hours, which are, as I learned, from eight a m to five p m. Then I walked down the road to the low Government building that houses the Immigration office, besides post office and police station. Here I had to pay fourteen dollars. My ignorance and lack of patience had cost me dearly.

Twenty-nine dollars! No use beating yourself on the head with it. Sometimes you have to pay for experience. I got over it and left Weech's to anchor out. There were only a few boats and I took up the first spot past the Fishing Club docks, opposite the official building. There is no dinghy dock at Alicetown and no beach to pull up a dinghy. At a concrete wall someone had tied a few rungs of a ladder to a protruding metal spike, which facilitated getting ashore, especially at low tide. I had a little, one-pound folding anchor, which I used to keep the stern of the dinghy away from the shallows and the outboard motor from getting stuck in the mud. Alicetown is a rustic place. Here nothing is done to welcome the cruising sailor who prefers to anchor, instead of renting dock space. On the other hand, nobody bothers those who are too cheap to pay for dockage or like the privacy of the anchorage. This was not the Tidewater Marina in Portsmouth, Virginia. This was "The Islands". Nobody cares. No problem, mon.

The anchorage shoals quickly toward the town side and there are numerous large and small rocks. On the other side, where Chalks seaplanes take off and land, is not much room before the wide expanse of shallows, which often dry at low tide. The land behind it is so flat that it gives no protection against the winds coming from the northeast and east.

The holding ground at a depth of eight to twelve feet was good. The strong tidal current and fierce winds that often come over the flat eastern part of North Bimini, make it necessary to set two anchors.

Alicetown, located on the southern tip of North Bimini, overlapping a portion of South Bimini, has an asphalt road on the harbor side. All the activities of any interest to sailors or tourists who come through Bimini, take place on this main road, about the length of a mile.

At the southern end is the "airport". I liked to watch the arrival of the big flying boats as they come out of the water and power up the ramp. Usually, some two dozen tourists arrive and another two dozen are waiting to board for departure to Nassau, or back to Miami. The arrival building is about the size of a small clinic or doctor's office. An Immigration official stamps passports and says, "Welcome to the Bahamas" to the new arrivals. In the shed, a Customs agent checks a list against the baggage, while porters of the few hotels and boarding houses are busy sorting the bags and suitcases. There are a few taxis and minivans on the island.

The Customs house is about at the halfway point of the mile-long road. Behind the Customs house is the commercial port with a shed and a sort of plaza for goods to be loaded or unloaded. Bahamian freighters, for instance *BIMINI MACK*, dock here once or twice a week, and on such days this place turns into a frantic frenzy. Trucks and pickups, cars and motorbikes with trailers maneuver among piles of boxes, crates and pallets of merchandise. Checkers with clipboards count cargo and at the same time try to answer the questions of receivers of goods. The noise is deafening. In the middle of this confusion, women and children offer drinks and ices colored with fruit juices, conch salad and fried pork or chicken. Dogs scurry around, looking for something edible.

There is a narrow sidewalk on either side of this main street, lined with rustic restaurants and bars, small grocery shops and souvenir stands. Toward the northern end are the Government House, the power plant and finally the telephone office. The road continues northward into the residential area, which is of little or no interest to visitors on the island.

A number of side streets, perpendicular to the main road, cross a steep hill and a residential street, and end at the beach on the ocean side. Facing west, there is nothing but fifty nautical miles of ocean that separates these Islands in the Stream from Miami. This ocean, however, is not standing still; for thousands of years it is moving steadily northward at a speed of two and a half to three and a half knots—the Gulf Stream.

I liked Bimini, and I felt as if I were slowly becoming one of the residents in Alicetown. I had, however, set my mind on Nassau, the capital of the Bahamas, and prepared for my departure. On 25 June, 1992, at six thirty in the morning, I started to bring up my anchors. I had trouble with the second one, the Danforth, which had lodged itself partially under a rock. I could see the chain and the anchor whose one fluke was jammed. I maneuvered the boat around to where I believed I could break the anchor loose by going forward full power. I gave the chain some slack and drove the boat full speed ahead. The bow went down, then sprang up like a cheetah after a prey. Just at the moment this happened, I thought, I either break out the anchor, or I lose the cleat to which the chain was fastened on deck. The cleat held and good old *TRITON 3* was the victor over the rock.

Anchor and chain on deck, I made my way past the commercial port, the docks with the deep-sea sport fishing boats and the marinas, and exited the harbor. After reaching the deep water, I hoisted the main sail and rolled out the Genoa. I headed for North Rock from where the Grand Bahama Bank opens eastward, allowing vessels with a draft under six feet to cross.

I was on my way to Nassau on Providence Island and turned to enter the Bank at North Rock. No longer in the lee of Bimini, I encountered a strong southeast wind and found it difficult to achieve reasonable progress. I made a quick decision to reverse course. Back to Alicetown; try another day. Nonsense, I just left the place, made all that effort with the anchor. Stick with the plan, go for it. Another quick decision. If I can't go east, I can go north to Freeport or any other place on Grand Bahama Island. What do I care, where I go? Get back on course, bypass North Rock and keep going.

This back and forth cost me about two hours, but that didn't matter to me. What bothered me, was my being indecisive. I usually did not waver, once I had made a decision. This was something new to me. Is this a weakness, or am I becoming more flexible, less rigid? I decided it was the latter; I was loosening up, becoming more like my friend Frank Gallardo. Go where the wind blows you. Well, that didn't mean I had to become a vagabond.

At the Moselle Bank it began to drizzle; a refreshing, light rain. I got my foul weather jacket, didn't need it yet, so I put it in the cockpit and closed the cabin hatch. Southwest of Isaac, the lighthouse in sight, I looked in the cruising guide for alternative harbors on Grand Bahama, since Freeport is commercial and perhaps not an attractive port.

When I looked up, an enormous, blue-black cloud came rolling toward me from the east, low over the water, which had turned into liquid lead. I sprang to the mast to take down the main. I had no time to tie it down on the boom. A gust hit me like a powerful fist. Hail pelted me, blinded me.

The sail blew out. My Genoa was still up. Back in the cockpit, I started to roll it in. It got stuck, fouled with the main halyard. There had been no time to belay it on the cleat. I let the sail fly for fear of being capsized, steered downwind to reduce the pressure on the beam and started the Diesel to improve steerage.

I was unaware of the thunder lost in the howling storm and the wildly luffing remnants of my mainsail. I did not notice the lightning bolts, was only preoccupied with keeping the boat from being knocked down.

Forty-five minutes later it was as if nothing had happened, except I was thoroughly shaken. The sea had not enough time to build and remained relatively calm. It turned cold; I was soaked; the foul weather jacket had remained where I put it. The mainsail was in tatters. The entire leach had separated from the body of the sail. Three of the four battens were missing. My brand new Genoa had suffered a tear at the clew, the grommet all but torn out. I turned off the engine, busied myself with clearing the halyard from the Genoa and tied my badly torn mainsail to the boom. Then I went back on my course for Freeport. A steady east wind blew at fifteen to eighteen knots. With my still serviceable Genoa I sped toward Freeport. By five in the afternoon I made landfall.

I continued along the south shore of Grand Bahama past Lucaya. The next haven was Xanadu, an expensive resort and yacht harbor. There was still enough daylight to make it to the Running Mon Marina. I called the marina on the radio for information how to enter the unmarked channel and asked if dock space was available.

"Come on in, straight forward. We got room for you." Welcome words.

I tied *TRITON 3* safely to the dock. It was like coming home after having been lost in a blizzard. I still could hardly believe what had happened in such a short time and felt like a changed man, in love with his boat, which had saved him.

There was a canteen on the premises. I had something to drink and a snack. Daylight was gone and the illumination in the yacht basin was not good. All marina personnel seemed to have left. I didn't know where the bathrooms were, so I showered on the boat and then sat in the cockpit. If this had happened on the trip with JP and Susi… Don't think about it.

I wrote in the logbook:

"15:00 T-storm. Gusts est. 60 kn. Hail. Main torn, Genoa light damage. 16:00 SE wind 15 kn."

The following two days I occupied myself with the repair of the mainsail and the Genoa. The leach, the aft edge of the main, had to be reattached. In several places I used new

157

Dacron material to replace or reinforce the sail where it was too badly shredded. I created two new batten pockets. The third one I could repair and the bottom pocket had remained intact. All the reef points had to be replaced. Every one of the quarter inch lines was frayed and completely unraveled. Once before I have had to repair the mainsail, but this time the damage was far worse.

Sitting on the cabin roof with my sail repair kit, I spread the sails out over the deck. Rain showers or thunderstorm downpours interrupted my work periodically. After finishing with the main, I started on the Genoa. There was not much work on it, but the brand new material was stiff and it was difficult to get a needle through the double and triple layers at the strongest corner of the sail, the clew. The stainless steel grommet was okay. I did have a sail maker's leather palm, the curved needles and the bee's wax for the thread, but I am no expert in sail repair and my hands were raw and swollen for days afterwards.

In a work shed at the marina, I found some wooden strips, which I could cut to the right lengths and use as battens. They were too stiff to my liking, but I was lucky to have at least those. I had started to cut up a plastic container to fashion some sort of battens but that material was much too flexible and would hardly have done any good.

On 27 June late in the afternoon, I sailed out of Running Mon harbor for a night passage to the North Berry Islands. The wind was good and I could sail a close-hauled course for Great Stirrup Cay.

Constant flashes of heat lightning were all over the night sky. By midnight, in the North West Providence Channel, I crossed the busy shipping lane and from then on there was wall-to-wall thunderstorms. I had taken in the sails early and proceeded under power; I didn't take any chances, especially with my weakened mainsail, although I thought I had done a pretty good repair job.

Before dawn I made out the steady red light on a tall antenna mast at Great Stirrup Cay, the northern end of the Berries, while thunder continued to rumble into the morning hours. At noon I motored into Great Harbor and put my CQR down near the little island of Goat Cay. Nearby was a local smack at anchor from which the delicious aroma of smoking fish came drifting over to me. There were a few other yachts anchored distant from one another and from me in this spacious harbor.

I enjoyed a leisurely day, but it was the season for thunderstorms and at night a fierce one hit while I was at anchor. Gusts broke in half the PVC rod that steadied the canvas awning over the cockpit. I had been too lazy to take it down before going to bed. The heavy downpour obscured everything around me. Goat Cay, the fishing smack, the other boats—nothing to orient myself by. In the morning I found that I had dragged at least half a mile. Luckily, I had enough room.

Early in the morning I set out for Little Harbor. I had read in the cruising guide of this remote, not frequently visited 'little harbor', which seemed to me just the place I would like. Located in the Middle Berries, it was an easy day sail from Great Harbor. The morning was sunny and hot. The wind was perfect for a beam reach. Without over-stressing the sails, I unreefed the main and used the full Genoa. At a constant speed of six knots, I arrived in the early afternoon at Little Harbor. Surrounded by a rugged, rocky landscape with rich green vegetation, the snug anchorage had room for three boats, and two were already there.

Dark clouds had gathered and just as I had my two anchors in place, the afternoon thunderstorm came down on me. That was no surprise; every day it was the same scenario: morning sunshine, hot by noon, sultry and humid in the afternoon, then gathering clouds and thunderstorms continuing into the night.

In the morning, I inflated my dinghy to pay a visit to Chester and Brenda, the two people who lived in two separate houses on a hill. At the foot of the hill was a short wooden dock. Steep steps led to a little plateau. The wooden houses did not appear to be more than shacks, but Chester and Brenda lived in unexpected comfort, with refrigerator and freezer, satellite TV and cozy amenities. Behind the two houses, separated by a little vegetable patch, was a small power plant, sufficient to serve both of them. Chester sold me a six-pack of Budweiser for twelve bucks and Brenda prepared a delicious conch salad. Brenda also baked a bread for me, to be picked up the next morning.

Some people from the other boats joined us and we all spent most of the day with Chester and Brenda on their hill, chickens and piglets running about. There was a picnic table and benches. We ate and drank and talked mostly about the weather, boats and sailing, but also about people we had met here or there while cruising in the islands.

"What do you do?" someone asked Brenda and Chester. "How do you make a living here?"

We learned that they lived here only six months of the year. "Another two people come here for the other half year. We live part-time here and in Nassau."

"And what do you do for a living?" someone else insisted.

"We own a business in Nassau," Chester said, walking away. Obviously, he did not want to say more.

"It's less than two hours to Nassau in the fast boat with the outboard you saw tied up down there," Brenda added. "We also visit people on the other islands. We like it here."

We did not find out more about them, nor why they didn't live in one house, and what they did or didn't do together. They revealed no emotional or physical involvement with each other. They could be cousins, brother and sister or just friends. Perhaps they would have answered, if we had asked, but we left it at that.

After two nights at Little Harbor, I sailed out of the place on an easterly course. I continued far enough on that tack to get a good angle on the wind for Nassau. There was only a light breeze and I resisted the temptation to turn on the engine. Even if I arrived at Nassau in the night, I should be able to find my way into the harbor. The biggest cruise ships enter this port, so the approach had to be well marked.

At last I discovered the sea buoy around midnight, lowered my sails and motored into Nassau, following the buoys. In the Bahamas, the US system of Aids to Navigation is in use. Red-Right-Returning: red buoys on starboard as you come in.

With Paradise Island to port and huge, white cruise ships on starboard, it was exciting to arrive at this largest seaport of the Bahamas in the dead of night. The city behind the towering passenger liners seemed dwarfed. It was totally dark on the water. I had no idea, how or where to find a place to anchor.

On the Paradise Island side I saw a large sailboat, which seemed to be at anchor. I approached carefully, only to discover that it was in fact at the head of a long pier sticking out from the shore. The pier was in complete darkness and I almost rammed right into it. After that scary moment, I didn't have enough guts to explore any further. I dropped the CQR, my main anchor, in seventeen feet of water and kept vigilance through the rest of the night. To stay awake and alert, I had coffee and thick slices of Brenda's delicious Bahamian coconut bread.

In the morning, a guy in a motorboat came by. He waved a friendly Hello.

"Good morning," I yelled and signaled him to come over. "Where do boats usually anchor in Nassau?"

"You're okay here, but most of the boats are over there," he waved his arm to the other side of the harbor. "Near BASRA, you know?"

I was familiar with BASRA, the Bahama Air and Sea Rescue Association, but I didn't know its location. "Where?" I asked.

"Straight across. Don't you see all those masts?"

I saw them. "Ah, now I see them! Okay, yeah, thanks a lot."

"You can also anchor a little farther up on this side, near Club Med. Some people like it there. I work at Club Med."

"Thanks. I might," but I wanted to be closer to the city, see what Nassau was like.

I found a good spot for *TRITON 3* near a dinghy dock among two or three dozen yachts. Next to the dinghy dock was a ramp for launching boats or even seaplanes that belonged to a boat yard or perhaps to BASRA.

Nassau had the appearance of a colonial port city, some of the buildings reminding of past glory and wealth. The principal commercial street, a block or two away from the waterfront, was crowded with local shoppers as well as tourists from several cruise ships. Clothing stores and souvenir shops, liquor stores, camera, jewelry and perfume retailers, restaurants, bars and an occasional local eatery line this busy street.

As I walked up side streets, I noticed that with every block farther away from the main street the city took on more run-down characteristics. With a park here and a memorial or monument there, poverty and neglect replaced the splendor of centuries past.

The Rainbow Bridge connects Nassau with Paradise Island. Underneath, on the city side, is Potter Cay, the docking place for the island traders. Bahamian freighters unload produce, meat and fish for local consumption. It is a colorful, lively place, a little like Bimini's commercial pier, albeit more orderly. There is a large market hall for wholesale and retail businesses.

On Potter Cay I ate fresh conch salad, concocted at one of the stands as I looked on, and I bought a snapper, which I took home and prepared in my galley.

On my second day in Nassau, I ferried water back to the boat. Across the street from BASRA was a birdbath with a pump, originally probably used to water horses. For fear that my plastic bottles might be stolen if left unattended, I took only four of them at a time to the pump. I filled them, carried them to the dinghy and went back to the pump with four more bottles. With twelve full bottles in the dinghy, I went back to the boat, emptied them into the tank and repeated the procedure twice more. That's a day's work, as far as I am concerned. Time for some serious sundowners.

On the Fourth of July, only two days after my arrival in Nassau, I felt the need to be out there again. Like The Flying Dutchman, I have to keep moving, restlessly and forever. I called the Nassau Harbor Control on the VHF to report my departure. This is either a courtesy or a requirement, I am not sure. I had not reported my arrival because at the time I did not know that I should. It didn't make a difference. I headed for Chub Cay, South Berry Islands. Chub is famous for sport fishing and there is an exclusive club adjacent to the boat basin.

There were some low clouds, some grumbling thunder in the distance, even light rain, but the general conditions were good. I made landfall in mid-afternoon, had Whale Cay and Bird Cay in sight, and at six thirty I anchored in the crescent cove inside Chub Point, a beautiful place with a white sand beach and white sand under the keel.

After a full day of enjoying this tranquil environment, relaxing, sunbathing and swimming, with only one other boat anchored close to the beach, I motored into the boat basin of Chub Club for lunch. I docked to fill up with fuel, went into the club's bar and asked for a conch salad and a beer, which came to the outrageous price of ten dollars. On leaving the fuel dock I misjudged, or rather did not see, a pile standing three feet from the dock and *TRITON 3* rammed it head on. Due to the slow speed, just coming off the dock, the damage was minimal. The bow pulpit was slightly pushed back with the result that my port lifeline, attached to the pulpit, had become slack. No big deal, but I hated to make such a mistake, and the attendant was watching.

Shamefaced, I left Chub, rounded Mama Rhoda Rock and took up my course for Northwest Channel Light. In a mild breeze, thunderstorms threatening in the hot, sultry afternoon air, I motor-sailed at a speed of barely five knots.

This part of the Bahamian territory, known as the Tongue of the Ocean, is the deepest water in this part of the world. Amidst the shallow depths of the Bahamas (Baja Mar, Spanish for shallow sea) is this deep gorge on the ocean floor, reaching depths of fourteen hundred fathoms, or 8,400 feet.

At the steel structure, marked on the chart as the Northwest Channel Light, the depth of several thousand feet changes within a few yards to only twelve to fifteen feet. What that steep wall down there must look like!

All shipping converges on this spot, and then again spreads out over the bank. The northerly route leads to Isaac Light via the Mackie Shoal; the central route passes south of Mackie to North Rock and Bimini; the third route goes via Russel Light, across the Bank, to Cat Cay and Gun Cay. Most recreational boaters use this route. I chose the one for North Rock and Bimini.

By midnight, Russel Light showed at a distance on port and at two thirty I had Mackie Shoal to starboard. I was sailing at a slow pace in light air. As dawn crept up in the east, a thunderstorm formed behind me. Before sunrise, looking back, I saw the frightening shape of a waterspout. The logbook reads:

"From a black cloud a funnel extended downward, like a garden hose, in the shape of a question mark, into the sea. I started the engine, ran at full throttle. Looking back every few seconds, the 'garden hose' coming after me, I kept steering a straight course, not knowing which way this phenomenon would go. Lightning was striking from the leading edge of the thunderhead. Ten minutes of helpless terror passed, then the waterspout dissipated, separating in the middle and blending into the background."

It was a bone rattling, teeth grinding, goose-bump causing experience.

Later, at Weech's dock in Alicetown, I told Jerry, the dock attendant, what I had seen. "What do you think would have happened, if the waterspout had caught up with me?" I asked him.

"I think you would have died," Jerry said in the calmest of island voices.

I stayed one night at Weech's and then sailed back to Miami. At Miamarina I paid five dollars for three hours at the dock, enough time for a lunch of sushi at Bay Shore, and informed Customs of my return. Via Biscayne Bay and Cape Florida, I sailed once again out into the ocean and arrived back home at the Roosevelt Bridge in Stuart on 11 July in the afternoon.

HURRICANE ANDREW 24 AUGUST, 1992

Michael Mahony always closed his Oyster Bar in the summer for several weeks. Every year in August he pilgrimaged to Milwaukee for the Irish Fest. I had come back from my Bahama trip on 11 July, a few days before Michael's summer vacation.

I could hardly believe that I was away for only three weeks. All that had happened did not seem to fit in such a short time. My arrival in Bimini in record time; the storm near Isaac Light; Running Mon Marina; Little Harbor with Chester and Brenda; Nassau; Chub Cay; the waterspout on Grand Bahama Bank, to name only a few highlights of my solo trip in the Bahamas. Michael was an eager listener.

I presented Sara with the finished poem, *Ballad of an Old Sailor*. She, too, was leaving Stuart, while the Oyster Bar was closed. Sara traveled to her native Mexico where she still had family. On her return, a month later, and after reopening the bar, she told me she had read the poem on the plane. "That was so sweet, thank you," she said and gave me a little peck on the cheek. I was happy that she liked the poem, which I had dedicated to her. Ever since, when I thought of her or spoke of her, I referred to her as the Mermaid.

TRITON 3 was in excellent condition. I re-examined the stitching on the mainsail and made some improvements. The Dacron cloth was strong and I did not need a new sail right away, but I replaced the temporary battens with new ones, made of varnished teak. I brought the still almost new Genoa to Mack Sails for professional mending.

Shortly before my Bahama trip, I had installed new deep cycle batteries. I did some regular maintenance work, like oil and filter changes. When it came to the engine's water pump, which showed a slow leak, I decided to install a new one. That was all the mechanical work I had to do, but I did not stop there. I varnished the entire interior mahogany woodwork and then proceeded to replace the hinges on all the doors, twenty-two pairs of shiny brass hinges.

With the exception of a few daysails on the St. Lucie and Indian rivers, I remained at anchor. My El Camino was a pleasure to drive and made it easy for me to get my purchases and provisioning done. I also undertook trips, alone or with friends, to explore the wider environs of Stuart and the St. Lucie, Palm Beach and Indian River counties, as well as Okeechobee. I sampled restaurants and bars, things I would not have been able to do without the car.

I had no intention to undertake another major voyage so soon. What I didn't want, though, was to sit at anchor and let the barnacles enjoy themselves covering every square inch of hull and keel, propeller and rudder. A moving boat does not collect barnacles, like a rolling stone gathers no moss.

On 18 August, I felt the time was right to go on a little trip. Without a plan, without a real destination other than somewhere south, I got my two anchors on deck and tied up at the city dock. It was a hell of a job washing the slime off line and chain, and then rinsing the muck from the deck.

The Roosevelt Bridge opened at eight fifteen and I went through. Without any wind, I motored along the Intracoastal and reached Palm Beach early in the afternoon. Not feeling tired, I continued without stopping through the Lake Worth inlet to open water. It was a sweltering afternoon; the wind was calm, the sea heaving lazily in a slow rhythm. I searched for a puff of air. There was none.

On the weather radio I heard something about a tropical storm far out in the Atlantic, five hundred miles east of the Antilles. It was the first one of the season. They had named it Andrew.

I continued moseying on down to Miami. Huh, I had to chuckle. Mosey on down was one of Lynn's latest expressions. The ocean was lazy, the boat was lazy, I was lazy—it would be another hot and lazy day. My mainsail remained under the cover, the Genoa rolled up. The Diesel did all the work, all the way from Stuart to Miami, without complaining.

It was August the 19th, my father's birthday. He had died almost ten years ago. He was a sailor, too, but I never had the chance to sail with him. I had told my father, after the war, about the day his boat appeared at the club in Rostock and that I had sailed it. At that time he had been in Norway, a captain in the Wehrmacht. Too many things, bad things, had happened by the time I tried to talk to him about his boat, his sailing experiences, his better years. My father no longer wanted an emotional connection with those much happier times of his life. I think it was too painful for him to remember.

At last Miami. I docked at the Miamarina for three hours, had lunch at the sushi bar in the market place of Bay Shore and then went on to anchor at Key Biscayne. The radio gave Andrew's position and predicted that the storm, if continuing its course and forward motion, would reach Florida in four to five days. On 20 August, hurricane watch was extended to the Bahamas and Florida's East coast. The area most likely to receive the brunt of the storm was between the Keys and Cape Canaveral.

It is a gamble: where would I be safer, here in Biscayne Bay, farther south, maybe Marathon; or in Stuart, perhaps even farther north? It was almost certain that Andrew would make landfall somewhere in south Florida. Should I toss a coin?

By some inclination, something like an instinct, I got underway at four in the afternoon on the 20th. Instead of taking the route through Miami's harbor and Government Cut, I chose the faster way around Cape Florida and out into the ocean. The wind was at five to ten knots from the east. The Gulf Stream seemed to be running at a very slow pace, almost not moving at all. I had never experienced that before. At the Municipal Marina in Riviera Beach I took on fuel not to get caught in a storm with my tank half empty. I arrived in Stuart twenty-four hours after I had weighed anchor in Biscayne Bay.

By then, Andrew had been upgraded to a category three hurricane.

The Stuart anchorage was no place to be in any bad weather, let alone a hurricane. I listened to the plans other sailors had. "We'll head up into the North Fork and put lines to the trees," somebody said. "I find it safest in the Boondocks, in the South Fork, among the mangroves," said another. I had a different idea. One guess was as good as another.

In the afternoon of 22 August, I left the anchorage and headed for the Palm City Bridge, and went on to the St. Lucie

Lock. In the event that Andrew's center would hit the area between Palm Beach and Port St. Lucie, the lock would remain closed to prevent a storm surge in the canal. Only a few boats were waiting at the lock when I arrived. Once past the lock, I continued for about a mile, looking for a spot offering the best protection from strong winds.

Rocks lined the canal. There were some trees close to the edge. Behind the tress I suspected orange groves. I stopped the boat near the bank on the right side, put one precautionary hook down and inflated the dinghy. I carried my CQR on a long line and fifty feet of chain across the canal, far past the middle. This was to be my main protection from the southerly quadrant. Climbing up the rocks on the near side, I tied two strong lines to trees, some fifty feet apart. My main Danforth went forward on a hundred feet of chain and line, and my auxiliary out over the transom. Every time a boat passed my position, I slackened the line that went across the canal almost to the other side. A tugboat came along and I let the line drop to the bottom. The tug's powerful screw, if it caught my anchor line, would certainly swing me around and take me in tow.

The sun was intense, the wind light from the northeast. After sundown it became gusty and later a thunderstorm developed. In the hours past midnight the sky cleared and in the total darkness of my surrounding, I could see a million stars. There was no indication that a major hurricane was coming this way. I remained vigilant throughout the night, observing every change in wind and weather. For this Monday morning, the forecast was wind gusts of up to seventy-five knots. Andrew was now a major hurricane.

24 August, 1992. I wrote in my notebook:

"Am I on the right side of the canal? Shouldn't I be on the other side? If the wind comes around to the east, I will depend only on my lightest Danforth. The wind is shifting. Too late now to make any changes. 1:30 to 2:00 thunderstorm with gusts, estimated at 25 knots. Heavy shower. I am okay, not even a lot of stress on the anchor lines. 3:00 to 4:00 another shower with gusty wind, then calm. 5:00 p m. Andrew makes landfall 25 miles south of downtown Miami, near Homestead. I don't know where that is; don't know Miami very well. Heaviest gusts in

thunderstorm. Heavy downpour. Tornado watch till noon tomorrow. Rainsqualls through the night, the strongest gusts at 40 knots, wind shifting more toward the south. 25 Aug. – Still raining, less gusty. In the afternoon the first breaks in the clouds. Tornado watch extended to 8 p.m."

In the afternoon it was safe for me to return to Stuart. The anticipation of the storm was more frightening than the storm itself, but that was hindsight. Andrew could just as well have hit the Stuart area. In that case I would probably no longer have had a boat. Where I thought I might be safe, a tree could have come down on me, or the boat could have been smashed on the rocks so perilously close on one side. What it all came down to, was luck. If I had decided to stay in Biscayne Bay... Unthinkable.

I anchored in my old spot, or close to it. Only boats unable to move had remained in the anchorage. Most had suffered minor damages. One derelict boat without mast or engine had washed up on the rocks at Shepard Park. It was the only total loss. Little by little, boats returned to the anchorage.

For a long time Andrew continued to be the topic of conversations.

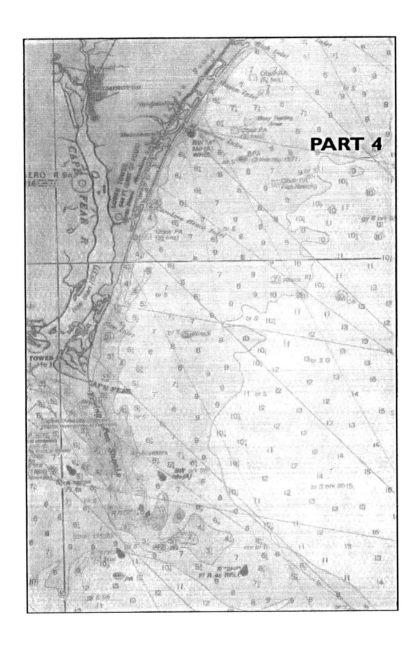

PART 4

PARADISE BECKONS

While Andrew was being discussed and commented on for days in Stuart, this hurricane had a much longer lasting effect on the area that received the direct impact. The devastation on Key Biscayne and Homestead was especially severe. The Dinner Key Marina was destroyed; most of the anchored boats there were total losses. Miamarina in downtown Miami had suffered serious damage and remained closed for a long time.

Andrew was the only major hurricane of the 1992 season, as I recall it. On 29 September, my logbook mentions tropical Storm Earl, which linked up with a cold front off Florida's East coast on 2 October. This storm came down the Florida peninsula with strong winds and heavy rain. Unsettled weather with tornado watches and record cold nights lasted through the first week of October.

On 16 October I left the anchorage to take *TRITON 3* to the Woodscove Marina at the Palm City Bridge for one-month dockage. I drove to New York to say goodbye to family and friends, for I was going back to paradise

The wish to make the Virgin Islands my home has been smoldering on my brain ever since I left the Caribbean more than two and a half years ago. I was determined to make the voyage alone, through the Bahamas.

The latest addition to my electronics inventory was the GPS, the Global Positioning System. These incredible new navigational instruments were developed for the military, but had recently found their way into the commercial and recreational realm. My SatNav had given me good service for six years, but was lately less than reliable. Old satellites were no longer replaced, and the SatNav gave fewer readings and at longer intervals. Sometimes I had to wait hours to get a fix, and that usually occurred when I most needed a position. Then the instrument started to turn itself on. I turned it off; a minute later it was on again. When I received information on the LCD screen that was completely out of whack, it was time to chuck it. Time for a GPS.

Those instruments were still rather new for the general public, and therefore expensive. Obviously, the prices would come down eventually, but I needed one now. I paid eight hundred dollars in November of '92 for my Garmin "GPS 50", a handheld device. A year later the same instrument sold for hundred fifty, and then I saw it advertised for ninety-nine dollars, because the model was discontinued. Too bad, but what the hell, I needed it.

I prepared for my voyage to the Caribbean, bought provisions in mass quantity, for which I had plenty of room since I converted one half of the fo'c'sle into storage space. The boat was ready, I was ready, but the weather was not. Until the beginning of December, one cold front chased another. When the weather improved, I came down with a cold, the flu or a strep throat. No, not again! Like November of '89, in the Chesapeake and the ICW, with Jon Reeve. I waited this one out until I felt well enough and left Stuart on 28 December in restored health, eager to go.

My GPS gave me great satisfaction. Once I had it programmed, the instrument gave my position instantly. I learned to put in waypoints and could see when I was off course and by how much. It registered speed, distance and time to destination. The instrument updated information constantly and the accuracy was amazing. My GPS was a toy as much as the most sophisticated instrument.

Lynn was in Miami to celebrate New Year's Eve at her daughter's. "Peter, give me a call when you get down here, so we can get together," she told me on the phone.

"Sure, I'll call you when I'm in Miami," I promised.

I remembered New Year's Eve a year ago at Julia's home in Queens. I had flown to New York for the holidays. JP, Susi and Julie had come from Paris. My brother-in-law and Fay were there. Carlos was away with his friends.

Lynn had called from Connecticut. "I will be in New York this afternoon. I would love to see all of you. Could you pick me up at Grand Central at three fifteen?" She invited herself for coffee into Julia's home. "I have to be back in Norwalk this evening," she added.

I picked her up at the corner of Park and 42nd Street, and I drove back to Queens with her. She was no stranger; everybody knew her from Susi's wedding. It became an entertaining kaffeeklatsch, Lynn quite at home, telling story after story.

"Lynn, when is your train leaving?" I reminded her. Didn't she say, she had to be back home in the evening?

Later again, "You have your schedule? When is your last train?" No reaction. She kept on telling stories. Something about her father, who had been an engineer on a merchant vessel. Some adventure he had in Brooklyn at one time. Very funny stories, most likely made up or at least enhanced. She knew how to spin a fascinating yarn. Midnight came, Champagne corks popped. Lynn showed no signs of fatigue.

In the basement was a spare bedroom, actually a small apartment with bathroom and kitchen. Lynn was put up for the night and in the morning, after a lengthy breakfast, I drove her back to Grand Central Station.

I remembered that as I sailed south to Miami, looking forward to celebrating New Year's Eve with Lynn at her daughter's.

After a night at anchor at Peanut Island, I left at noon on the 29th for Miami. It turned stormy in the night and I had a rough time of it. In the pre-dawn hour I sailed into the harbor. The Miami Beach Marina at Government Cut had no space available. Miamarina had not reopened since hurricane Andrew. The Marriott Marina was full, Dinner Key still closed, with the devastation all too visible. The anchorage outside the marina was strewn with wrecks. All the marinas I knew in the area were either shut down, or fully booked. I had no choice but to anchor at Key Biscayne. In the afternoon of New Year's Eve I went back to the Miami Beach Marina. All slips were taken. I tied up at the fuel dock and bought a few gallons of diesel, just so that I could use the telephone. The attendant told me, after eight o'clock I could move my boat to the end of the fuel dock for the night. I called Lynn.

"Hey, Peter! You can't believe what's going on here! The whole apartment is turned upside down for the party. Guests will be arriving any time now. Krissy's boyfriend just came in with two bags of ice cubes. The hors d'oeuvres are ready and the champagne is on ice. Give me a call tomorrow, but not too early. We'll probably sleep late, or have a hangover. Gotta go now."

Okaaay, so much for my New Year's Party. Now I can toast me and myself. What a Bitch, with a capital B. Happy New Year to You! Call you tomorrow, after the party? Yeah right, I don't think so!

I never saw or talked to Lynn again. She must have gotten the message, although I doubt that she was capable of feeling any remorse or regret. As far as I know, she never made an attempt to contact me either.

On New Year's Day, although I did not have a regular slip, the marina charged me forty-two dollars, one fifty per foot. I left Miami Beach Marina and anchored again at Key Biscayne. I would have liked to sail directly to Bimini, but the weather was not right, too unstable. Calm followed gusty, shifting winds. Hot sun under blue sky changed abruptly to balmy heat and thunderstorms. It was the kind of uncertain weather I avoid if possible.

Three days of stormy weather followed. Exposed on three sides to the open expanse of Biscayne Bay, the boat went from rolley-polley to mechanical bull. The steep, breaking waves reminded me of Cat Island. What little protection Key Biscayne used to provide, was further reduced since hurricane Andrew had removed all the trees. *TRITON 3* plunged her bow into the seas and then reared up like a stallion on his hind legs. I had my two main anchors at a hundred feet of chain and line in a water depth of six feet, a scope of almost 20:1. I wasn't going anywhere.

Late in the afternoon of 4 January, I left the bay and sailed out through the channel at Cape Florida. The weather had improved and a fine wind blew out of the southeast. At Fowey Rocks I had a fairly good angle on the wind and began my eastward tack. The sea was not quite as smooth as I had hoped and the Stream was running faster than I expected. At nine in the morning I made landfall near North Rock. After some good sailing during the night I now had to employ the Diesel in order to reach the entrance to Alicetown. I was not sure whether the authorities might charge me overtime if I arrived during the lunch hour; therefore, I waited until two p m before approaching Weech's dock.

It was the year 1993. Three years had gone by since I had made St. John my home and then had to leave it again. It could take me a month to get back there, two, perhaps three months. I didn't care, as long as I was going in the right direction.

The officials at Customs and Immigration received me with the stern professionalism, which their bureaucratic officialdom required. They took their work seriously. I had arrived during office hours and no fee was due. I took *TRITON 3* to the familiar anchorage.

Seven days I remained in Bimini and renewed my taste for the island life. Sufficiently acclimatized, I started out in the morning of 12 January, destination Nassau by way of Northwest Channel Light and Chub Cay. At North Rock, I turned east and entered upon the Bank.

I remembered June of last year when I had tried the same route. Unable to make good a course across the Bank, I had sailed north into one of the most horrifying thunderstorms. As a result, I limped into Running Mon Marina, shaken and with shredded sails.

This time I did very well, heading straight for Northwest Channel Light. Two sailboats had come out of Alicetown with me. They took up a more southeasterly course and were out of sight in a couple of hours. I passed Mackie Shoal on the north side and, as the wind had all but died before midnight and the sea was calm, I anchored in open water on the shallow Bank.

I started to open a can of herring in tomato sauce for a late evening meal, when a ship approached full steam. I could not make out the course, only that it was a freighter. The navigation lights were confusing. At one moment it seemed the vessel was coming right at me, then again I wasn't sure. I switched on all my lights, started the engine and raced forward to get my anchor up. I could not lose a second. Turning to starboard I got out of the way. As the vessel passed at close range, I saw her faulty navigation lights. What I had identified as one of her range lights turned out to be a naked bulb that shone through the open door of the galley.

That was a close one. I forgot all about being hungry. Collisions with Bahamian freighters are not rare. I had just narrowly escaped one.

Under power I proceeded in the warm, calm night. The structure that was the Northwest Channel Light, consisting of steel beams, was a twisted, broken mess. Andrew had done a thorough job. A buoy with the same light characteristics had been planted at a short distance as temporary replacement.

I anchored close to the old light structure. Although rolley-polley, I managed to fall asleep. It was safe here; no vessel would come so close to this heap of metal. I awoke in the blistering heat of a totally calm morning and prepared a lunch of corned beef and rice. Not being in any hurry at all, I lounged lazily, made entries in the logbook, and wrote down my nightly encounter with the Bahamian freighter in my notebook.

The sails remained under their covers. It was calm all day long. In the afternoon, under power, I made it around Mama Rhoda Rock and into the crescent anchorage at Chub Cay. It had been a hot, windless day and the night did not bring any relief. I rigged my ladder and went for a swim to cool off.

I had good memories of Little Harbor. Last June I had spent one whole day with Chester and Brenda and some visitors on their little hill. With no deadline, no appointment in Nassau or anywhere else, why should I not go back to Little Harbor? There was a light breeze blowing from the southeast, just right for what I had in mind.

Around Chub Point by nine a m, I sailed along Frazer's Hog and Whale cays and then along the South Berries. I noticed it first at Whale Cay: something was wrong. At Sister Rock the GPS had me sailing over land. Marking my position on the chart put me right on top of Whale Cay. A little later I found myself west of Bond Cay on the chart, instead of east. My GPS was off by three quarters of a mile—or was it the chart? Where was the mistake? The rest of the way I sailed by eyeball, which was not at all difficult. The Berry Islands are a string of rugged little cays and islets, the entire topography like the open page of an atlas. North of Frozen Cay I took my sails down. There is one solitary rock in the middle between Frozen Cay and Little Harbor, as if saying, "Welcome! You have arrived."

As soon as I had my two anchors set, I got to work on the chart. I checked various GPS positions and concluded that the chart was wrong. I had often heard that some charts in the Bahamas were inaccurate, but so far I had never noticed it. I decided to write a letter to the chart company.

It was still early in the afternoon. On my way to the dock, I stopped at the only other boat at anchor, a gorgeous Gulfstar 52, to say hello. Two elderly couples were sitting in the cockpit under their Bimini awning, drinking wine. They were from Delaware on a two-month cruise. "We're really from Delaware," one of the ladies assured me. "Wilmington." She felt she had to explain that. Many boats are registered in Delaware for tax reasons. If you own a three hundred thousand dollar yacht...Well, figure out the tax saving.

I was disappointed. Chester and Brenda weren't there. Another couple, or perhaps not a couple, lived there instead. They took turns, six months here, six months in Nassau. I didn't spend much time on their hill and rowed back to my boat. In the evening the people on the Gulfstar asked me to come over for a glass of wine. Oh, nice people, I thought. I did row over, and I felt a little uncomfortable. They were such snobs. One of the gentlemen kept making condescending, self-aggrandizing remarks; the other made speeches like lecturing me about all kinds of things. As much as I found out, one of them was a scientist or researcher at Dupont, the other a professor at some Ivy League school. The women attempted to tone down their husbands' arrogant attitudes. I didn't stay long, pretended to be exhausted. "Singlehanding, you know," I explained.

One of the nice old ladies asked, "Would you like to take back a lobster and some fish? It's fresh, you know."

"Oh, thank you very much, I am well provisioned. Very kind of you." I was already in my dinghy and I didn't want to appear needy. What do I care, take the damn lobster.

"Please, you would do us a favor. We can't eat it all, it would spoil."

"Well, if you put it that way, I'll take a piece of fish."

179

"It's snapper, already filleted." She brought out a big Ziploc bag with at least three pounds of fish in it and a whole lobster, wrapped in white paper.

"Too much!" I said, protesting. "I'm alone, I won't be able to eat all of that." Man, how many meals can I get out of that?

"Take it," said the professor or the scientist. It sounded like an order.

"Okay, well, thank you." I wanted to get home with my treasure and have a feast. The fish? The lobster? What will it be tonight? I unwrapped the lobster. Oh, great! It was already cooked.

My neighbors sat in the cockpit until late in the night. The anchorage is small and the boats were pretty close together. I really didn't want them to see me eating their crustacean. Maybe they would call over and ask, "How is it?" or something. Then I would have to yell back, "Very good, thank you again!" and that would spoil it all. So, I sat below, in the stifling hot cabin with just my little fan going. Let them think I have air conditioning.

Early in the morning I heard their electric winch groaning and the anchor chain rattling over the capstan. Sure, they just push a button and the anchor comes on board. I stayed below, didn't feel like waving goodbye to them, or worse, having to say something nice. But that lobster sure was good.

I saw the Gulfstar disappear around the rocky point out into open water, under power, of course, although there was wind. Why don't people like that buy motorboats?

My next destination was Nassau. If wind conditions, southeast fifteen to eighteen knots, remained steady, I would arrive there in less than twenty hours. Therefore I saw no point in leaving Little Harbor earlier than in the afternoon. *TRITON 3* was now the only boat anchored in this cove, in midst of mountains covered with abundant green vegetation. I dinghied to the little wooden dock to pick up the bread I had ordered the day before and, back at the boat, I deflated and stowed the dinghy. What did I have for lunch? Snapper, of course.

Out of the cove of Little Harbor, I continued east. The longer I kept on this course, the better an angle on the wind I would have for Nassau. Before nightfall, I tucked in a reef in the mainsail. The wind was steady and strong from the southeast. The Berry Islands became a faint silhouette before disappearing entirely in the gathering darkness. At that time I tacked and steered directly for Nassau.

A cruise ship at night is an impressive sight. As long as the ship is under the horizon, a glow, as if from a big city, illuminates the sky, sometimes reflected from low clouds. The glow disappears when the ship's lights become visible. Through binoculars it looks like a real city.

As I sailed toward Nassau, three of these giants came out of that port in intervals, leaving one or two miles between them. All three of them traveled north in the wide thoroughfare between the Berry Islands and Eleuthera, the Northeast Providence Channel. They looked majestic to me, as they crossed my bow at a safe distance. They really were like floating cities, a sight to behold. The forward extension of the decorative strings of lights cruise ships display while in port, were turned off to afford the personnel on the bridge an unimpaired view. It was a challenge for me to distinguish the navigation lights on these vessels, in the abundance of their illumination.

As the floating cities passed into the night behind me the glow of the city of Nassau rose out of the night ahead of me. I was on a collision course with a container ship that had come out of Nassau an hour after the cruise ships. It is true that a sailing vessel has the right of way over a power driven vessel, but in practice it is not reasonable to expect a huge ship to change course for a twenty-eight foot sailboat. At least, I wouldn't take that chance. To avoid collision at sea, I was forever vigilant, day or night, to detect ships the moment they rise above the horizon.

Most sailors are familiar with the horror story about a supertanker that came into port with parts of the rigging of a sailboat hanging from the bow. The collision was never noticed on board the big vessel. The rest of the sailboat and the crew were never found.

I entered the port of Nassau at six in the morning, together with a giant cruise ship. There were a few early risers standing at the railing of the ship's decks, eight or ten stories above me. Some of them waved down to me and I waved back. Did they perhaps think, I had to be crazy to be on the ocean in such a small boat, or did they envy me? I certainly did not envy them; I would not give up the freedom I experienced for all the entertainment, good food and luxury on that ship.

I anchored near the launching ramp and close to the dinghy dock in front of BASRA, the Bahamian Air and Sea Rescue Association, and announced my arrival over the VHF radio to Nassau Harbor Control. A strong, gusty wind had come up. The sky was clear, but the barometer was falling. I did not go ashore, wanted to take nap, but I was too worried. There was not a lot of room for me to have my anchors at a scope greater than 1:5. The anchorage was packed, and two boats were very close to me.

The barometer continued to fall. In the morning of my second day in Nassau, a tugboat, maneuvering a barge loaded with sand, was trying to get to the ramp. I was in the way. The captain asked me to move my boat. Easier said than done. One of my anchors was almost under the barge. I couldn't get to it, so I put a mooring ball to the line and hoped that I would be able to retrieve my anchor later. The other anchor I left in place, but I moved the boat upwind as far as the rode allowed and let down my auxiliary Danforth. That put me at the edge of the deep water. I considered this a temporary solution.

The barge was halfway up the ramp, like a landing craft, and the tugboat left. I was able to recover my anchor, while stevedores began unloading the barge.

The weather continued to act very strangely. It was calm one moment, then suddenly gusts and rainsqualls came out of nowhere. I had not planned for a long sojourn in Nassau, but the weather kept me pinned down and my temporary position became a permanent one. The following morning, the tug came back and pulled the empty barge off the ramp.

I listened to the forecasts on my VHF radio. Gale warning was in effect for Northwestern Bahamas, including New Providence. In the night to 26 January, my barometer had dropped to twenty-eight point six. The atmosphere was thick, loaded; thunderstorms rumbled in the distance. It was like waiting for an air raid in the war.

I had set a third anchor with plenty of chain, reaching far into the channel. On the 27th, the barometer had dropped further and dark clouds rolled in. At ten in the morning the first strong gusts came through the harbor. A motorboat started dragging her anchor and fouled the line of my auxiliary. The skipper of the Canadian boat close to me got into his dinghy and came to my assistance by first putting the motorboat on one of his anchors, then I got into my dinghy and he helped me free my line from that of the motorboat. Afterwards I repositioned my Danforth.

All this was going on in winds of up to thirty knots, heavy showers and whitecaps on the water. Soaked to the skin from rain and dirty harbor water, exhausted, cold and hungry, I checked frequently to make sure that my anchors were holding. The storm was most powerful on 28 January. I had never before seen my barometer showing pressure as low as on that day. It hit the low mark of twenty-seven point five and remained there for at least six hours.

Then the weather turned cold. The wind shifted to the north and the barometer started to rise quickly. February came in with record low temperatures. Two weeks had gone by, much longer than I had wanted to stay in Nassau. I was well enough provisioned with canned goods, pasta and freeze-dried meat and vegetables, beer and soft drinks, but I was low on water. I had not been able to get to the pump across the street from BASRA because of the weather. On 3 February, conditions had improved significantly and I could get underway. I stopped at the fuel dock on the Paradise Island side to fill my Jerry cans with diesel and to replenish my water supply.

I started out of Nassau harbor via the eastern exit, but before reaching Porgie Rock, I chickened out. It was still blowing hard and this route was unfamiliar to me. I anchored under the eastern tip of Paradise Island and got away early the following morning. At Porgie Rock I turned south, following the cruising book guidelines, and began crossing the Yellow Bank.

Numerous black rocks and boulders, imbedded in the pale yellow sand, seemed so close as if the keel might hit them, but the depth sounder read nine to twelve feet. The water was so clear, I could see the shadow of the boat on the bottom.

In a fine northeast wind of ten knots and under sunny skies, it was an excellent sail toward the northern end of the Exuma chain. Ship Channel Cay came into view first, then Allen's Cay and Highborn. I had chosen Allen's Cay Harbor for my overnight anchorage. Thousands of iguanas inhabited Allen's Cay, a big attraction for many sailors stopping here. I didn't care much for the reptiles and stayed on board, enjoying my supper and a couple of sundowners.

From Allen's, I tried to reach Sampson Cay the following day, but I had to struggle hard against some strong wind from the southeast. I had to reduce my Genoa to a tiny triangle, and double reef the main. I passed Norman Spit at noon and headed for Elbow Cay. It was still early in the afternoon when I reached the Hawksbill anchorage. After the rough sail from Allen's Cay, I was glad to have found a nice, calm and well-protected place to anchor.

Early next morning I sailed out of beautiful Hawksbill. On the chart there appeared to be no place for me to anchor until Sampson Cay. It was a gorgeous day, with rather light wind. I had to make Sampson in daylight. When I could no longer sustain a speed of three knots under sail, I turned on the engine. I came around Twin Cays and steered into a beautiful, large cove, high mountains to the east and north, a couple of cottages to the south and a narrow entrance to a shallow lagoon.

On 6 February, 1993, in the evening, I made the following entry in my notebook:

"I am not really that much of a nature lover, like some people. I cannot admire a landscape for hours. I have seen the Grand Canyon, breathtaking; the Andes in South America, spectacular; a tropical sunset, fascinating for a moment or two. Sampson Cay is a different matter. I am anchored in the cove, the harbor of Sampson Cay, which is open only to the west. South of my position is a gap, too shallow for sailboats, which leads to an inner harbor. Next to that narrow gap are a couple of picturesque houses and a wooden dock. All around the rest of the cove are steep walls of rocks, shooting straight up from the water.

It has been a sunny day, there were only a few thin, high clouds. At six o'clock I watched the sunset through the western opening. The sky turned a yellow color, then salmon-pink, finally fiery red, silhouetting black rocks over the calm sea.

"At the same time, in the east over the high rocky shore not more than fifty feet away from me rose the silver disk of the full moon. I didn't know which way to look: the setting sun in the west, or the big, rising moon in the east. The masts of a few sailboats, at anchor not far from me, stood out against the red sky. On the other side, the moon had given the black rock wall a silver outline over the rugged top. I let my dinner get cold and my drink get warm, not to miss a second of the magic nature offered me. It was awesome display, overwhelming. My words are inadequate to describe the sight, to which I was treated at Sampson Cay. It lasted not more than a few minutes, but I was in awe for a long time afterwards."

I had wanted to visit Sampson Cay for some time. Marcus Mitchell lives there with his family. Marcus, originally from Boston, had established his salvage company on Sampson Cay. Dennis O'Reilly had called him to the rescue, when he had sailed his *CHANDELLE* onto the reef at Samana Cay.

I went by dinghy into the shallow lagoon and saw a bunch of children at play on a meadow. The rustic house looked comfortable, inviting. I knocked. Marcus was home.

"Marcus!" I said. "Remember me?" I saw his wife coming up behind him, looking over his shoulder.

"You look familiar, remind me." He was tall and thin, as I remembered him.

"Peter. You will not remember me by name, but you might not have forgotten the CHANDELLE, run up on the reef of Samana Cay, back in May of '86. Skipper Dennis O'Reilly."

"Yes, I remember that very clearly. Sturdy boat. English, a Cutty Hunk, am I right?"

"Yes, that's right," I said. "You thought it would take about a week to drag the boat inside the lagoon to a place where she could be pulled over the reef. You could only work at times of high tide."

"I think we did it in four days. She only suffered minor damage, a few gashes in the hull. She made it in one piece. A strong boat."

"Lambertus DeBoer, remember him? He and I flew out with you to Nassau. I felt bad about leaving Dennis alone with one of your men. But he was such a stubborn asshole, I didn't want to be around him any longer than I had to, especially in that situation. Lambertus couldn't stay, had to get back to his job in Toronto."

"Yeah. Lambertus was his name? A big guy. Well, you know, O'Reilly was crushed. His insurance had expired. He called his broker several times via the marine operator. There was nothing he could do. The whole salvage operation cost him ten thousand dollars."

"You know, I called him in Boston a couple of weeks later, wanted to know how it went and whether the boat was okay. He was mad at me for leaving the boat. He didn't want to talk to me."

"He was grumpy the whole time, not that I blame him. But once we got him over the reef into deep water, he was okay and sailed the boat to Lauderdale for repairs."

"Marcus, I would have stayed with him if he hadn't been such an idiot. It was because of his stubbornness and stupidity that we ended up on the rocks. I had been at the helm before him and I had changed the course by ten degrees to make sure we would clear the reef. When he took over from me, he went back on the old course. I came out at midnight and happened to see the dark shape of the reef and breaking waves. I called him up. 'Dennis, come up here, quick!' He stuck his head out and yelled, 'Diesel on!' Lambertus turned the key. He shoved me out of the way, turned the wheel hard to port and that's when it happened."

I relived the moment as I told Marcus, the awful crunch, the grinding as the hull settled in an angle on the reef. "We tried to back her off," I continued, "rocking the boat at full power. It didn't work. We were solidly lodged, the tide running out."

Marcus said, "he told me, he had wanted to pass Samana Cay on the east side, the weather side."

"Yeah," I said, "and then he tried to blame me for what happened. He said, if I had turned hard to port the moment I saw the reef, instead of calling him first, we might have avoided it. But Marcus, had I done that, and then struck the reef anyway, he could have blamed me for the whole thing."

"Oh yeah, sure. And how! He would have accused you, maybe sued you, for steering the boat on the reef."

I nodded and said, "He came all the way from England with the boat and then ended up on the rocks in the Bahamas. Well, as it turned out, he and the boat were okay. Did he pay you?"

"Oh, he has money, owns a lot of real estate in Boston. He paid me, no problem."

His kids yelled from the lawn and his wife pushed past us in the doorway. We shook hands and said goodbye. "Are all theses planes yours?" I asked.

"I have three of them now. The one over there is the oldest. You flew to Nassau in it."

I rowed back to my boat thinking he probably owned all of Sampson Cay. Marcus was still young, in his thirties. Five kids, and I thought his wife was pregnant. Maybe, someday he moves back to the States, a rich man.

Later that day I had dinner with Woody and his female companion of the *GOLDEN ECHO*, out of Annapolis and the singlehander Stan from Toronto, on *LAPIS*. They had asked the woman, nanny to Marcus's children, to prepare dinner for us. She was glad to do so for sailors who stopped at Sampson Cay. She lived in one of the little houses near the Mitchells. She had converted the screened-in porch of her cottage to a sort of restaurant dining room with a long, rough table and benches on either side. We had lamb chops, very well prepared, peas and carrots, mashed potatoes and a couple of bottles of red wine.

The evening was great fun. We swapped stories of our adventures and the plans ahead of us. *GOLDEN ECHO* and *LAPIS* were traveling together.

We stayed one more day at Sampson and then took off, the three boats together.

While *GOLDEN ECHO* and *LAPIS* continued down the Exuma chain, I stopped at the Happy People Marina of Staniel Cay, and I was glad I did. Only a three-hour sail from Sampson, I tied up before lunchtime at the marina dock that accommodated three medium sized boats. It was immediately clear to me, I would never find friendlier, more content, happier people anywhere in the islands. From the moment I passed my dock lines to someone, I was treated like a friend. Not that they lavished services, assistance or anything on me; it was a sincere friendliness, as if saying, "We are glad, you could come!"

In the night of 9 February, while at the dock, a heavy thunderstorm broke loose over the Exumas. The incredible amount of twenty-five inches of rain was reported. I felt that it must have been somewhat exaggerated. Twenty-five inches in one night? Is that even possible?

I had invented a special rain catcher, which I used to fill my one-gallon jugs with water. The canvas awning with a spout built into it, slung low over the forward hatch, looked more efficient than it was. The strong gusts spilt most of the water in directions other than the spout, and I had to sit on deck holding the bottles so that the wind wouldn't blow them away. I didn't have a very good time, sitting in the torrential downpour to collect a few gallons of water. Anyway, it turned out that the water wasn't even clean enough to use for drinking or cooking. So much for my invention. The couple next to me, on the powerboat that looked like a miniature tug, thought the rain catcher was very clever. They studied it and they were going to make one for themselves. Better luck to them!

I was so well received at Staniel Cay that I became one of the happy people myself. I sat in their little, red church, witnessing a baptism. I watched a pig being slaughtered and saw a typical Bahamian sailboat under construction, designed and supervised by Kenneth Rolle. Ken owned and managed the marina, and his wife, Theaziel, ran the restaurant and the Royal Entertainer's Lounge. The restaurant had five tables and the lounge was a small empty room. Theaziel cooked on request. The Rolles, one of the most significant names in the islands, are prosperous, friendly and, most of all, very happy people.

On the small, wooded island to one side of the marina, domestic pigs were set free to roam and feed. From time to time, one or two people would take a boat over to the island and bring back an animal for slaughter. While I watched an operation of that sort, I hoped to secure a nice piece of meat for myself. I was, however, disappointed. All the meat was destined for the stores, the Yacht Club restaurant and some of the households.

After two days at the dock, I anchored for one night off the beach between the Happy People Marina and the Yacht Club of Staniel Cay. A blond black man, an albino, who had been present at the pig slaughter, met me on the beach in the morning.

"Did you get a piece of that meat yesterday?" he asked me.

"No," I said, "I did not."

He said, he was sorry about that. "I'll get you a lobster, if you like." In the afternoon he showed up with a nice, big lobster.

"What do you want for it?"

"Nothing. I saw you waiting for a piece of pork and I thought they should have given you some. That's all."

I gave him five dollars and he was very happy. I boiled my lobster before I left Staniel Cay with the nicest memories of any of the Bahamian islands.

I headed for the Galliot Cut. It was a hot, sunny day. A good breeze came up from the southwest. I rounded Harvey's Point and before I anchored at Little Farmer's Cay, I ran into trouble, twice. Inside the ample anchorage, I first ran aground on a sandbar. I flagged down some Bahamians passing in a motorboat. Using the main halyard from the mast top, with an extra length of line added to it, we fastened it to their runabout. They heeled my boat over so that the keel came off the bottom. Then they pulled me into deeper water. Twenty dollars for fifteen minutes work, they didn't complain.

The second mishap was caused by the line I had tied to the halyard. I forgot that I was trailing the line through the water and it got stuck in the propeller. I had to get into the water and unwind it. The nylon three-strand was badly chewed up and hard to remove. This was the job I hated the most, having to get into the water. What got me even madder was that I had caused it by being careless.

In the far corner of this anchorage were two boats, side by side. On coming closer, I recognized them as *GOLDEN ECHO* and *LAPIS*. I anchored close to them and later we all had drinks on Woody's boat.

Both Woody and Stan left early the following morning. They tried to make it before nightfall into Georgetown, Elizabeth Harbor on Lee Stocking Island. I was also sailing to Georgetown, but preferred to sail at night to make sure, I arrived at daylight. At Little Farmer's Cay there is a cut through the chain of the Exuma Cays into the deep water of the Tongue of the Ocean. With the last light before sundown, I sailed through the cut. Deep Water! I was tired of seeing the bottom, rocks and boulders, sometimes with inches to spare under the keel—and sometimes no inches.

I had a fantastic sail through the night and heaved-to off Conch Cay. It was an hour before sunrise. At the entrance to Elizabeth Harbor, between Conch Cay and Channel Island, I was again in shallow water and it became tricky. Following the waypoints I had programmed into the GPS, I headed straight for the sandbars. Another mistake in the chart! I couldn't see where the deep water was. Guessing, and luckily without touching bottom, I made it into the anchorage.

There were hundreds of boats. Holy crap! Why did I come here? Motoring through the harbor, looking for a place to put down my anchors, I estimated there were about three hundred boats in this place. It was a couple of weeks before Race Week in Georgetown and many more boats were expected. I found a spot not far from a wide beach of yellow sand. Boats were packed in closely. Two anchors down, I got my dinghy ready to carry out a third one to keep my boat from swinging. People on neighboring boats watched me, with looks of skepticism and curiosity and amusement, but ready to pounce on me the moment they felt I infringed upon their territory. I found hostility rather than camaraderie.

The chart with the approaches to Georgetown and the harbor itself was faulty. As in the South Berry Islands, I found an error of half to three quarters of a mile. I would definitely have to write to the chart manufacturer.

Most of the people on the boats around me seemed to know each other. They probably came together here every year. There was constant chatter on the VHF. "Meet me at the beach for volleyball." "Are you going in later?" "Come over for a swim." "Cocktails on our boat at five!" "Can we bring the kids?"

I found myself surrounded by partygoers, rude kids speeding with high-powered dinghies through the anchorage, noisy and inconsiderate Canadians, French, Germans and Americans. I didn't see *GOLDEN ECHO* or *LAPIS* anywhere.

After Sampson Cay and the Happy People of Staniel Cay, this was dreadful. Far from the town, I was anchored on the opposite side of Georgetown. Once here, of course I wanted to see what it was like. I had to cross a stretch of nearly a mile of choppy water. I did not find a rustic little tavern, a quaint cottage where I could get a meal or a coconut bread, nor someone on the beach offering me a fish or a lobster. No one gave me a friendly smile, saying, "okay mon" or "no problem" as I passed in front of their houses. What I found was something resembling a supermarket, with packaged goods, frozen fish and meat, canned fruit juices, imported Wonder Bread and milk in cartons. I bought some groceries, wrapped them in my foul weather jacket and headed back to the boat. Careful as I was, motoring slowly against the choppy seas, I could not avoid getting myself and my purchases soaked from spray. Georgetown, one of the most popular places in the Bahamas for cruising sailors and race enthusiasts, was not worth a second visit to me.

On the third day after my arrival at Georgetown, I sailed out of Elizabeth Harbor. With the corrected chart, it was piece of cake. Once again in deep water, past Conch Cay Light, I took up my course for Cape Santa Maria on the northern tip of Long Island. The wind was light. Under full sail, I covered the distance of twenty-five nautical miles in eight hours, an average speed of only three knots. I anchored in the lee of the Cape. Peace and quiet after that mad place, Georgetown.

From Cape Santa Maria to Port Nelson on Rum Cay was another short hop. In the morning of 18 February, there was no wind at all. The sails remained under their covers. Under power, I rounded the sand spit extending far out from the north point of Long Island. All day long, not a puff of wind rippled the water and the sun was beating down from a cloudless sky.

Conception Island came into sight in the distance by mid-morning and Sandy Point of Rum Cay appeared over the horizon a little later. I anchored at Port Nelson off the

Government dock. Two and a half years earlier I wanted to visit this island, but after hitting a rock or a coral head on approach, I did not insist and sailed to Conception Island instead. This time I had no problem.

The calm weather was the precursor of another cold front, which pushed south from the continent with winds of twenty to twenty-five knots. *TRITON 3* securely anchored, I rowed ashore and beached the dinghy. The dock was far too high for me to reach. Port Nelson was so much more my style than Georgetown. Rum Cay had a population of fifty-three. There was a landing strip for small planes. I found the little hut with a wooden board nailed over the door, Post Office burnt into it. The woman in charge of the mail has irregular 'office hours'. When I came by, she was hanging laundry out to dry on a nearby tree. I had bought some postcards in Georgetown and wanted to send them off to the States.

"I don't have no stamps. But you give me de money, dey put them stamps on in Georgetown or Nassau," the woman said. "De freighter come by tomorrow, or I give 'em to de pilot, if he show up," she added. None of my cards ever made it to their destination.

I love that smooth island dialect, although often I can't understand it. I definitely do not understand a word when Bahamians speak among themselves. I met young George Gator, who sold me a take-out dinner from his kitchen, called the Two Sisters, and the very old Hugh, a fine gentleman of eighty years, with whom I had a long conversation. He knew a lot about this island as well as all the others. He had relatives, and there must have been a hundred of them, spread out over all the islands. Unfortunately, I could understand only a fraction of what he was telling me.

The island freighter arrived from Nassau. It was the most important day of the week, like a feast day. Half the town's population gathered near the pier where the ship docked. Crates and bundles and baskets with fresh vegetables, meat and poultry, and an occasional piece of appliance or part of machinery were unloaded. Tanks and bottles of all sizes filled with propane gas were exchanged against empty ones. The crew took their meal in the pub near the foot of the dock and then the ship left again. The event, anticipated for a week, was over in a couple of hours.

Port Nelson on Rum Cay became one of my favorite places in the Bahamas, but I had to move on. San Salvador Island was the next stop in my itinerary. In the blustery weather on 21 February, I expected to be able to make the trip in daylight hours. As I came out from the lee of the island, a sharp wind met *TRITON 3* and I resolved to stick a reef in the mainsail and roll up one third of the Genoa. It was a sunny, warm day with a steady wind of fifteen to eighteen knots. Sails sheeted in closely and the boat heeled over, I had a terrific ride on the long ocean swells that roll in unencumbered all the way from Africa. San Salvador Island lies farther out into the Atlantic than all the other islands of the Bahamas, and most cruising sailors pass it by. Precisely those far out places, the less traveled and less visited islands, held the greatest attraction for me.

Shortly after Rum Cay disappeared, San Salvador came out of the waves ahead of me. It was Sandy Point, the islands westernmost end. Quickly I came closer and in an hour and a half I was in the lee of the island. I took down the sails and approached the harbor entrance of Riding Rock under power. The cruising guide warned of cross currents in the channel leading into the Riding Rock Yacht Basin. The harbormaster gave me instructions on the radio for entering between the jetties. At five p m I tied up at the concrete seawall.

The dock master, I forgot his name, was not a very accommodating individual. "You can stay here only for one night. The place is booked for a dive boat and a deep sea fishing vessel. They come in tomorrow and by then you have to be out of here," he told me quite clearly.

I came here to get to know this island, and now I wouldn't even have a full day? San Salvador Island has no natural harbor. Riding Rock, the only sheltered basin, is an artificial harbor, protected by a seawall and jetties. On the east side of the island is the open Atlantic, and there are a few flat saltwater lagoons. The south end, at Sandy Point, offers no shelter at all. That leaves me with only the extreme northern coast, Grahams Harbor.

SAN SALVADOR ISLAND

On the afternoon of 22 February, 1993, the dockmaster at Riding Rock Marina told me to vacate the place at the concrete dock, where *TRITON 3* had been since I came in the day before. Diving enthusiasts frequent San Salvador Island, which lacked a natural harbor, and Riding Rock Yacht Basin is the domain of sport fishermen, looking for the adventure of catching, and releasing, the biggest game fish.

I had gone out of my way to visit this island, where Columbus supposedly made landfall five hundred and one years earlier and studied my chart and the cruising guides. The only possibility for me was Graham's Harbor. At the northern tip of San Salvador Island, Christopher Columbus had discovered a 'harbor', which he described as large enough "to hold all the ships in Christendom". The problem was that the reef enclosing this harbor had only one narrow entrance.

I worked out the approach carefully, programmed waypoints into the GPS, measured the precise distances between them and calculated the courses to make sure not to miss that passage.

Determined, yet apprehensive, I left the safety of Riding Rock. The wind was steady from the south. I sailed with just the Genoa exactly nine miles to the northern end of the island, from where the reef extends northward. I rolled up the Genoa, turned on the Diesel and looked for the only opening in the reef that leads into Graham's Harbor. I stood high on the cockpit locker behind the wheel, to have a better view.

I saw the narrow gap. To either side of it waves were breaking over jagged rocks. I turned sharp to starboard and steered directly into the opening. Is this it? Is this where I have to go through? Should I look for a wider entrance? Too late now. White water to either side of me, my senses focused on the center between the rocks, I passed the most crucial point and then looked back to see the gap behind me. I was in.

My heart was throbbing in my throat, the adrenaline level in the red zone. The water was relatively calm, the depth sounder read twelve to fifteen feet. There were rocks everywhere on the bottom, imbedded in white sand, some the size of cars, others much smaller. Following the course I had worked out earlier, I approached the beach on the far side, turned toward it at the appropriate waypoint and dropped my first anchor in seven feet of water.

At that moment I smelled exhaust fumes. Smoke came into the cockpit from the engine compartment, through the cabin and out the companionway. At the same time I heard the automatic bilge pump working. I turned off the engine.

Before examining the problem, or the cause of it, I let the boat fall back and set my second anchor. Then I hauled in the slack of the first anchor to position the boat midway between them, the classic Bahamian method.

I don't know what made me keep my cool. Usually I totally freaked out over engine failure. I told myself, it was probably just a hose clamp that had sprung loose or perhaps a hose that burst. It had to be somewhere in the exhaust system. I'll check it out later; first let me bask a little in my success, having navigated skillfully through that reef.

I surveyed my surroundings, which good old Christopher had called a harbor. I found myself about one hundred fifty yards from the beach. There was a short, dilapidated concrete dock. To the east, where the beach ended, a rocky cliff rose from the water and continued northward for about two miles where the rocks sank below the water and formed a reef, indicated by waves constantly crashing over it.

Toward the west, the beach stretched for some two miles in an almost straight line. The reef, jutting out at the end of the beach met the other reef at a distance also of about two miles. Thus, the beach, as the base, and the two reefs formed a triangle. That was Graham's Harbor.

I wondered how Christopher Columbus found this place and the only narrow passage, without charts, cruising guide or GPS. It diminished my accomplishment.

My position in Graham's Harbor, as noted in my logbook, was 24 degrees 07 minutes north latitude, 74 degrees 28 minutes west longitude. I felt quite secure in this spot, although it was not as calm as I had hoped, protected against wind only from the south.

As if delaying the discovery of the engine problem, or to strengthen myself for it, I had my breakfast in the morning before opening the engine compartment. It became immediately clear to me what had happened, and it was more serious than a busted hose or a failed clamp. The cast iron exhaust connector, or mixer, where exhaust and cooling water mix, had completely disintegrated. I stared at a gaping hole. Repair was out of the question. I needed a replacement part.

I got out my tools. Removal of the bolts that held the broken part to the manifold was easy. As I unscrewed the mixer from the exhaust hose, it broke into three pieces. Nothing but the paint, or the rust, had held it together.

I had to order the part from JAZ Marine in Palm Beach, authorized dealer for Universal; I just needed a telephone.

As I inflated my dinghy, a car stopped at the little dock. Some people had come to look at a small motorboat, tied up at the old dock, which I had not noticed before. I rowed to the beach; the dock was too high, with jagged pieces of concrete and steel rods sticking out.

The driver of the car was the first person to hear about my dilemma. He said his name was Patterson. "My car is a taxi. I take you anywhere you want to go for ten dollars. I help you with everything you need. Don't worry. First you need a phone? I get you to a phone. No problem." He spoke a civilized English, very calmly, with only a hint of island accent.

"Okay," I said and got into his Ford Fairlane. "Take me into town. I have to make a call to the States. Are the phones working here?"

"Of course they are working, he said indignantly." I shouldn't have asked. It was almost an insult.

We drove a short distance on the asphalt road. "There's a phone right here, don't even have to go all the way to Cockburn Town," said Patterson. He pronounced it Coburn.

I called JAZ Marine. Bruce answered and I explained my problem to him. "The part number in the Universal parts catalogue is (I gave him the number). It's called the exhaust mixer, or something like that."

"I know what it is, but we don't have it in stock. I've got to order it from the manufacturer. Might take a few days, a week tops."

"That's okay. Go ahead." I gave him my credit card number. "Send it to my name at the post office in Cockburn Town, San Salvador Island. Mark it 'Hold for pickup'."

That was easy. Patterson was waiting. "Now let's go into town," I said as I got into the front passenger seat. "Let's find a place to have a beer."

There were several working telephones in Cockburn Town. The most convenient one for me to make future calls was in the building with the post office, the police station, the Commissioner's office and a clinic with one doctor and one nurse. There was a restaurant with a grocery store attached to it, a bar across the street and a gas station—all owned by eighty-three year old Jake Jones, whom I met later. Also a bakery, or rather a woman who baked Bahamian coconut bread, or any other kind, in her home. A couple of churches. A museum, a library and several commemorative stones and monuments reminding of Christopher Columbus' arrival at this island in fourteen hundred ninety-two.

Someone gave me a ride back to Graham's Harbor. I didn't see much of Patterson in the days and weeks to come. Anybody with a car was happy to stop and pick me up. People were friendly and liked to talk to a stranger. Never again did I have to pay for a ride.

I had ordered the part for my Diesel and was confident that I would be able to install it myself. With the right part, I didn't have to be a skilled mechanic to tighten a few screws and bolts. In the meantime I could relax and enjoy the island life.

At Jake Jones's grocery store I noticed cartons being folded and stashed away. New produce had arrived from Nassau. The freighter, here called the mail boat, had been in Cockburn Town the day before. I entered the store. The fresh fruit was already sold out, except for plantain. I didn't want any.

"Is there any meat?" I asked the girl. "You know, beef?"

"No beef," she said, "only chicken, pork, hamburger and steak."

I didn't lecture her about the hamburger and the steak. "Let me take a look at the steaks."

The frozen, individually wrapped steaks, each about eight ounces, were marked three dollars, not bad for island prices. I bought two of them.

On my way back out of town, a woman in a jeep stopped. "Want a ride?"

She worked for the new Club Med being built just north of the town, and she was from Luxembourg. We spoke German. "Club Med opened a few months ago. So far there are only accommodations for about thirty-five guests," she told me, "but it's going to be a major village. They'll call it Columbus Island and it will be for five hundred people."

On our way we passed Riding Rock Marina. A dive boat and a deep sea fishing boat occupied the concrete dock where *TRITON 3* had been. Adjacent to the marina was a two-storied inn. A short distance farther north was the airport. Construction was going on there, too. If Club Med was to receive up to five hundred guests, the airport would have to be able to handle at least midsize jets.

My Luxembourg friend drove me all the way out to the dinghy, about ten miles north of Cockburn Town. On our right we passed a group of low buildings and I was about to ask what that was.

"This is a field station, in which several universities participate. It's mostly for marine related studies. It's really a small campus. Used to be a US Navy tracking station during World War II," she told me.

Half a mile farther she dropped me off. "Thank you," I said. "Here's my dinghy."

"Is that your boat out there?" She asked. "It's so small! With that you sail on the open ocean?" I had been asked that question many times before.

"Oh yes," I laughed at her surprise. "Size doesn't matter. It floats just like the bigger ones."

"Well, good luck! See you around."

I waved goodbye and she drove off. I never met her again.

Every day I rowed ashore, sometimes to get a ride into town, at other times just to get off the boat, walk and explore this northern end of the island. Besides Cockburn Town, there are only a few outlying settlements, some solitary dwellings and the lighthouse on Dixon Hill. One paved road encircles the island. The interior is mostly wilderness.

After one week of my solitary existence—I had not seen another boat—I went to the post office. "I am expecting a package. It will be marked for pickup."

"Nothing here for you." The woman at the counter said, almost apologetically. Two days later, still nothing.

I had set a third anchor the day after my arrival in Graham's Harbor. I was quite exposed to all weather, except from the south and it was a rough anchorage even in the best conditions. On 1 March, the wind turned north and made my life on the boat very uncomfortable. Fine weather returned after a few days, but on the 12th a gale center formed over the northern Bahamas. A powerful storm hit the islands with winds of thirty to thirty-five knots and gusts of over forty in thunderstorms. It rained day and night. Tornado watch was in effect and it turned very cold.

For three days I had not been able to get off the boat. When the storm calmed a little, I was eager to go ashore to inquire about my package at the post office. There it was! I got the package, but something was wrong. It was much too heavy. After paying one hundred percent duty on the declared value of fifty dollars, I opened the box right there and… Oh, no. What's this? This had to be for an engine twice the size of mine. Right away I called JAZ Marine.

"Bruce, that's not it at all. Didn't you order it by the catalogue number?"

"You must have an old catalogue. This is the right number. Can you adapt it?"

I said, "impossible. Can't make it fit at all. Don't have even enough room. The diameter of the connection to the manifold is not an inch and a quarter, it's more like two inches. Don't you have a cross reference to the new catalogue?"

"Not any more, this goes back at least three years. You've got to make a drawing of the part you need with the diameters and all. Send that to me and we'll see."

Oh, man, this is not good. "All right. I have to see what I can do. What about this piece of crap you sent me? I guess I can return it when I get back to the States, right?"

"Sure. We credit you when you bring it back. But we will have to charge you for the other part, when or if we get it."

"Okay. Let me get the drawing done. I'll mail it to you tomorrow."

I got a ride back and started out in my dinghy, the wind blowing thirty, thirty-five knots. How am getting back to my boat? I could not make it straight out, I had to come up with a method. Under the protection of the high cliff, I first rowed north, actually away from boat, until I reached a point from where the wind would push me in the right direction. As I came out from behind the rocks, I felt the real strength of the wind. I didn't have to row, just steer with the oars. If I missed the boat, I'd end up a couple of miles away on the beach. I manipulated the oars. Man, how am I going to do this? Now! A few more feet. Now, ship the oars! I stood up and got hold of one of my anchor lines. I held on to the line, pulled myself up on the gunnel and tied the dinghy to the stern.

It was still stormy the next day and I thought of the stunt I pulled the day before. I'm not going to do that again! It was a day to take it easy. I made a fairly good drawing of the part, with a description and the measurements, and a day later the weather was a lot nicer. I sent the drawing off to JAZ Marine and had the feeling this place would be my home for quite some time.

Some fellows came to the dock and tried to get the motorboat going. I took the dinghy in to talk to them. "I would like to get some fish some day. Aren't you guys going fishing?" They were busy with that boat, didn't pay much attention to me. They couldn't get the motorboat started and left.

A couple of days earlier I had seen several of the students from the field station climbing up the rocks that formed the cliff. I was curious and went up there one morning. What a view I had! *TRITON 3* looked so tiny from the height that I thought, how did I come this far? I turned around. There was the enormous expanse of the ocean and I felt a great loneliness coming over me. The vast ocean on one side, the rugged, forbidding reef enclosing the harbor on the other—no wonder, there are no other boats here.

Jammed between jagged rocks at the steep northeast coast, I saw the rusted hulk of a Japanese freighter, a reminder of the perils that await anyone venturing out onto the indomitable sea. I sensed a silence around me, an aloneness with raw nature, yet in my ears was the pounding of the waves crashing against the rocks, waves that for a million years were coming across thousands of miles of ocean.

What am I doing here? Is all this meant to be witnessed by man? Does man not belong in cities, with skyscrapers, traffic and crowds? Is this not meant for Nature alone? For waves eternally breaking against an uninhabited shore? For winds gusting forever, bending resisting branches of trees and shrubs scarcely thriving in the crevices between the rocks? For a lone bird sailing on the wind, hardly flapping a wing? For creatures in the deep blue water beneath the white crests? For the sea grass and the precious coral? My mind wandered. If I stayed any longer, could I find my way back to reality?

I met Patterson again, a nice guy, but not too reliable. He was semi-educated, went to school in Nassau, he told me, and he had a good knowledge of interesting facts about the islands and their history. The help he promised me, "Anything you need," I did not get. "I'll send the guys out in the boat. You will have fish, conch, anything you like." There was a fresh water pipe with a faucet near the dock. "I'll have the water turned on for you. My cousin works for the Public Utilities Company." He also said, "That case of beer I'll drop off for you next time I come out here." None of those things happened.

I developed a friendly relationship with the staff at the field station and had permission to take all the water I needed. I bundled my twelve empty plastic bottles together with rope, slung them over my shoulder and walked the twenty minutes to the field station. At the pump in the yard I filled my bottles and then carried them, four at a time, back to the dinghy.

I had met Don Gerace at the post office a few days earlier. Don, a man of small built, a few years younger than I, was the dean at this university outpost. I saw him many times, in town or in his office. We talked for hours. He was an authority on the island, on Columbus, on meteorology and the marine environment. A fascinating conversationalist, with a great sense of humor, he took much interest in my predicament and offered his help in any way he could.

"Don't rely on the postal service. You may never see your spare part. And think of the shipping cost," he said. "I have an airline, it's called Red Airline, out of Palm Beach. Flies in here once a week. Tell your people to send it to Red Airline at the airport and I guarantee you get your package this Saturday." Red Airline consisted of one turbo prop.

I called Bruce at JAZ Marine. He didn't have the part yet. "When you get it, send it to Red Airline at Palm Beach International. Don't ship it through the mail."

It was St. Patrick's Day. A new storm center had formed over South Florida, with a front extending through the islands. There were white caps throughout the harbor. It was magnificent to watch the seas breaking over the reef. My anchor lines were as tight as guitar strings, the boat was bucking like a mechanical bull. Chafing gear wore through in an hour. Even if I had received the spare part that Saturday, and if I had been able to repair the engine, I could not have sailed out through that reef.

In the night the lights on shore went out. The storm had knocked out the power lines on the island and it was confusing not to have a reference point in the total darkness. Looking over the cliff, I could see the beam of the lighthouse on Dixon Hill, maintained by its own power source: two flashes every ten seconds. In the morning the weather improved and I did my laundry in the dinghy, which had collected enough rainwater. Then I hung my clothes on the lifelines to dry.

For some time I had agonized over the question whether to continue my voyage to the Virgin Islands, or to return to mainland USA, but I avoided dwelling on that subject. On Saturday I expected to receive the right part via Red Airline. I had to decide what to do. During these weeks in Graham's Harbor I had lost my enthusiasm for the long voyage ahead. I was not looking forward to the difficult portion of the trip against the trade winds to Puerto Rico. I weighed pros against cons. My decision would have to be final, with no looking back and no regrets. If I stuck to my original plan, it could either be out of strength of character, or stubbornness. If on the other hand I had a change of heart, it could be common sense, or a weakness. I knew that whatever my decision, I would have to live with it. I needed more time to think. First concentrate on the engine, I told myself, then make up your mind.

Somebody in a pickup truck stopped and drove me to the airport. It was Saturday, 20 March. A group of students with backpacks waited to fly back to Palm Beach. The plane came in as expected at one o'clock. Some twenty students got off and a lot of baggage was unloaded.

I waited at the Customs office, and yes, there was a package for me. I had to sign some papers, the inspector had to sign and stamp others. Again fifty dollars changed hands and then I had my package. I rode in one of the vans with the students back to their campus at the field station. Excited as I was, I opened the package on the way, and again I looked at something not quite right. The piece did remotely resemble my drawing, but the flange that had to fit into the manifold seemed too big. I was determined to make it work; somehow I had the inkling that I could. Don Gerace had given me permission to use the workshop at the premises. Whatever materials and tools I found there were at my disposal.

I returned to the boat with the replacement part for the broken mixer, which I had to fit with a piece of pipe or tube of some kind to make it compatible with the manifold. Not being much of a mechanic, I had no other choice.

The manifold had to come off the engine block. There were eight bolts to be removed. I carried a good set of tools, but my main concern was not to strip the threat of the bolts. By applying penetrating oil and letting it work for a while on the bolts, I minimized that risk. Another concern was gasket material, which I hoped to find in Don Gerace's workshop.

Carefully I started loosening the bolts, spraying more of that penetrating catalyst when they were not turning freely. All eight bolts came off intact and I removed the manifold from the block. Everything depended on finding what I needed in the pile of scrap metal and junk at the field station.

It was an enormous help to have free reign over the entire workshop where the vehicles and machinery belonging to the campus were serviced. Among the teaching staff was a young engineer, who supervised a couple of local part-time mechanics. This weekend the place was all mine.

Early on Sunday morning I put the new mixer, the manifold, hose clamps, a piece of exhaust hose, the bolts, Permatex (liquid gasket), and tools into my canvas bag, and took off for the shop on campus. The young professor in charge of the mechanics department showed me around in the work place and pointed to a pile of scrap metal where I might find tubing. With a friendly "good luck" he left me alone to work on my project. I laid out my stuff on the workbench and went to look for discarded pipe or tubing. Almost immediately I saw a piece of copper pipe, three inches long. It measured one and a quarter inch outside diameter. How is this possible? Did someone put it there for me to find? This is incredible! This couldn't be just luck. If I believed in miracles… Never mind. Gamblers call it beginner's luck. Maybe it's the same thing. I thought I had grown wings. I was in an indescribable, euphoric mood.

The copper tubing made a tight fit, Permatex served as a sealant. The manifold with the new mixer looked like one unit. My piece of rubber hose did not fit, but I found one of the right diameter. I cut a six or eight inches long piece off and fitted it over the flange at the exhaust end of the mixer. On a shelf above the workbench I found gasket material from which I cut a piece for use between manifold and engine block.

I was ecstatic over my success. In less than two hours I was on my way back to the boat. I thoroughly cleaned the surfaces of engine block and manifold and placed the carefully cut gasket between them. I paid extra attention to apply the same torque on all eight bolts that held the two components together, tightening them one by one in a cross pattern. Permatex and double clamps made sure that the rubber flange connecting the mixer to the exhaust hose was a tight fit. The entire system was ready for the test shortly after twelve o'clock.

One whole month I had not used electricity to save the battery power needed to turn over the engine. I have not allowed myself the luxury of light at night and did not use the fan.

The moment to turn the key in the ignition had finally come. Although there was no reason why the engine should not run, the sound of the Diesel coming to life gave me such a pleasure that tears welled up in my eyes. It was a beautiful sound. Cooling water together with exhaust fumes came out through the transom pipe. There were no leaks of water or fumes where I had contrived one adapter between manifold and mixer, and another one between mixer and exhaust hose.

Overjoyed I let the engine run, sat in the cockpit and celebrated with my favorite island concoction, rum and guava nectar with a splash of lemon. Then, again the question came to my mind that had plagued me for days and weeks. Deep inside of me, I had already reached a conclusion, but the time to put my decision into action had arrived: tomorrow morning I would start my voyage back to the United States.

I told myself, this is my life. I have not always chosen the easy way, but this time I would. And, don't forget, I still had to bring *TRITON 3* out through the reef.

One more time I had to row ashore in my dinghy. I owed a great deal to the people at the university outpost and I wanted to thank them for their generosity and assistance, for their interest in my situation. The young professor had told me in the morning that he and his wife would celebrate the birthday of their daughter, who was one year old. I had no present for the baby other than a red bandanna I had never worn. With my gift, wrapped in white tissue paper, I went to their door and knocked. They appreciated the humble offering and wished me smooth sailing. Don Gerace was not on the premises. I had thanked him the day before at the airport and would definitely send him a card from Nassau or my first port in the States.

Back on the boat, I reflected on the last thirty days. I had wanted to visit this island and did so more thoroughly than I had ever expected. I rode out many days and nights of extremely bad weather. I saw and experienced nature in her crudest form. Without the comfort of light, I had spent evenings and nights in darkness. I had proven myself as a so-so mechanic and had the good fortune of having met with friendly and helpful people. The month in Graham's Harbor of San Salvador Island has enriched my life as a sailor in many ways.

THE EASY WAY

I chose the easy way. Ahead of me was the prospect of a great sail downwind through the islands. From the moment of my decision, I no longer had a conflict within myself. The matter was settled and I concentrated on getting out of Graham's Harbor. Only one more night in this remote, solitary place, which had been my home for thirty days.

It rained heavily during that last night, but no storms were forecast. The sky over the rocks had been red at sunset, a good sign. *Red sky at night, sailors' delight. Red sky in the morning, sailors take warning.* According to that old wisdom, I should have fair weather.

At dawn the sky was pale blue. I concentrated on studying the reverse course through the gap. Although the distance was not more than two miles, I could not find the exit, even with the binoculars. I had to rely on the waypoints in my GPS in reverse order. The opening between the seas breaking over the rocks would come into sight before I reached it.

I stowed the dinghy and then brought up my Danforth. I ran into trouble with the CQR. That anchor had found a four-inch thick rope on the bottom and did not come free. Damn it, I should have rigged a trip line, with which to pull the anchor up by the crown. Shit! Can't leave my best anchor here. If I were a diver... but I am not. The boat was directly over the anchor, the chain going straight down; the water was so transparent, I could see the problem clearly.

I had to inflate the dinghy again, and launched it over the side. From the dinghy I reached down into the water and hitched a strong, braided nylon line as low as possible to the chain. Back on board, I took a few turns with that line around my starboard winch and started cranking. Inch by inch the anchor came off the bottom. Back in the dinghy, I tied another line lower down on the chain and cranked that one up. Twice more I had to replace the line lower on the chain before the anchor broke the surface. With it came the rope that was thick enough to moor a battleship. How the hell can I get my anchor free? Once more I had to get into the dinghy. I tied a line to that monster rope and belayed it on the stern cleat. Then I released the anchor chain. Problem solved! The anchor swung free and I let the rope sink to the bottom where it had been for who knows how long. Could it be that Christopher Columbus had forgotten one of his mooring ropes?

This backbreaking job has worn me out. The procedure took two hours of hard labor. During spells of stormy weather, I had sometimes wondered why my anchors were holding so well. Now I knew. The dinghy stowed away again, I pulled up my third anchor and finally got underway.

At two o'clock in the afternoon of Monday, the 22nd of March, all three anchors were on board and I began my exit from Graham's Harbor. My eyes were fixed on three things simultaneously: the boulders on the bottom, the depth sounder and the GPS. As the narrow opening between white water breaking over black rocks came into view, my eyes latched on to that all-important spot. A tidal current running through the gap threatened to twist the boat off course and I had to handle the wheel very cautiously, counter steering to keep the boat in the center of the gap.

With great relief I looked back at the reef. The depth sounder showed MSD, a reassuring Mostly Super Deep—a little joke by the people at Datamarine, the manufacturer of the instrument. Depths greater than 125 feet did not register on the LCD.

The scary reef behind me and smooth sailing ahead, I set the Genoa. I could be back in Palm Beach or Stuart in a matter of a week or ten days. Or, since I had all the time in the world, I could extend the voyage indefinitely. Due to the delay in my departure from Graham's Harbor, caused by the snag with Christopher's rope, it was late afternoon when I passed Riding Rock Marina. At Cockburn Town, wind and sea were calm enough for me to anchor near the concrete dock for island freighters, or mail boats. The first leg of my return trip was to be to Hawks Nest, Cat Island, which could take as long as twelve hours.

I said goodbye to San Salvador Island in the morning. It was raining, and with the wind blowing hard from the east, I made excellent time. Seas were building to six to eight feet. Before noon I sailed through a rainsquall and in less than four hours, Cat Island rose above the waves and two hours later I rounded Columbus Point and Devil's Point.

Hawk's Nest Creek turned out to be a dark, narrow entrance, with trees overhanging the water's edge on both sides, making it a completely calm and quiet anchorage. About a hundred yards inside was a side arm leading to the deserted and dismantled Hawks Nest Marina. I wasn't sure about the depth and possible hidden obstructions there and chose to anchor in the middle of the solitary creek. By five thirty it was dark and in the low cloud cover and soft drizzle, soon no light penetrated into this ominous hole. Everything was black—the water, the trees, the sky—and there was no sound, not even the flutter of a bird. I have never anchored in a place as scary and mysterious as Hawks Nest, lost in a haunted fairy tale forest. In Graham's Harbor I had been isolated and alone. During the entire month I had not seen one other boat, but the loneliness I felt in this black, creepy, haunted hollow gave me goose bumps and for the first time the thought of pirates came to mind. This seemed to be the perfect hiding place for smugglers or drug runners.

The next day I made the short hop to Fernandez Bay, Cat Island, where I relaxed in the afternoon and remained overnight. There was a long, beautiful white beach and calm, shallow water. Two other boats were at anchor there, far apart from one another. I remembered Cat Island from three years earlier when I had anchored at The Bight during a nasty storm. This time it was different, there was hardly a ripple on the water.

I left early the following morning for Little San Salvador. On the way I met a local fisherman, but he had no fish. So, once more no fish for dinner. I lived on the water and had no fish for weeks. Where have all the fishes gone? I hummed.

I stayed in West Bay of Little San Salvador for the afternoon. An elderly couple from New Hampshire anchored their boat at a short distance from me. They came over in their dinghy to say hello. We exchanged a few words about the weather, where from, where to, hope to see you again and good-bye.

At dusk I left in a light breeze for Highborn Cut. It was motor sailing much of the way. At nine p m I passed the southeast point of Eleuthera. There was supposed to be a light, but it was not working, as so many in the Bahamas. By midnight a nice breeze had sprung up and I was making four knots. An island freighter crossed my wake at a safe distance. Two hours later I passed the buoy in the middle of the Exuma Sound. As the dawn colored the eastern sky, I entered Highborn Cut. First I anchored just inside the cut, but later one boat left the anchorage and I found a spot for *TRITON 3* near the dock.

The inner harbor, if you can call it that, shoals at a short distance beyond the dock. There is not much room for more than two or three boats. I was nicely settled in six feet of water over a sandy bottom, when a boat from Montreal anchored so close to me that our anchor lines crossed.

I did not quite understand what made Highborn so popular. There was a short dock with a fuel pump and a little shack where you could buy a T-shirt and a candy bar, but there was no shop or restaurant and no settlement. The nearest grocery store, I was told, was thirty-seven miles away, on Sampson Cay. I've been at Sampson Cay, but there was only one little shop. Is that what they call a grocery store here?

A small cruise ship, an ugly catamaran, from Ft. Lauderdale, came in and tied up at the dock, leaving no room for any boats. About thirty tourists came ashore. For what? I had no clue. Perhaps it was ideal for diving enthusiasts.

I stayed one day longer at Highborn Cay than intended. A front was approaching from the north. As it turned out, the front never made it as far as these islands. I missed a beautiful day with just the right wind for my next destination, Nassau. Instead, I had one more day with nothing to do. That was fine with me, however, I had to spend the evening and the night enclosed behind screens in my cabin, defending myself against the most ferocious mosquitoes. On the bright side, a fisherman sold me a beautiful, big lobster. Finally proof that these waters were not barren. I ate the whole thing.

Early on the third morning at Highborn I maneuvered my boat around to retrieve my anchor from underneath the French-Canadian boat and left after a brief thunderstorm to cross the Yellow Bank on a straight course for Porgie Rocks. Averaging five knots, New Providence was in sight shortly after noon. There were heavy black clouds in the distance, but the developing thunderstorm stayed well to the north. Not taking any chances, I took down my sails and approached the Rocks under power. Several boats converged from various directions for the approach to Nassau.

I stopped at the fuel dock near Potter Cay under the Rainbow Bridge to top off my tank with diesel and proceeded from there to the anchorage at BASRA. I reported my arrival on the radio to Nassau Harbor Control as soon as I had set my two anchors.

Nassau was already quite familiar to me. I liked to walk through the town and to the docks where the huge cruise ships tie up. Thousands of tourists stroll through the duty free shops and buy high-priced cameras, jewelry and perfumes, convinced they got a bargain. For the tourists, Nassau was mostly that one shopping street, parallel to, but one or two blocks removed from, the harbor. The other attraction, of course, was across the steep Rainbow Bridge on Paradise Island, with the casinos and modern high-rise luxury hotels.

For the cruising sailor the city is convenient. Grocery stores, ship chandlers, post office, bars and restaurants are all in walking distance from the anchorage. On Potter Cay I enjoyed a fresh conch salad, prepared while I waited.

To get to know the outskirts and surrounding areas of Nassau, I boarded a public bus to the eastern part of New Providence Island. Outside of town, I saw some beautiful homes and mansions, manicured lawns and well tended gardens, little gleaming white churches and the St. Augustine Convent. On Fox Hill, nicely fitted into the landscape, was the prison with a section marked 'For First Offenders'; I found it funny that there were separate accommodations for them. Montague, high on a cliff, provided a spectacular view over the eastern approaches to Nassau, with Porgie Rocks in the distance.

After a couple of days I left Nassau. Several cruise ships arrived, to take the place at the Prince George Wharf, vacated last night by others of these giants—a constant coming and going of these floating hotels the size of cities. The port of Nassau can accommodate up to seven of them at one time.

Leaving Nassau behind, I settled on my course for Chub Cay. As it was still early in the day, I passed Chub and headed straight for the Northwest Channel Light. My progress was good and in the early evening I entered the bank together with an island freighter that had come up behind me. The light structure had not been repaired. It was still there, twisted and torn, the way hurricane Andrew had left it. The flashing buoy next to it had taken over the duty of showing mariners the way.

I set a course of 300 degrees and, with a fine south wind, I beam-reached toward Mackie Shoal. Later I had to tuck a reef in the main sail. The wind increased steadily, giving me some excellent sailing. After midnight, Mackie was behind me and I took down my main sail and continued under reefed Genoa alone. I had made such good time and was in no hurry. I wanted to approach North Rock in daylight.

Bimini was in sight shortly after six in the morning. By then I was pounding into four-foot choppy seas with a southwest wind of twenty knots. Two hours later I powered around North Rock. From then on I had wind and seas dead against me. I followed another sailboat into the calmer water along the beach. At noontime, twenty-nine hours out of Nassau, I was in the anchorage of Alicetown.

Giving myself a whole day of leisure time, I prepared to leave for Miami in the morning of 3 April. I would have liked to stay a day or two longer in Bimini, but I had run out of propane gas and at night my supper consisted of a half-cooked meal of pasta and tuna fish. At seven in the morning I sailed out of the harbor and before ten, Bimini, the Island in the Stream, was out of sight.

In the light wind, progress was slow, I did not see the skyline of Miami before five in the afternoon and it was dark when at last I distinguished the light on Fowey Rocks against the backdrop of the city.

To add one more challenge to the voyage, I chose the Cape Florida Channel, which is well marked with lighted buoys, but difficult to discern among the many buoys warning of the shallows. I love the thrill of night sailing, and when by midnight my CQR went down at Key Biscayne, I felt the satisfaction of yet another successful completion of a passage.

On Sunday morning, I was disappointed to find Miamarina still closed—I had long anticipated a nice lunch of Sushi at Bayfront—and sailed into the Marriott Marina. A slip was available and I stayed overnight in relative luxury.

In no hurry to reach Stuart, I strolled over to Bayfront Park. I wanted my Sushi and postponed my departure until after lunch.

By sunset I was off Boca Raton and between eight and eight thirty that evening I had a most amazing sight. At a distance of two or three miles, in the reflection of the rising moon on the water, I saw a tugboat towing a huge battleship. Shivers went down my spine, as the silhouette of this powerful ship, symbol of Naval strength, passed slowly and in absolute silence under the bright full moon. Then it disappeared into the darkness beyond. The memory of these five or ten minutes remains with me to this day. I had the sad thought that this proud vessel would soon be mothballed or reduced to scrap metal.

I sailed into Lake Worth Inlet at midnight and anchored at Peanut Island. In the morning, just getting underway, my engine stalled. The shaft had caught a vent hose and ripped it to shreds. The wire coil had wound itself around the shaft and rendered it incapable of turning. With the momentum, I barely reached the Coast Guard dock and asked permission to tie up. I started cutting away the wiry bird's nest that had disabled my engine.

"How long do you need?" A guy in uniform shouted at me. "We need the dock, our boat's coming in."

"I am having a hell of a mess to deal with. The shaft is fouled. You got a wire cutter handy? It would make the job a lot easier and faster."

"No, we ain't got no tools like that. I can give you a hand and tow you around to the inside. I need that dock free."

"Okay, let's go then." We worked the boat around the pier. For the next two and a half hours I wound and unwound, tore and cut with the inadequate tools I had for a job like that. I didn't care for the air hose, which supplied ventilation to the engine compartment; it was a dispensable accessory.

Around eleven o'clock I was ready to resume the long and tedious stretch to Stuart via the Intracoastal Waterway. With the wind from the north and the current against me, which is so often the case, I reached the Roosevelt Bridge not before eight o'clock at night and I stayed at the Stuart city dock overnight.

Suddenly, a revelation hit my brain like a lightning bolt. I had completely forgotten to report my return from a foreign country to US Customs. By law, notification must be made immediately upon arrival, from a place where the vessel could be inspected, if the official should decide to do so. Severe penalties, ranging from fines to imprisonment and confiscation of the boat, could result from such neglect.

I had actually arrived in Biscayne Bay on the night of the 3rd and spent another night at the Marriott Marina. Then I had sailed to Palm Beach, anchored at Peanut Island for the third night, then docked at the Coast Guard Station, of all places, for almost three hours and spent another night in Stuart.

It was on my fourth day back in the USA that I motored anxiously to the marina closest to the St. Lucie Inlet, the Sailfish Marina in the Manatee Pocket, and made the phone call to Customs. The official on the other end of the line made no unusual inquiries and I did not have to give specifics about my time or place of arrival. Thus, to my relief, without having to lie, he gave me my clearance.

A huge weight was lifted from my shoulders.

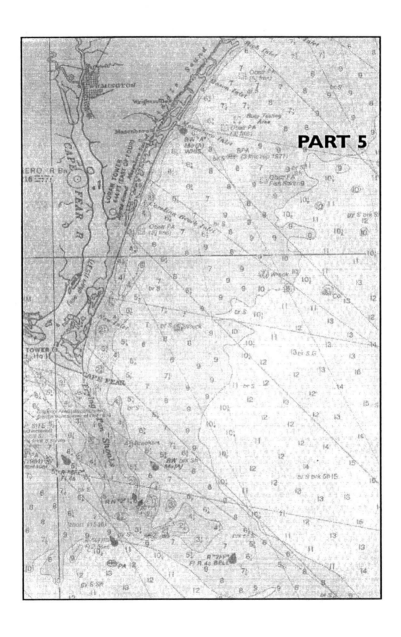

RIVERPOINT HARBOR

My life, from school to retirement, has not been one straight line. There were bends and curves and detours. The end of World War II left me at the age of seventeen without a clear view or idea for my future. After trying my hand at repairing dentures in a dentist's laboratory and, closer to my ancestral roots, learning the fur trade in Frankfurt, I functioned as a fur salesman in my father's failing business. When the opportunity to emigrate presented itself in the form of a letter from a distant relative, I did not hesitate and shipped out to Ecuador, South America. For two years my work had to do with importation of industrial goods and heavy machinery, before going into business on my own. For three years I traveled through the provinces, selling anything and everything, even kitchen sinks.

In 1960, married and with a daughter, I took up residence in New York where in 1962 my son was born. After a year and a half with an automotive parts import firm, I joined a Far Eastern company. For twenty-four years I worked in the Foods Division in the New York office of one of the largest trading concerns in the world.

At the age of fifty-seven and divorced, I accepted an early retirement offer. In a short speech at my farewell reception, I pointed out, "I am retiring to change my life style" and embarked on a life on the ocean, a life of as much freedom as it was possible to find. The sea has represented that freedom for me since childhood.

Now I was back in Stuart. I had not returned to Paradise. How did I feel about it? I rejected the notion of failure and told myself that my paradise could be wherever I wanted it to be.

So, was it too much to ask for some comfort? I thought not. Returning from Graham's Harbor, San Salvador Island in the Bahamas, I longed for a more comfortable life and rented a slip for *TRITON 3* at the small, rustic marina just north of the Roosevelt Bridge, known as Riverpoint Harbor. There were finger piers with slips for twenty-six boats. The monthly charge for dockage, with added live-aboard and electricity fees, was reasonable. I lived henceforth in what I considered great luxury.

I had reading light, could run a large fan, watch Television on my little portable black and white set and plug in my refrigerator/freezer on 110 Volt shore power. In the little green building on shore were showers as well as washer and dryer. What I did not have was air conditioning, but I was happy with what I did have.

A friendly atmosphere prevailed at the dock. Several boats in this marina were home to their owners. There were no rich people living at Riverpoint Harbor, though some of the yachts, mostly sailboats, were bigger and more luxurious than others. Almost all of the residents had jobs or a business to run. I was the exception. I was retired.

Most of the boats at Riverpoint Harbor never moved an inch away from the pier. Some of them lacked an engine or were otherwise unseaworthy; others were constantly in the process of being repaired or improved. Yet, this was not a rundown place. All of the residents at the marina wished or intended to leave some day on a voyage to far away places. Work one more year, make some money, fix up the boat, then take the wife and the kids and sail to Tahiti, Australia or the Med. Dream on! You either do it, or you don't. You've got do it now, or it remains forever a dream.

TRITON 3 was not one of the boats that never moved. I often undertook overnight trips or some weeklong excursions. When the wind was right, the Indian River offered some excellent sailing. Returning to Stuart, it was always nice to know that my slip at Riverpoint Harbor was waiting for me. There was always somebody ready to give me a hand when I pulled up to the dock.

I busied myself with improvements to the boat, and there was never a shortage of routine maintenance or repairs to be made. I built a boom gallows, a contraption on which the boom rests when not in use. Relieving the topping lift, it holds the boom in place and prevents it from swinging with the boat's movements.

Another clever addition was the davits for the dinghy. On the transom I installed two sturdy hardwood brackets, fitted them with a pulley system, and adapted the dinghy with slings, on which to lift it out of the water. I no longer had to deflate and store the dinghy for every little trip. Well, it didn't work the way I had hoped. I could not pull the dinghy up with the motor attached, and even a short shower made the dinghy too heavy for the davits. Still, the davits were not totally useless; besides, they looked good and made a real cruising boat out of *TRITON 3*.

On September 12, standing on the dock at Riverpoint Harbor, I watched the launching of the Challenger from Cape Canaveral. It was a Sunday and most of the marina residents stood on the dock or on their boats to witness this amazing sight. A huge firecracker, with a long yellow-orange flame, leaving behind a white plume, rising, rising... Rising toward something we can hardly imagine.

That same day I left Riverpoint Harbor for Riviera Beach. I had an appointment for Monday morning to haul out at Old Slip Marine. *TRITON 3* needed fresh bottom paint. The travelift hove the boat out of her element and the pressure washer removed slime, grime and barnacles, and revealed a phenomenon I had never seen on a boat. The entire surface below the waterline was covered with rock hard, white worms, thin as angel hair spaghetti, each about half an inch long. Yard personnel and bystanders alike had never seen anything like it. Where did I pick those up? Graham's Harbor? Hawks Nest?

There was one man, who had seen those worms before. He was Cowboy, and there was nothing Cowboy hadn't seen. A tall, thin old black man, he was the yard's factotum. Cowboy, never moving faster than in slow motion, did everything at the Old Slip boat yard. Management assigned him to work on my boat. This was to be the first time that I did not paint the bottom myself. Cowboy was my man.

"I seen dem worms befo'. Dat wus at Cairo, down Egyptway." He spoke as slowly as he walked. "Dem's called de toobs. No prob'm. I git's em off," and he set to work. Broad scraper in one hand, hose with slow running water in the other, he sat on an upturned bucket and started methodically working away on 'them toobs'.

I watched for a while and he amazed me with the progress he made. He worked at the same even speed through the rest of the morning, through lunch, through half the afternoon.

When I came back from a late lunch at a diner, he was just finishing the job. Persistence gets it done. Not speed. Wow, something from my school years popped into my mind: *Gutta cavat lapidem non vi sed saepe cadendo.* A drop holes the stone not by force but by steady falling.

"Cowboy, you're a genius. How do you do it?" I wondered whether he knew Latin. "I thought you'd need couple o' days to get them toobs."

"I seen most evyting. Traveled out Indiaway, China, Fiji. Nutt'n I ain't seen. Sat wid de King of Samoa, danced a jig wid de Princess. Spoke deir lingo too. Dey wus friends wid de King George of de Brits. I known dat ole boy too. Chewed tobacco all de time. Gone to see 'em at Buckinam, him an' de ole Lady Queen." His work done for the day, he stood and talked. Where does he get this stuff? Even to make it up, didn't he have to have some knowledge?

"Where else have you been, Cowboy? You've seen a lot, haven't you?" I egged him on. "You hobnobbed with kings and potentates, have you seen presidents, too?"

"I seen 'em. Saw de Pope too. Pius de Twelfd gave me dis." He pulled tarnished silver cross out from the neck opening of his overalls. "He say to me, 'have a safe voyage, my chile.' Dat's why I'm still here, an' I'm comin' up on eighty-five dis winner." He pushed the hood back from his forehead and scratched his short, wiry gray hair. "You wan 'er wet sanded? Pick de paint you want on her. Talk to Sandy in de shop. I finish up tomorrow."

"Eighty-five? Why, that's amazing, Cowboy!" To me, he could be sixty or a hundred. "And, yes I want her wet sanded. I'll get the brown Interlux Bottomcote. Don't bother with the boot top, go right up to the gel."

"Take it easy." He walked off in slow motion.

"Good night, Cowboy."

I hooked up to the electrical cord Cowboy had left me. My refrigerator was running. I climbed the ladder and sat in the cockpit with a cold one, high and dry, overlooking the yard. Activities were coming to an end. Floodlights kept the yard well lit and the gate closed at six o'clock. Riviera Beach was not a safe neighborhood. I plugged in my little old TV and watched

Jeopardy. Then I wrote down in my notebook some of the conversation I had with Cowboy. What a character! What a dreamer! What a talent! He tells it all in a totally plausible, believable way. He's not bragging at all.

I went to take a shower in the bathroom behind the office building and storeroom, and then went to bed. Where did I get dem worms? Never been to Cairo.

At eight in the morning I went for breakfast at the diner and when I returned, Cowboy was already at work. Sitting like the day before on his bucket, his arm moved like a pneumatic rod. The wet sandpaper under his palm seemed to smooth the hull as if by magic. Everything he did, he did in slow motion and the effect was astonishing. Absorbed in his work, he didn't bother to answer my "Good morning." He did not stop to wipe his brow, until the job was done.

I talked to Sandy at the office and ordered one gallon of the brown Bottomcote so that in the afternoon Cowboy could paint the hull below the waterline.

I couldn't wait to hear some more of his stories. At lunchtime I found him sitting in the shade under a boat, eating a sandwich. He didn't join any of the other workers at the yard. They had probably heard his stories and I could imagine that they made fun of him. In me, he had an eager listener.

"How's it going, Cowboy?" How can I get him to talk? "You still travel much these days? I've been to the Caribbean, the Virgin Islands, Bermuda, Venezuela, all over the place, but nothing like you."

"In de Far East. Chindao an' Shanghai." He just gave me the names of some places he'd been to, for real or in his fantasies, but then he got into it again. "In Taipei I call' on Changkaishek an' de Missus. Had me to dinner an' all dem ministers were dere too. Dey aks'd me all 'bout Western places I's seen an' what's it like in America. An' I tol' 'em all I knows." He swallowed the last of his bread with a gulp from the water bottle. "Gave me a letter fo' Mr. Roosevelt."

"Did you bring him the letter?"

"No, dey tol' me he wus dead a'ready. I lef' de letter wid de man who open de doo' an' den I never heard no mo' 'bout it." He seemed to regret that.

221

"Have you been back to Formosa, then?" I asked him.

"Fo'mosa? No. Been to Tokyo an' Kyoto. Da's in Japan, what dey calls Nippon dere. Ole Hirohito's a good man, but dat kid o' his, no damn wort' a fart."

"You've met them?"

"Didn't stay, though. 'Cause dat idiot son." He got up. His lunch hour was over. "Now, Churchill an' Bismarck an' all dem big brains, da's somet'n' else. Dem you can have a conversion wid," he rumbled on as he walked back to my boat.

I could not figure this man out. Names and places most high school kids don't know are to him familiar as if they were his relatives and his neighborhood. And the stories? They are so real to him that he tells them in the most casual way. I went over to watch him paint. He was concentrating on putting the tape down along the waterline, perfectly straight. I stood around for a while, until he was ready to pour paint into the tray and start rolling the Bottomcote on. He did not talk when he worked. I went to get something to eat. After that I stopped at a ship chandler's to pick up some cable I needed to replace the main connection from the battery to the starter motor.

Cowboy was more than half finished with painting when I came back. He ignored me as I climbed the ladder to the cockpit. I busied myself with some chores I could do only while hauled out: cleaning the through-hulls and the impeller of the speed log.

"Leave dem tapes on. I dun paint'n, 'cept fo' some touch up," Cowboy told me as I came down from the boat. "I finish tomorrow mornin'. Then I's got to do dat trawler over dere." He walked off.

"Cowboy, don't forget to put that zinc on for me. Sandy will give it to you."

"Not to worry." He was already five feet away.

On the morning of the following day, Cowboy had another job. I was not in a hurry, still had to work on the head, the stuffing box and the steering quadrant. After lunch, Cowboy fastened the zinc to the shaft, touched up the waterline and left the tape for me to remove.

The travelift was busy that afternoon. "We splash you back in tomorrow morning," they told me at the office, as I went

222

to pay my bill that came to four hundred forty-eight dollars. Not bad. I would not have saved much by doing the job myself. Old Slip would not have sold me the paint at the discounted price and would have charged me a standard yard fee. Besides, it would have taken me twice as long, and Cowboy probably did a much better job.

Cowboy was working under the trawler on the other side of the yard. I didn't have the chance to talk some more with him. Maybe he ran out of yarn. I hope, he stays in his fantasy world when he goes home at night, alone, so he would not have to face the shock of reality.

Launch time was nine thirty the following morning. Forty-five minutes later, I was through the inlet and sailing north in a beautiful southeasterly breeze. With the smooth, freshly painted hull, I was hitting eight knots. Avoiding the ICW entirely, I sailed all the way to Fort Pierce and anchored for the night at Faber Cove. Another beautiful day followed and I had a great time sailing the Indian River south to Stuart. I did not use the engine, except to negotiate the bridges, until I approached Riverpoint Harbor and maneuvered into my slip.

On my next trip, two weeks later, I sailed the Indian River to Fort Pierce and out into the ocean. The weather was stifling hot, the humidity must have been a hundred per cent and the wind became absolutely calm. The air was so laden with moisture that a mist developed and before I reached Bethel Shoal, under power, I was enveloped in gray fog. I had set no goal for the trip, just wanted to be in open water. All around me was an ominous quiet, foreboding bad weather. I turned around and motored back to Fort Pierce where I anchored overnight. The atmosphere continued saturated with oppressing heat and humidity.

I started out in the morning. Barely underway in the Indian River, dark, low clouds gathered and it began to rain hard. There were some boats ahead of me. The downpour became so heavy, I all but lost sight of them, and could no longer see the markers to guide me. I slowed the engine. Two boats had stopped and dropped anchors close by the side of the channel. A strong thunderstorm developed.

Passing under the power line that crosses the Indian River from the Indian Point Power Plant, the thought occurred to me whether it was more likely to get struck by lightning under a high voltage electrical power line, or less so.

I have since asked many people this question, without receiving a conclusive answer: does an overhead electrical cable attract or deflect a lightning bolt? Would it endanger a boat passing underneath, or protect it? I got answers from yes to no to makes no difference. I wish, I could ask my Australian shipmate Jon Reeve, the electrical engineer, the scientist. I can hear him now: "a scientist sits at a desk, a scientist does research, a scientist does not answer stupid questions." All the same, I liked the man. We had made a good team.

Equipment on board *TRITON 3* included lightning deflectors via the shrouds from the masthead to the chain plates and down to below the waterline. There has always been dispute over the wisdom of having such devices on a boat. While some sailors maintained that lightning rods invite lightning and do more harm than good, others said that a bolt passes harmlessly through the deflector, bypassing vital parts on board. I had made it safely through many thunderstorms. Whether that was due to the lightning rods or in spite of them, I guess I will never know.

On one of my trips in the fall of 1993, I lost my watch. It had been a retirement present from my Japanese coworkers. They had sent me this fine Seiko Silverwave from Tokyo in February of 1985. That was eight and a half years ago. As I was in the process of hoisting my mainsail, my wrist was caught in the reefing line, which tore off the watch. I saw it sliding off the cabin roof, hitting the deck and bouncing over the side. I tried hard not to pay too much attention to this loss, and went on with the task at hand, as I navigated through the St. Lucie Inlet.

In my mind, I can still see the insignificant splash the watch made as it disappeared beneath the waves. I sailed to Biscayne Bay, spent some time in Coconut Grove and Miami Beach, and I bought myself a cheap replacement.

A week later, I returned to Stuart. It was a calm night. I often sailed without my lights on when alone on the water as far as I could see. Passing the Fort Lauderdale harbor entrance a couple of miles offshore, a boat of the Coast Guard circled me. I called over, "what's the matter? Am I doing anything wrong?" Then I realized, I had forgotten to turn my navigation lights on. Quickly I grabbed the red and green flashlight from the cockpit locker and put it on the cabin roof.

"Your running lights were not on when we spotted you," a guy in blue uniform shouted back.

"Batteries are low. That's why I use this substitute. Sorry, if it's not bright enough."

The boat came alongside. "You didn't have that on either when we first saw you."

"Well, it's hard to see. I apologize." Being polite has helped me out of trouble before.

"Keep your running lights on, especially here, where you can expect traffic in and out of Port Everglades. Have a good trip."

"Thank you. Good night."

I continued on my way, giving brightly lit shrimpers engaged in night fishing a wide berth. At two in the morning I was at the St. Lucie seabuoy. At first I did not dare going into this tricky inlet in the dark, but then, I didn't want to wait four hours for daylight out there in rolley-polley conditions either. I poked my way in carefully. This is the spot where I lost my watch last week, I thought for just a fleeting moment.

Julia decided it was time to give up residence in Queens and move to an easier year-round climate. She had bought a house in Jacksonville, Florida. I drove to New York to assist with the packing and organizing the transition.

Everything was ready for transport to the Sunshine State when the enormous moving van showed up, with the exception of two mattresses for us to sleep on the last night.

The two mattresses fit perfectly into the cargo space of my El Camino. In Virginia, a torrential downpour interrupted our journey to Julia's new home in Jacksonville. I feared the mattresses would be soaked, but the tightness of the vinyl cover over the bed of the car (and my packing skills!) kept them perfectly dry.

I spent a few days in Jacksonville, helping Julia with the task of moving in and getting settled.

From then on, the family came together in Jacksonville for visits and holidays. We had cut our ties with New York.

BIMINI

I had lately watched the temperature gauge indicating a slightly high engine temperature. The Universal Atomic Four normally ran at 140 to 145 degrees. When I saw the needle go up to 165, I knew that something was wrong and I replaced the thermostat. Thereafter the temperature did not climb beyond 150 degrees. I installed a new Oberdorfer Water pump and, confident that *TRITON 3* was now in fine condition, I left Stuart on 19 May for a cruise to Bimini. Carlos and Linda, looking forward to a special vacation, were my invited guest crew for this excursion. They had booked their flight to Palm Beach for 21 May. Our rendezvous was to take place at one p m at the Municipal Marina in Riviera Beach.

Three hours away from Riverpoint Harbor, at Peck Lake, my temperature gauge showed 165 degrees. Somewhat alarmed, I anchored and let the engine cool down. After a couple of hours, I closed the seacock and examined the pump. There was nothing wrong with it, except for some dirt and sand on the impeller. I cleaned and reinstalled the pump and remained at anchor overnight in Peck Lake.

In the morning everything seemed to be all right, but I stopped at the Jupiter Marina to consult a mechanic about the overheating problem. The shop was closed, it was Saturday. The mechanic could not get into the shop and was unable to do any work on the boat. He suggested removing the thermostat, which I did. I continued along the Waterway. The PGA Boulevard Bridge was closed and, due to mechanical failure, did not open. I had to spend the night tied to a concrete pier at Seminole Boat Yard. Many boaters, waiting on either side of the bridge, turned back, their weekend ruined. Although the gauge indicated that my engine temperature was not rising above 160 degrees, I was still concerned. There was no mechanic available at this marina.

On Sunday morning, the bridge still did not open. The trouble with the engine and the malfunction of the bridge had dampened my mood considerably. I called a taxi and drove to Riviera Beach to meet Carlos and Linda. They arrived on time from the airport.

"Stay in the taxi," I greeted them. "The boat's not here." I got into the backseat with them. "Problem with a bridge. I couldn't get to Riviera Beach." I gave the taxi driver directions to Seminole Boat Yard, twenty minutes away.

I explained to them, "if they don't fix the damn bridge we can't go anywhere except back to Stuart," but kept the other problem to myself.

At last, late in the afternoon, the bridge opened to let us through. I hoped that the malfunction of the cooling system could be taken care of at Old Slip Marine on Monday morning.

We took *TRITON 3* into a slip for the night. "There is a slight problem with the cooling system." I made it sound like nothing too important. "Maybe a mechanic can take a look at it before we head out."

For the rest of the evening and the night I tried to make the best of the situation with good food and drink. Riviera Beach is no place to roam around any time of day, let alone a Sunday night. They didn't mind the delay. Sitting in the cockpit, in the semi-tropical ambiance, was a big change from their daily routines and we enjoyed each other's company. I told them about Cowboy. "Maybe you meet him tomorrow. He's a real character." I related a few of his stories. Carlos and Linda laughed at my attempts to imitate Cowboy's speech and slow movements.

On Monday morning the mechanic at Old Slip said, "There is really no quick fix to the problem. Thermostat removed, pump working well, there must be an internal obstruction," exactly what I had feared all along. I bought and installed a filter for the raw water intake, to prevent further clogging of the system. I asked about Cowboy.

"He's out sick, but he'll be here tomorrow, maybe this afternoon. He never stays out for more than a day. He ain't never gonna quit until he dies."

We missed Cowboy and took off in the afternoon. "We will use the engine as sparingly as possible," I said. "The problem is what it has always been: time. Remember, what I have always told you? If you don't have the time, let's not go?" Of course, I did not want them to lose their vacation, long in the planning.

228

As soon as we came through Lake Worth Inlet, I shut down the engine and Carlos helped me get the mainsail up. It was Linda's first time on a sailboat, in open ocean water. The weather was hot and the wind light.

Without the use of the engine, the Gulf Stream would take us to Grand Bahama Island, instead of Bimini. "We have to get across the Stream," I told them. "With so little wind, barely making three knots, we'll end up in Europe." We pushed ahead with the Diesel, temperature rising to 180. I turned it off. "We'll give it another push in an hour, let the thing cool off first." In this way we sailed and motored through the night. Linda got a light touch of seasickness. I felt bad about that. I felt responsible for giving them a good time.

"Come here, Linda, take the wheel and watch the compass. You're in charge now." That'll take her mind off being sick, works every time.

In the morning we ended up at Isaac Light, far north of Bimini. As we approached, a U.S. Coast Guard Helicopter circled above. I called on the VHF radio. "U.S. Coast Guard Chopper. Triton 3. Do you have any instructions for us?"

"Triton 3. Small freighter or fishing vessel on fire at Isaac. Two POB (persons on board). Can you give assistance? Over."

"Will give assistance if required, but so far have not seen the vessel or smoke or any POB." That's all I need, engine overheating and rescue two Bahamians whose boat's on fire. Carlos found this very interesting.

"Stand by, Triton 3." Pause. "Two people on Isaac Rock. We'll do the rescue. Thanks for your assistance."

"Glad to help. Triton 3 out." I knew the regulation. If able to render assistance, any mariner is under obligation to do so. We were too far to witness the rescue, but as we closed in on Isaac, we saw some smoke rising from the other side of the rock, behind the lighthouse, but nothing else. We found the calmest spot at the southeast tip of Isaac and dropped the CQR. Carlos and Linda immediately jumped into the water to cool off, while I rigged the ladder, to get them back on board.

Although the boat rolled and pitched in the open roadstead, we had a nice day and evening. Linda was no longer

229

seasick. What my young shipmates wanted, complete relaxation and play, carefree lolling about on deck, in the water, or falling asleep under the cockpit awning, they took full advantage. I was happy to see them enjoying every bit of it. For supper I prepared a new specialty of mine: garlic soup. I knew, they liked garlic, but this was perhaps a bit too much for them. The meal consisted of beef consommé, shredded carrots, Italian style bread crumbs and minced, fresh garlic, with a few whole cloves thrown in, slowly cooked and simmered until the garlic was quite soft. Buttered Cuban bread on the side.

"Ice cold Coronas go best with it," I recommended. "Tomorrow we'll eat at the Red Lion in Alicetown, I promise. Anything you want. Lobster, grouper, steak, chicken. You name it." If they made any complimentary observations about the gourmet dish I had served, I must have missed them.

In the night, a rainsquall got me out of my bunk. I struggled with the awning, rolling it up in the strong wind and stowing it below before it would rip to shreds. Then I checked on the anchor, concerned that we might drag onto the rocks, if the wind changed. The squall was of short duration. I took off my wet T-shirt and crawled back into my berth.

In the morning, as we left our rough anchorage, Carlos spotted two waterspouts. Luckily they were far away. We got underway with reefed main and Genoa in a strong wind and I was glad to give my guests some excellent sailing.

"This is where I had that terrible thunderstorm three years ago, I told you about. Right here, between the Moselle Bank and Isaac. Ripped my main to shreds. I will never forget that afternoon."

"Wow. Could anything like that happen today? I mean, this is pretty strong wind, isn't it?" Carlos loved a good adventure, the rougher, the better; still there was concern in his voice.

"Naw, this is nothing like that. This is a beautiful, steady wind of maybe twenty knots," I said. "Hey, Linda, you want to take the helm? Get a feeling for what real sailing is like?"

"Thank you. Oh, this is great! I feel the power of the wind, and how the boat responds to it. It's like flying!" She loved it. After a while she said, "Now you take it, Carlos."

Carlos took over. "See that? We just hit eight point three knots," he said excitedly.

"Yeah, watch the speed limit!" I joked. There is nothing more invigorating than taming a strong wind, standing behind the wheel of a boat, feeling the resistance of the rudder to your touch, as you slice through the waves. There were some clouds, a brief shower but the wind remained steady all the way to North Rock. Then we were in the lee of North Bimini, but did not need the help of the engine until we turned into the channel for Alicetown. I took down the mainsail and rolled up the Genoa.

"Carlos, line up those two stakes, one on the beach, the other farther inland among the shrubs. You see them? Don't get off course. To either side of the range we run aground."

In the early afternoon, we docked at Weech's in Alicetown. Carlos and Linda headed for the showers, while I walked with the passports and forms to Customs and Immigration. When I came back, Carlos and Linda had spread the awning over the cockpit and, fresh out of the showers, they were already enjoying the island life.

"Dad, we will be here for only two nights. Can we stay at the dock, instead of anchoring? We can come and go, don't have to rely on the dinghy."

"Okay, you tourists!" I mocked them and asked Jerry, Weech's dock attendant, to assign us a slip. I, too, was glad not having to anchor, but didn't tell them that. Then we walked to the ocean side. The beach was our playground. Swimming, snorkeling and Frisbee playing under the hot sun tired us out.

"I don't really like the beach. Too much sand," I complained. "You bring it back in your clothes, your shoes, it's all over the boat. Everywhere sand. In the cockpit, in the cabin. I like to swim off the boat or the dinghy, not the beach. No sand!"

As promised, we had dinner at the Red Lion Inn, a rustic restaurant near the water, and had a table by the window. While we ate we watched the rats scurrying about this way and that among the rocks and the junk piled up in the yard at the water's edge.

"Mom wouldn't be able to eat here," said Carlos. "She would be terrified." But we enjoyed watching as the animals played and searched for food scraps.

Tired, but not yet exhausted enough to go back to the boat, we walked along the main road to the End of the World. In the wooden shack with a dirt floor, we had a Heineken and looked at the old T-shirts, bras and bikini tops and bottoms that hang from the walls and the ceiling. "A lot of people must have walked back to their hotels or boats in the nude," said Carlos. "What do you say, Lin…"

"Don't even go there!" Linda protested.

Then we stopped at one of Ernest Hemingway's favorite saloons, where he might have written parts of his novel *Islands in the Stream*. A heavy downpour kept us long enough to have a couple of beers in the crowded bar. Black and white photos of the famous writer covered the walls.

The Tour Guide

After a long day in the sun and an evening with good food and several beers, it felt great to step on board without having to get into the dinghy and row out to the anchored boat. "I could get used to this," I told them, "but I allow myself such luxury only when I have guests. At other times it's a hard life. Mild tropical breezes, moonlit nights, swaying palm trees, island rhythms from the shore—sure, but that's not all. I work my fingers to the bone, splicing rope or mending sails, working on the engine, scraping barnacles off the hull, getting the anchors back on board." I didn't want it to sound like complaining, so I added, "it's all part of the romance of sailing and I don't want it any other way."

Carlos and Linda at the helm

I compared my life to theirs. Crowded Manhattan, screeching subways, offices in skyscrapers, telephones and typewriters and computers. I have done it myself long enough. This is my reward. Theirs will come, too.

On day two in the Islands in the Stream we went by ferryboat across to the South Island of Bimini. There is only a small settlement where the boat dropped us off. We found our way to the beach; or rather, a dog showed us the way. This mutt, the size of a German Shepherd, got attached to Linda, the dog

233

lover. As our tour guide, he ran ahead, then waited for us to catch up. On the way he took a bath in a pond to cool off and in the end he led us to the place where the range markers for the channel are. As soon as we reached the beach, he turned around and walked back to the ferry landing.

In the morning of the following day we had to say goodbye to Bimini. I had planned for a nice, long cruise without any need for the engine, once out of the harbor. From Bimini to Fort Pierce we crossed the Gulf Stream by sailing west with the prevailing wind, while the current pushed us northward. It was a perfect solution.

At the end of a beautiful day and night sail, we came through the Fort Pierce inlet by daybreak and docked at a private pier to make the all-important phone call to customs. There was only the stretch of the Intracoastal to Stuart ahead of us. We hardly had the need to run the Diesel since leaving Isaac for Bimini three days earlier, but this last day, in the Indian River, we had no choice. In five anxious hours of engine on, engine off, with the gauge climbing to 190 degrees, we made it safely into Riverpoint Harbor.

Linda looked good with her black hair framing her sunburned face, and Carlos was thoroughly suntanned. He took on a dark complexion in an hour or two in the sun. "With that wild hair and your beard you look like a Greek fisherman," I told him. They were a handsome couple.

That evening residents and guests at Riverpoint Harbor staged a big beach party. "You came back at the right time," they greeted us. There was food on the barbecue grill. Coolers with beer stood between the picnic tables and a bar was set up with bottles of booze, ice buckets and sodas. A band, comprised of one of the marina residents and his friends, played rock-and-roll into the early morning hours.

On Sunday morning, 28 May, we had to get up before daylight. I had to drive Carlos and Linda to the airport in Palm Beach. With less than two hours of sleep, and no breakfast, we carried their bags down the dock and put them into the trunk of my car, a white Chevy Caprice. The El Camino had outlived its usefulness after Julia's move to Jacksonville. The car did not start—the battery was dead. What happened? Now, that it's real important, it doesn't start? Six o'clock on Sunday morning, how can I get them to the airport? I nearly panicked. After the party, everybody was asleep. Whose car can I borrow? Impossible.

"Dad, don't freak out. Let's calmly think, what we can do. Can't you borrow a car?"

I shook my head. By sheer power of concentration, I remembered the telephone number painted in big, black numbers on yellow cabs around town. But there was no phone here, the office was closed. Jon's boat, the *PEGASUS*, has a phone on board, but he's not home. I looked after his boat when he was away and I knew the combination to the lock. I grabbed a flashlight, ran to the end of the dock and climbed aboard the *PEGASUS*.

"Car service? Yes, I need a taxi right away at Riverpoint Harbor, just north of the Roosevelt Bridge. It's an emergency!" I was out of breath. "Only one? And that is where?" I listened. "On the turnpike? How far? Can you get in touch with the driver?"

Carlos said, "Dad, calm down. It's going to be all right."

"Yes, I'm holding," I said back into the receiver. "What? Ten to fifteen minutes? Okay. Please, tell him to hurry. What? Ah, to Palm Beach International. Yes. We'll be at the side of the road. A hundred dollars? Okay, okay. Thank you."

We put our bills together and, between the three of us, we had enough. "Let's get the bags out of the trunk and wait out by the road." We did that and then stood there on the pre-dawn Sunday morning. It was quiet, there was no traffic. The first car that came along was the taxi.

"Wow, that was fast! You're going to make it in time." We stuffed their bags into the trunk and, after a quick hug from both of them, I shoved them into the backseat. "Bye, I'll call you!" I shouted as the taxi drove off.

Relieved, I went to bed to get a few of hours of sleep, and woke up by ten. There was the party going on at the beach. The couple on the trawler *SHIP HAPPENS* and their neighbors had brought out Champagne and orange juice. They were drinking Mimosas.

"What the hell went wrong with my car?" I asked. "Anybody know?"

Nobody knew, nor did anyone care. With jumper cables from the neighboring pickup truck, I got my car started and I drove straight to Sears. That weekend, batteries were on sale. I bought a new DieHard and drove back to the marina.

"Oh, Peter, by the way, I found the rear door of your car open late last night. I closed it," Marty, the dockmaster, said as I walked to my boat. He had also been at the party last night.

"What? Why didn't you tell me? I just went out and bought a new battery which I probably didn't need."

"Sorry. I don't know, must have slipped my mind. Or you were gone already."

Let it go, I told myself. I had no appetite for a Mimosa, but drank one anyway. Finally, I could relax and reflect on last week. They are just about now landing in Newark. They probably slept on the plane.

We really had fun. The sailing was great. Bimini was no disappointment for Carlos and Linda. Coming home to a party was a great finale to our cruise. A little bit of panic... A lot, actually, this morning when the car didn't start.

What had bothered me all that time, though, was the overheating of the engine. That problem had to be addressed before anything else.

I called a diesel mechanic. He came and removed the pump. "Nothin' wrong with the pump. Just needs a new impeller. This one's chewed up pretty bad." He looked at the thermostat, which I had just put back into its housing.

"Good," he said. "You gotta flush out the whole cooling system. I ain't gonna do that. Suppose she can't take the pressure and somethin' else breaks. Then you've got to buy a new engine. Might as well do that anyway. She's what, fifteen years old? That's a lot."

Yeah, a lot of bullshit. The man left without putting the pump back together. Some days later I got a bill from him, which I didn't pay. He had done nothing but take the pump apart, then left it for me to deal with.

Jon of *PEGASUS* and I did what the mechanic refused to do. I reinstalled the pump and we reversed the flow of the cooling water. Turning the engine over for two seconds, Jon collected in a jar the water that came out of the open intake flange.

"Will you look at that? Gravel, shells, even tiny shrimp," I exclaimed.

"It's hard to believe any water got through the narrow passages in the engine block at all," Jon said. "That should take care of your problem."

In a matter of minutes, we reinstalled the hoses and put the system back together. I switched on the engine. The temperature registered between 140 and 145 degrees. A simple cure for a big problem!

WAITING FOR PEGASUS

The hurricane season of 1995 was a busy one. In August, Erin and Tropical Storm Jerry were of concern to the Treasure Coast, bringing heavy rain, thunderstorms and tornados with them.

There were plenty of named storms that year. Roxanne lasted a whole week in October. She came as a tropical storm across the Yucatan Peninsula, grew to a hurricane over the Gulf of Mexico, then swept across Florida. Thirty inches of rain fell in some areas of the Treasure Coast. At Riverpoint Harbor, the boats were riding high above the dock, which was under a foot of water.

The winter months were stormy, too. The Great Blizzard of January '96, that dumped two and a half feet of snow on New York, brought a record low temperature of twenty-nine degrees and winds of thirty-five knots as far south as central Florida.

Between storms and cold fronts, I undertook day sails and overnighters. The engine temperature did not exceed the normal range. All pumps were working properly, through-hulls were tight and the rigging fine-tuned to optimum performance. I caulked a leak above the starboard cupboard in the galley that had bothered me for a long time.

One more thing had to be done before another voyage. A fresh coat of bottom paint was necessary once a year, so I made an appointment for *TRITON 3* at Old Slip in Riviera Beach.

Jon Kreeger and I had been talking of a Bahama trip together. Jon has not moved his boat *PEGASUS* for about two years. He had difficulty finding a part needed to repair his generator. "I am not going anywhere without my generator," he said, and kept searching from Florida to Washington, Maine to Texas for a connecting rod of some sort.

"That old generator of yours... Get a new one and be done with it," I told him. We planned to sail down the Keys, then head over to the Bahamas, but he was stubborn about his generator. Maybe, I thought, he didn't really want to go cruising.

I was impatient, wanted to get going. "Look," I told him, "I'll go ahead. We stay in touch and you can catch up with me when you're ready." I've been sitting at the dock for months, only now and then sailed a little sailing on the river when the weather allowed it, but that did not satisfy me. I wanted the open ocean, islands, real sailing.

"They're ordering the parts from Italy. I'll get them in a week, ten days tops, and I'll join you."

That didn't convince me. "From Italy, huh? What's that generator, anyway? A Maserati or something?" Then more seriously, "okay, I'll give you a call from Riviera Beach, then Miami and after that from Marathon. From there I'll go across to Bimini." I hoped, but doubted, that he would meet me at one of those places.

I sailed out of Riverpoint Harbor on 4 March 1996. Haul out was scheduled for the next morning. The weather had become stormy again. Forecasts predicted winds of thirty knots and wave heights to reach twenty-five feet in the Gulf Stream. This did not affect the work at Old Slip in Riviera Beach. Cowboy wet-sanded the hull in the morning and painted in the afternoon. He either did not remember me, or he did and was not in the mood to spin more of his yarns about kings and foreign places. Perhaps he had told me all he knew. He sat on his bucket and worked silently. When he was done, he just said, "Keep de rest of de paint fo' touch up," and walked away. I would have liked to hear more of his fantastic stories.

The storm off Florida's east coast caused high seas and prevented launching for a week. I wrote in the logbook:

"Heavy rain, cold NW wind, seas 18 to 25 feet in the Gulf Stream."

When finally the sun came through, several boats were scheduled for launching ahead of *TRITON 3*.

I telephoned Jon. He was still waiting for his generator parts from Italy. "Yeah, good luck!" I said.

After hanging out in the boat yard for a week, I sailed through the night to Miami. The weather was cool, the air clean and fresh as so often after a storm. The boat performed excellently, under sail as well as under power. The newest addition to my already extensive ground tackle was a Fortress, said to be the best lightweight anchor. Made of hardened aluminum, the model I chose weighed only nine pounds. It was recommended for boats of up to thirty-six feet. I used my new anchor for the first time in Biscayne Bay.

After several days riding out cold front after cold front as if on a mechanical bull, I ventured through the channel at Cape Florida. Barely out through the intricate buoy system into open water, choppy seas came at me so that I had no chance of making any significant headway. The stress on the equipment and on me was not worth the struggle and I turned back into the relatively calm Biscayne Bay.

I had not spoken to Jon since my arrival in the Miami area and called him from a phone booth at Crandon Park. Jon wasn't ready. Parts coming from Italy... Yeah, right.

Tumultuous conditions kept me for three more days at anchor in Biscayne Bay. I had set a second anchor and both were on a rode of over a hundred feet. Like Cat Island in 1990, six years ago—and no other boat in sight. Occasionally my bow dipped into a wave scooping up water that ran along the deck and washed overboard at the transom. I really had enough of that, when at last I saw a chance for a second attempt.

Early in the morning the wind was light from the west, but became stronger by the hour. Close-hauled, I sailed past Bowls Bank for Fowey Rock. At noontime I took down the sails and continued under power, head-on into breaking seas.

A big yacht that had followed me at a mile distance turned into Caesar's Creek, Key Largo, and promptly ran aground. Her crew struggled to get free, eventually managed to heel the boat over and get her keel off the bottom. They decided to sail back to Key Biscayne.

I fought for another hour with hardly any progress before turning around. Downwind, I reached Caesar's Creek in a matter of minutes. Carefully I attempted what the bigger yacht could not do. Aware of the strong current, I steered into the marked channel past the spot where the other boat had run aground. Once in the creek, the water was comparatively calm.

In the wilderness of Caesar's Creek, at the north end of Key Largo, it was difficult to find a spot without grass on the bottom. The Fortress was no good on grass; slid right over it without getting a bite. I tried the CQR. At last, after a couple of hours, I got it buried in a depth of thirteen feet. The hard work finished, I noticed how cold it had become. The radio announced, "expect freezing temperatures statewide for tonight." It was the right time for a grog, Rum, hot water, sugar, a hearty dinner of beef stew and, to insure a good night's sleep, more grog. Settling down for the night, I slipped into my sleeping bag, put on my watch cap and gloves. I woke up several times, listening to the wind howling in the rigging, but the water in this creek was calm and the boat hardly moved. All around me was rich, thick vegetation.

In the morning, limbs stiff in thirty-five degrees Fahrenheit, I didn't leave my sleeping bag until nine-thirty. After oatmeal and hot coffee, I took my anchor on board and exited through the cut into the deep water of Hawks Channel. The wind was steady from the northwest at about fifteen knots, but became gusty later. With reefed main and Genoa, passing Rattlesnake Key, I headed for Rodriguez Key.

Even though the sun was strong, the air had not warmed much. The wind came from the frigid north where people were still digging out after recent snowstorms.

Since it was still early in the day, there was no reason for me to stop at Rodriguez. The next place to anchor, Tavernier, was within my reach. There I found a wide-open, shallow bay. Carefully I approached in water not deeper than six feet, still far from land. Under the keel was white sand, promising good holding ground, but I did not dare come closer to the shore. The wind had become much calmer and there were hardly any waves. When the depth sounder read five feet, I let my Fortress down. It had been a fine day, with some very good sailing, in spite of the cold wind. I had worn my foul weather suit, watch cap and gloves all day. At last, in this calm bay, I could shed my wintry clothes and relax in the cockpit with a sundowner of rum and cranberry juice. It was time for warm weather to return to Florida.

It really was warmer when I woke up in the morning. The wind was light, still from the north, but it had lost its grim bite. I put my dinghy in the water and attached the motor to the transom. Curious about Tavernier, I went for a long ride, taking my empty water jugs and Jerry can for diesel fuel with me. Coming into the narrow creek, I found a fuel dock, a dive shop, a Jet Ski rental place and a souvenir and T-shirt shack, and not much more. Still, it was a quaint and charming place.

On the way back to *TRITON 3*, anchored way out there, looking small and lonely, I came upon a flat boat with two men standing in it. Handling long poles, they seemed to be searching the bottom for something. I thought I might be disturbing their activity, shut down my outboard motor and rowed closer.

"Lost something?" I called over to them. "What are you looking for?"

"Sponges." One of them answered. He rested for a moment, leaning on his pole. The other man continued with his work.

I came alongside to take a look at the critters they had in the bottom of their boat. "They don't look like what I've seen in drug stores." These things were unsightly, slimy, full of sand with green weeds hanging about them. There was about a dozen of them.

"They're alive. They've got to be cleaned and processed, before you can use them in the bathtub."

"Interesting. Thanks, and good luck." Later I learned that Tavernier was one of a few places where natural sponges were still harvested.

For the next leg, Tavernier to Marathon, I calculated a full day of daylight hours. The weather had still not warmed up much, but the sailing in Hawks Channel was good. There were shallows to avoid, but courses were well marked with buoys and light towers along this barrier reef, one of the longest of the North American Continent, that separated Hawks Channel from the Atlantic Ocean. There was Hen and Chicken Rocks, then the Alligator Reef with a white tower on it; a little farther, Tennessee Reef. I passed the high bridge at Channel Five and remembered my cruise with Frank Gallardo four years earlier. East Turtle Shoal at noontime, and two hours later East Washerwoman. Before four o'clock, I was on my final approach to Boot Key Harbor at Marathon.

It was a challenge to find a spot to safely anchor in this popular, always crowded harbor. There seemed to be even more boats than when I came here in 1992. I tried first near the Dockside, where I had anchored with Frank. There was no room. Most of the better-looking, seaworthy yachts occupied that side of the harbor. The farther away from the Dockside, the crummier the boats. Mean looking people observed my every move as I circled through the anchorage. I felt like an intruder upon their turf. "Now, what's this newcomer like, where's he gonna put that boat of his? Don't even think of coming close to me. I kick your butt if you anchor here. There's no room for guys like you." That's what I read in their faces.

It was a weekend. They were all hanging out on their boats. Men, women and children. Dogs, too. I saw an open spot, in the middle of the packed anchorage. Slowly, suspicious about it, I motored towards it. Woom, I hit something. There had to be a wreck down there. I expected to hear applause or cheering, but they were all silently enjoying my predicament.

At last, I chose a spot that seemed suitable. I prepared two anchors, the Fortress and the CQR. I dropped the CQR close to a fairly decent looking boat with one man on board, then pulled back into a space between two boats as far as my rode permitted, and let my Fortress slide down. By hauling in the slack on both anchors I made sure they were set, put the engine in reverse and satisfied myself that my anchors were holding.

Not a single person on the neighboring boats had waved a welcome to me. There was an atmosphere of hostility around me. If one of my anchors dragged, I could not hope for assistance. If my boat were to drift into another, there would be war. I had to be absolutely sure my anchors had found good holding ground. The show I had given them by maneuvering and placing my anchors should at least have told them that I knew what I was doing. By the time I came to rest, it was almost dark.

Sunday morning I put the dinghy in the water and carried my main Danforth out on a hundred fifty feet of chain and line. Back on board, I hauled in on the line, gaining more distance from my closest neighbor. Satisfied with my anchoring design, I mounted the motor on the dinghy and went across the harbor to Dockside to buy a ticket that entitled me to dock the dinghy for a week and to draw unlimited water. One phone call to Julia let her, Susi in Paris and Carlos in New York know where I was. Sundays were always the big communication days.

Then I called Jon Kreeger. He had no news for me about his generator and I thought he used the generator just as an excuse. I gave up on him, but did not say so. The whole thing turned into a joke for me and on April Fools Day I wrote to him:

"On the 14th I will leave Marathon. We will rendezvous at midnight in the middle of the Gulf Stream at the coordinates 25 degrees N lat., 80 degrees 30 min. W long. From there we continue together to Alicetown, Bimini." I am sure he knew I was just teasing him.

I called The Cat. "Guess where I am. I'm on the phone," I told her, but the old joke was no longer funny. I wanted to find out if any remnants of our former relationship still existed. There was a thread, but it had worn thin. She had moved on; I was doing the same. Besides, she would never leave New York, and I would not move back there.

Winter still did not want to yield. Cold fronts were pushing down from the north, colliding with low-pressure systems over the Bahamas and the Western Caribbean. I experienced a bad storm in the night of 2 April. Rain squalls, packing winds of thirty-five knots, had me standing at the helm, engine in slow forward against the wind, to make sure I would not collide with any of the wildly swinging boats. Wet and cold, I was on watch through the night. Most of my neighbors were also up, while those on permanent, secure moorings did not care what was going on around them.

I also had some good days while I was in Marathon. Besides the Dockside Bar and Restaurant, where I always met with lively company, I found several good local eating places. Ship chandlers, general shopping and post office were conveniently nearby. One weekend I attended the big Marathon Seafood Festival, held on a large meadow. The Fishermen of Florida and the Marathon Chamber of Commerce sponsored this annual feast. Tents and kiosks, set up for the weekend-long event, offered everything from smoked to fresh fish and seafood. Beer was flowing freely.

Three weeks I spent in Marathon, surrounded by unfriendly people, and I had no idea why they were so hostile. They had not exchanged a single word or gesture with me from my arrival to my departure and, to the best of my knowledge, I had not shown any ill will toward any of them.

No word came from Jon and early on the 14th, I began work on my anchors. There was no easy way to get to all three anchors without drifting into one or another boat. I drew a diagram and studied the position of my anchors in relation to wind and tidal currents. The solution was to put the Danforth on the mooring ball. For this maneuver I had to use the dinghy. The first anchor to come on board had to be the CQR, which I could retrieve by falling back on the Fortress. Then I shortened the rode of the Fortress. It was time to hook the boat up to the Danforth. I rowed my dinghy out to the mooring ball, attached a line and, back on board, I pulled up the Fortress. No longer in need of the dinghy, I lifted it out of the water onto the davits.

My neighbors watched this complicated, intricate piece of work silently, but with skepticism and puzzlement. Their faces showed criticism and amusement. I felt as if I were on stage, performing a difficult magic trick. Satisfied with my performance, which unfolded flawlessly and without so much as an unnecessary step, I turned on the Diesel and hauled up my last anchor, the Danforth. A swan among ugly ducklings, *TRITON 3* moved gracefully away from this place without a goodbye or a farewell, without a hand raised in salute, without a smiling face. The show was over, but there was no applause. After almost two hours of giving free entertainment, I left the stage and my audience without looking back.

I stopped at the fuel dock to top off my fuel tank and then headed out. A strong wind hurried me toward East Washerwoman. Between Coffin Patch and Tennessee Reef, I crossed the barrier reef. *TRITON* 3 was in the deep water of the Florida Strait.

A swan among ugly ducklings... Was that the reason for their hostility? Their envy?

One hour past midnight at the coordinates 25 N lat., 80.5 W long, I called on the VHF "Pegasus, Pegasus, Pegasus. Triton 3.

Over." I repeated my call twice. Of course, there was no answer. It was just the conclusion of my private joke. What if Jon had answered, "Triton 3, I am here, waiting for you. You are late!"

I felt the effect of the Gulf Stream, the balmy air and the northward pull. In the light breeze, dodging a number of freighters, I had to turn on the engine. To cross this busy shipping lane, I steered directly for one huge container vessel and passed closely behind her stern through the turbulent water, churned up by the propeller. The next big freighter was only two miles behind. At the speed of eighteen knots, that's a matter of less than ten minutes. I let out a sigh of relief when the range lights and the green running light of those monsters indicated that I was out of harm's way.

In the morning mist, the island of Bimini rose above the horizon. Dolphins played alongside the boat, jumping out of the bow wave and diving back in gracefully. They crossed over from one side to the other closely under the keel, setting off the depth sounder. Watching them perform their antics I wondered, do they mind that we humans infringe upon their habitat? Are they showing off like acrobats? What do they think of these strange objects in which we travel?

BACK IN THE BAHAMAS

Twenty-four hours after leaving Boot Key Harbor at Marathon, I filled out the Customs and Immigration papers Jerry handed me. Official business settled, I took *TRITON 3* to the anchorage.

I had grown fond of this island and wanted to stay for a week or longer. There were always some six or eight boats at anchor and when one or two left, others arrived. One day I spotted the most unlikely flag to fly on the stern of any vessel. This was the red-white-red national ensign of Austria. I rowed over to talk to the skipper. He was an elderly man from Vienna.

"Yes, Wien," he told me. "We sailed the Danube and the canals of Europe." He continued, "We came across the Atlantic, wintered in Puerto Rico. Now we are on our way up the east coast of the United States."

That's real sailing. What I do is small stuff. "And in a boat not bigger than mine," I said. "It's the first time I see the Austrian flag on a boat."

His crew was as unlikely as his homeport. She was a very beautiful and friendly young African woman. "I want to see New York," she said enthusiastically, showing a splendid set of gleaming white teeth.

The next morning they were gone. It's so hard to make lasting friends among sailors.

An Ericson racing sloop came in and anchored close to me. On the transom was the name *STIR CRAZY*. The young man on board donned snorkel gear and fins and dove to inspect his anchors. Then he swam over to greet me. "Hi, I am Roy Gordon."

"Hey. Peter. Pleased to meet you. You are real particular about your anchors. I like that."

"I like to dive. Want me to take a look at your anchors?"

"Oh, that's okay. But, if you like to dive, why not. Thanks."

He went down, stayed longer than I thought good for anybody. Then he came back up, shook the water out of his hair and told me, "The chain of your CQR is hooked under a rock. You won't be able to get that anchor free when you want to leave."

Something like that had happened to me once before in the same spot, I remembered. "Can you dislodge it and bury the anchor for me, so I'll be safe?" I asked him.

"Be glad to," he answered and down he went. After sixty seconds he surfaced next to my boat. "I dug it in real good for you," he said. "You're not going anywhere."

"Thank you, that's very nice of you. Come over for a beer when you're ready."

"Okay. See you later." He swam back to his boat. A young woman waited for him in the cockpit. They didn't have a dinghy. Their transportation was by snorkel and fins.

A little later Roy climbed up my ladder. "We don't care much to go ashore," he told me. They had come from Dinner Key, Coconut Grove to Bimini for the weekend. He was a nurse and his girlfriend an artist of some kind. "What," he burst out when he saw me having a cup of coffee, "you drink Instant? You are German and you don't have a coffee maker? It's a sin for a German to drink Instant!"

I opened a bottle of Kalik for him. "I don't always drink Instant," I said and told him of my primitive way of pouring boiling water over ground coffee in a strainer into my mug.

On Sunday morning they both swam over to my boat and climbed the ladder. I had asked them to come for a Triton 3 pancake breakfast. He pulled a Bodum Plunger from a pouch around his waist. "Here," he said, "at least you can brew some half-decent coffee now." He spotted my can of Maxwell House. "Let's make some right now."

I got the kettle going and he took over to show me how to use the Plunger.

"I can't accept that. What will you do without your Plunger?"

He shook his head. "Nonsense. We'll be back in Miami tomorrow. I have a real coffee maker at home. This one's only for the boat. I'll be happy to know you can drink good coffee now. Don't worry about me."

"All right." What a nice guy! I told him about my experience in Marathon while we were eating pancakes á la Triton 3. "Those horrible people were ready to pounce on me."

"Oh, Marathon? I had no trouble. I know what you mean, though. You just gotta win them over. I give 'em a big smile and say 'Hi' when I swim past them. What do I care if they're such miserable bastards?"

Boy, I can learn a lot from this young fellow. "Have you been to Staniel Cay in the Exumas?" I asked him. "Now, there are friendly people. You would fit right in." I told Roy and the girl all about the Happy People of Staniel Cay.

"We haven't been anywhere yet, except the Keys. This is our first time in Bimini."

I knew they would make friends anywhere, with that easygoing, nonjudgmental attitude of his. The girlfriend was clinging to Roy all the time without saying much. She was pretty and sexy, but that hanging on his arm and around his neck all the time… Who's gonna get tired of whom first?

In the evening they waved goodbye as they left for a night crossing back to Miami. I kept that Bodum Plunger for years. Roy Gordon has made a lasting impression on me.

Summer had begun in the islands with hot days, sweltering nights and afternoon thunderstorms. Squalls accompanied by strong gusts of wind had prompted me to set a third anchor.

One of my propane bottles was empty. Propane was not available in Alicetown. I sent my aluminum cylinder out to Nassau on the island freighter *BIMINI MACK*, which docked at Alicetown every Thursday. I was skeptical: would I ever see my propane bottle again? But a week later, among all that loading and unloading of cargo, and countless big and small propane tanks and cylinders, there was my little aluminum container. I had tagged it with a cardboard sign, but somebody wrote TRITON 3 in big letters with a red marker directly on the cylinder. Amazing, how in all that confusion nothing seemed to get lost.

Before leaving Bimini for Nassau, I changed the engine oil and filter and had difficulty getting the engine to run. It started all right, but stalled. Again and again, I tried to bleed the system of air. The idea of spraying WD 40 into the air intake popped into my head. Every time the engine was about to stall, I gave her a little shot and she revived. After several times squirting that miracle lubricant, the engine ran smoothly on her own. What a discovery! Great stuff, that WD 40.

Carlos and Linda had arranged to meet me in Bimini on 14 June. There was plenty of time for me to do some sailing. Stormy weather, however, pinned me down for a week. The wind blew at twenty to twenty-five knots straight out of the east.

The day I left Bimini, the wind moderated, became mild and variable and died by midnight. A lot of traffic was criss-crossing the Bank, and those fast Bahamian island freighters were a real menace to slow moving craft. I knew that first hand.

I approached Northwest Channel Light together with another sailboat. To break up the monotony of the lazy, slow night, I called her on the VHF. "Sailboat approaching Northwest Channel Light. TRITON 3. Over."

"Yeah, TRITON 3, what's the matter?" Snappy way to respond; probably one of those delivery captains.

"The light is supposed to be a three second flash, but it flashes five seconds. Did you notice? Over."

"No, I didn't. So what? Who cares."

Arrogant bastard. Can't do a little friendly chitchat in the middle of the night? What would Roy Gordon have said?

"Have a real nice day! TRITON 3 out." The boat passed the faultily lighted buoy ahead of me and took up a course for Nassau. I steered for Chub Cay.

When I left Chub days later, I wasn't sure whether to sail to Nassau, or pay another visit to Little Harbor in the Berries. I let the wind decide for me, and as I came around Frazer's Hog, it was in favor of Little Harbor. Past Whale Point, TRITON 3 heeled sharply in brisk northeast wind and five-foot seas. In an exhilarating three-hour sail, I reached the entrance to Little Harbor, indicated by the rock with the seas furiously breaking over it.

Three boats were at anchor and I had no choice but to put my hook down way outside in rough, unprotected water. There was a lot of grass on the bottom and I had a hard time getting my anchor to dig in. I spent an uncomfortable night, being tossed about in my bunk.

In the morning I rowed ashore. Instead of Chester and Brenda, there was again the other couple. People from the boats at anchor and some Bahamians were hanging out on the little hill, chatting and drinking cold Budweisers. I asked the female resident to prepare some cracked conch for me, which she did.

One of the Bahamians left to make a quick visit to neighboring Frozen Cay. I asked him, if I could take a ride with him. "No problem, mon." We got into his Boston Whaler with a huge outboard on its transom. He puttered slowly through the anchorage, then opened up the throttle. The boat lifted the bow and quickly settled on a plane, skimming over the waves at forty-five knots. I have never been anywhere near that speed on water!

Back on the hill of Little Harbor, I stayed until dark talking, drinking beer and eating my cracked conch.

In the morning after a restless night, I awoke with what felt like a concrete block in my stomach. I was sick and terribly weak. It was a great effort for me to get out of my bunk. I could not eat or even drink anything. My belly was rock hard and I could not go to the bathroom. I wanted to take advantage of the great weather for my sail to Nassau and don't know how I managed to go to the foredeck and get my anchor up. Nevertheless, I got underway. Surely, the cracked conch had turned my stomach into one solid brick. I was debilitated to the point where every movement was an effort.

As soon as I passed the rock and the seas breaking over it, I put the boat on autohelm and went to the head. After a bowel movement of something resembling black tar, I felt better, but still extremely weak.

Even so, I hoisted the reefed mainsail and rolled out the Genoa. On a close reach, I had a fantastic ride in fifteen to eighteen knots of easterly wind. The chain of the Berry Islands, except Little Harbor, was out of sight in less than two hours. A freighter came up from behind and for a long time it seemed we were having a race. I went to the mast and shook out the reef. My speed jumped to over seven knots.

Only ever so slowly, the freighter pulled ahead. This was one of the glorious experiences that occur so rarely. Despite my weakened condition, this eight-hour sail between Little Harbor and Nassau remains in my memory as one of the best days in my sailing life.

On the afternoon of 17 May, 1996 I arrived in Nassau. What a fantastic sail it had been from Little Harbor, rarely doing less than seven knots. Racing a freighter—but how sick I was! I had no doubt it was from that cracked conch. The woman at Little Harbor probably used the same oil to deep fry conch over and over again, until it became indigestible.

I had not eaten anything all day and did not feel up to the task of setting a second anchor. Tomorrow is another day.

I heated the contents of a can of Campbell's Chicken Noodle soup, the least offensive food for an injured stomach. Comfortably settled in the cockpit under the awning I slowly recovered my health.

Much of my time in Nassau I spent ashore, rummaging through marine supply stores, stocking up on duty-free liquor, buying fish at Potter Cay and groceries at the supermarket up the hill, past the post office.

One day, some skippers of boats in the anchorage organized a luncheon in a restaurant near the Prince George Wharf. They had engaged a speaker from BASRA to say something about safety and courtesy in the harbor, the need to leave room for commercial traffic and barges, and so on and so forth. The reason or purpose of that gathering, which cost me fifteen dollars—drinks not included—did not become clear to me. It was a diversion, though, from my regular routine of eating in one or another of the local pubs, or preparing my meals on board.

Nassau had become quite familiar to me and I liked it. In the evenings, I sometimes went to the Hammerhead Bar where this evening I met with some young businesswomen. While drinking a few Heinekens, I learned the rudiments of playing Dominos from them.

Twelve days after my arrival in Nassau, I left port. My destination was Andros Island. I was curious about the largest of the Bahamian islands, which is almost at sea level, without any elevations, and crisscrossed by numerous cuts and creeks. The only settlement on Andros that I know of is Nicholstown near Morgan's Bluff. Not often do cruising sailors come to this remote island, and that is exactly what attracted me to it.

I sailed along the north coast of New Providence. Soon the east wind deserted me and turned west. Why is the wind always turning against me? For the night I anchored between Goulding Cay and Simms Point. The sea turned lumpy and there was some rain and a thunderstorm after midnight.

The following morning I sailed for Morgan's Bluff, located at the northern tip of Andros Island. Conditions were actually pretty good. A little complaining once in a while seems to help. I cut diagonally across the Tongue of the Ocean. With thousands of feet in depth, this phenomenon lies amidst the islands of low elevations and generally shallow water of the Bahamas; hence the name, Baja Mar, Spanish for shallow sea.

There were showers over Andros as it first came in sight. I closed in on the island and proceeded toward the bight at the northern corner, Morgan's Bluff. The approach was well marked, the entrance into the wide bay protected by jetties. In a shower of torrential proportions, cutting down visibility to a few yards, I came into the bight. The surrounding land has an elevation of only a few feet and provides little protection. I let my CQR and the Fortress down in nine feet of water. I had chosen a place close to the western beach, seeking what little shelter there was. One yacht came in right after me and anchored in the opposite corner, close to a concrete dock.

The next morning the wind came around to the northeast and increased to twenty, twenty-five knots, and later in the day to over thirty. It was impossible to leave Morgan's Bluff against such weather; I had to ride it out. There wasn't much to do other than sit on my mechanical bull and watch the lines tighten and slacken as the boat kept swinging on her anchors.

On the third day at Morgan's Bluff, I was bored and in need to stretch my legs. Confident that my anchors were holding, I inflated the dinghy and rowed ashore. There was one house, which had the looks of a deserted tavern. A pickup truck pulled up and a few men were standing around, talking.

"What's Nickolstown like?" I asked.

"Not much there, mon. We'd take you, if you wanna go."
With that they went into the cool, seedy tavern.

I didn't feel good about leaving my boat alone as long as
the wind and intermittent rainsqualls continued. "Thanks," I said.
"If it's not worth it I rather get back to my boat." We had a beer
together in the empty lounge of the tavern and they paid no
further attention to me. After a while I returned to the boat that
pitched heavily in the choppy seas at her anchors.

A freighter came in and docked against the concrete sea
wall, just inside the jetties. Andros Island was the major fresh
water supplier for the capital, and twice a week the freighter,
converted to a tanker, carried water to Nassau.

The seas that broke over the jetties and came rolling in
looked as if they were ten feet high. That's what it says in my
logbook, *"ten foot seas..."* They might have seemed that high to
me at the time; actually, five to six feet was probably more
accurate, but they were scary. How can I get out of here?

In the afternoon I went ashore again, this time to the
nearby beach. I had removed the seat and the lid of the head and
took it with me. With nothing better to do, I had decided to paint
it with the maroon spray paint left over from some touch up job
on my El Camino. Why not use it, and why not on my toilet
seat? I guess such a crazy idea can come easy, sitting in
Morgan's Bluff, pinned down by the weather.

On Sunday, 2 June, the wind, still from the northeast,
had decreased to ten to fifteen knots. Seas were still breaking
over the jetties, but it was time for me to sail on. I had
considerable trouble getting my Fortress off the bottom. The
point of one of the flukes was stuck in the chain of the CQR. I
had to pull up both anchors together. The Fortress, which carried
a lifetime guarantee, came on board with one of the flukes
twisted out of shape.

I battled my 'ten-foot seas' between the jetties. Sticking
her bow into the steep waves, *TRITON 3* again and again was
knocked to a standstill. I was proud of my eleven horsepower
Diesel engine for pushing on and getting me through. Out in the
deeper water, the seas became more manageable. I rolled out one
half of the Genoa and kept the engine running in order to gain
distance from the Joulters Cays, north of Andros.

Back in the Tongue of the Ocean, the short and steep seas became nice long swells. I headed for Chub Cay, which was in sight long before Andros and the Joulters Cays were lost below the horizon. Chub, Frazer's Hog, Whale and Bird Cays were all spread out before me.

Anchored at the far side of the marked channel into Chub Harbor, the delicious aroma of smoked fish emanated from a nearby pontoon launch. I rowed over in my dinghy.

"How about a nice fish for my supper?" I talked to the two men on board and obtained a big piece of smoked grouper for two dollars. They were happy, and I was happy.

Carlos and Linda were due to fly to Bimini on 14 June. I still had two weeks to kill. There was nothing for me to do at Chub and I'd rather wait for them in Bimini.

I headed for Northwest Channel Light and passed the lighted buoy on the outside, leaving room for the island freighter *BIMINI MACK* and a tug pulling a work barge, both of which had come up from behind me. As the sun was dipping into the sea, I sailed past a sailboat at anchor near the old twisted structure that once was Northwest Channel Light. I came close enough to shout over, "Enjoy your meal," as her crew was having dinner in the cockpit.

Most cruising sailors and sport fishermen prefer to cross the Grand Bahama Bank from Northwest Channel Light to Cat Cay, via Russel Light. I have so far avoided this route because of the shallow water, in some places not more than five feet. My Bristol 27.7 has a draft of four and a half feet and I preferred to sail via Mackie Shoal in deeper water.

But I felt it was time for me to explore the more conventional route. At midnight, I was at Russell Light, the halfway point between Northwest Channel Light and Cat Cay. The depth sounder showed less than ten feet and the water got steadily shallower. I met a sailboat on the opposite course, reassuring me I was on the right track.

Early in the morning, heading into Cat Cay Harbor, I called out to an attendant, "What is the charge for a slip?" In

1992, with JP and Susi, we had taken a slip and JP had paid the dockage fee.

"Dollar fifty a foot," was his answer.

That's forty-two dollars for *TRITON 3*. There are better ways to spend forty-two bucks. I waved goodbye to the man and sailed for Honeymoon Bay at the northern end of Gun Cay. Honeymoon Bay was open to northerly winds. I found a calmer place in a small bight on the west side of Gun Cay and dropped an anchor. Then, tired from the night crossing, I took a long nap.

I was not in a calm anchorage; it was not an anchorage at all. Exposed to the long ocean swells, *TRITON 3* swayed and rolled gently, pleasingly, keeping me all day long in a state of drowsiness. Sleepy and lazy, I was not in the mood for work in the galley. For my evening meal I opened a can of corned beef and a package of crackers. The heat, the soft motion and a glass of wine induced a light, conscious sleep through the night.

By nine in the morning the sun was already burning down on me and in the light breeze it became brutally hot. I spanned the awning over the cockpit, rigged the ladder and went for a swim.

The wind was still very light from the north. With the mainsail under its cover, the Genoa rolled up and the awning spread over the cockpit, I left Gun Cay under power and anchored three hours later in Alicetown.

Bimini felt almost like home to me, and I liked it. It reminded me of Cruz Bay, St. John. Over three years ago I gave up on returning to the Caribbean. I was not unhappy with that decision, but the Islands in the Stream would always only be a substitute for the Virgin Islands.

I lived the leisurely island life. On most days I took the dinghy ashore, had something to eat and a beer in one of the less touristy places. Once I watched some fishermen weigh a tuna they had brought in. The scale read over six hundred pounds. They cut up the fish at the dock and most of the meat went to the restaurants in town. I asked if I could buy a piece of it but, as at the pig slaughter at Stanley Cay, they ignored me. The following day, a boat came in with a Maco shark. I was able to get a chunk of two or three pounds, for free. I had to trim off a lot of blubbery, unsavory meat and what was left, was not very good.

The stuffing box—the device that keeps water from coming in where the propeller shaft exits the hull—was leaking again. Since I had it rewound with Teflon at Steadman's in Key West, back in March of '92, I had to tighten it more often than ever, on this trip alone three times. So much for Teflon, supposedly the best material to keep water out.

Excitedly I awaited the day on which my visitors were to arrive. The last few days had been rainy, but on the morning of 14 June, the weather was gorgeous. I went to the 'airport' to receive them, but they were not on the noon flight. Did something go wrong? There was no way for me to get in touch with them. At Chalks, I checked the passenger list for the second flight of that day. Their names were not on it. I had so looked forward to this day and didn't know what to do.

Dejectedly, I walked the dusty road back to the dinghy when a girl on bicycle came after me. She wore the white blouse and blue skirt, Chalks uniform. "The computer found their names," she said. "Hess, that's how she pronounced it, Carlos and Linda, right?"

Things do work out in these islands. "Yes," I said, "that's them. Where are they?"

"They're on the next flight. Arriving two thirty." She turned her bicycle around and started back.

"Thanks. Nice of you to come all the way after me!"

"No problem," the standard island reply for "You're welcome."

The plane was on time and set down smoothly on the water. Then, straining under the powerful engines, the big flying boat rolled up the ramp to the asphalt apron. I watched the passengers step down from the plane as cargo handlers unloaded the baggage.

I saw them! We waved, but before we could greet each other with a hug, they had to be processed through Customs and Immigration.

From their visit the year before, they knew to bring as little as possible. Carlos carried a small duffel bag, Linda a backpack.

"We'll walk down the road, about a mile."

"What, a mile, in this heat? Let's take a cab." Carlos, not used to tropical climate, insisted on taking one of the waiting minivans.

We spent a lazy afternoon on board. Carlos liked to putter around the anchorage in the dinghy. At night we went for dinner at the Red Lion Inn. Linda, the animal lover, fondly remembered the rodents. "How are the rats? Are they still here?" She really seemed concerned about them.

"I don't know. I never come to the Red Lion alone," I said. "You want to ask the waitress?"

The waitress, a real Bahama Mama, pushed her bulk over to our table by the window and we ordered. Linda did not ask about the rats and ordered the grouper. Carlos asked for a steak and I had the same as Linda. Before heading back to the boat, we stopped at one of the bars Ernest Hemingway used to frequent.

"We were here last time," Linda remembered. "Islands in the Stream; you think he wrote it here?"

"I don't know. I never read it, but I'll pick up a copy. Some say it's one of his best works, as good as The Old Man and the Sea. It was published after his death."

After a leisurely pancake breakfast in the morning, I accompanied Carlos and Linda to the beach. We played, swam and sunbathed for hours.

On our way back to the dinghy, I stopped at Weech's to ask Jerry if he had a slip for *TRITON 3*. "Bring her in," he said. Carlos and Linda preferred the dock over the anchorage.

Back on board, we lifted the dinghy onto the davits, got the anchors up and motored into the slip Jerry indicated for us. The first thing the two landlubbers did, was head for the showers. Then they hit 'the town', Alicetown that is, while I had the boat to myself.

I had come to realize how much I enjoyed being alone on board. Nobody to consider, when and where to go or how long to stay in any place—the freedom from all restraints I valued so highly, and I remembered all the individuals I've had on my boat.

Well, I never had real bad company on any of my trips. Among the worst I count Johanna, who was scared being on a boat and had no sense of humor. Then there was Thomas Nagel, the Bavarian truck driver. He quarreled over every little thing. And what about Michael? The only thing on his mind was to put his condoms to use, and as many of them as possible. Chris Nielsen, poor fellow, just couldn't take it and left me stranded in the Dominican Republic. Aaron Lester I remember as the kid with an attitude and an overweight and overbearing father. What about Lynn Thordahl? She's in a category all by herself, intolerably selfish, yet adventurous, funny and entertaining.

My best crew, of course, was Jon Reeve, the Australian engineer with a superiority complex, who helped me sail *TRITON 3* to the Virgin Islands. His compatriot, Paul Weir, was agreeable and easygoing. We had a good time together. Frank Gallardo, more friend than crew, left all the decisions to me. "It's your boat," was his devil-may-care attitude as we were cruising the Florida Keys. "I'm your crew, I do what you tell me." He was too relaxed to get his brain cells working. We are friends to this day.

One person I will always remember with special fondness is Chris deBoer. Chris carried more than a huge fishhook in his personal baggage. A melancholy, sadness— memories of bad experiences, made him one of the unforgettable characters I have come across in my sea travels. I wish I knew that his life took some happy turns.

Outstanding as crew, of course, was Susanne with her love for sailing, boats and the ocean. She and JP, Julia, as well as Carlos and Linda, were guests rather than crew, and I loved to have guests on board—guests for a day or two, or a week.

Providing a good time for Carlos and Linda gave me great satisfaction and I had planned to make the most out of the few days they were able to get away from their city life. I was happy that they had come back for a second vacation aboard *TRITON 3*.

We left Weech's dock on a calm, hot day and headed for Honeymoon Harbor. The sky was cloudless, the sea had hardly a ripple on the lightly undulating surface. We kept the awning over the cockpit and used the Diesel for the mere two-hour trip. I chose the same spot where I had been less than two weeks before, on the ocean side of the northern tip of Gun Cay. Only a narrow sand spit separated us from the Honeymoon Bay.

We landed the dinghy on the beach of fine, white sand and had the whole place to ourselves. The shallow bay was ideal for their exploration under water, snorkeling between the rocks and watching a great variety of fish.

"You should try this, Dad," said Carlos. "You don't know what you are missing. The colors of the variety of fishes are amazing. Here, put this on." He handed me his mask.

"I don't stick my head under water, you know that."

"I can't understand you. You live on the water, but don't know what's under the surface."

"I know what's under the surface: more water and fish. They belong there, I don't."

Carlos and Linda thoroughly enjoyed this remote and solitary place, so different from the crowded streets, subways, busses and offices. They returned to the boat late in the afternoon, sun drenched and with a deep tan. It was the last day before we had to sail back. I allowed each of them a full gallon of fresh water to rinse the salt from their bodies. My skin was so conditioned from years on the boat, I couldn't possibly get a darker tan, and salt was ever present in the environment in which I lived.

"Dad, don't drink all that beer; you'll be totally dehydrated. Drinking alcohol in this heat is the worst you can do," Carlos lectured me. He and Linda drank water or iced tea.

"I don't like water; it doesn't taste good. Anyway, beer is mostly water." I knew he was right, but still... "I am doing this for years, and see how healthy I am."

"Yeah, you want to stay that way, you better listen to me. And that sun... No shirt and no sunscreen lotion... I don't know how you can live this way." They were both covering themselves with copious amounts of lotions.

I was glad both of them cared for their health. "I live a healthy life style and am in better shape than most people my age. I know you are right, but look at me: do I look sick?"

"No, but what about five or ten years from now?"

"Five or ten years, please... at my age, I don't think that far ahead." With that last remark of mine the discussion ended. Carlos shook his head. Linda knew better to stay out of it.

They had no appetite for a big meal that evening, and I was not in the mood for cooking. We feasted on the Bahamian bread I had bought in Alicetown. Especially the coconut bread, a little sweet and with a nutty flavor, was a novelty for them and very good with cheese or cold cuts and almost like cake when eaten plain or buttered. Baked in small quantities in home bakeries, without preservatives, the bread gets moldy in a couple of days and is best eaten while fresh.

During our last night in the islands, my guests slept through a thunderstorm while I hurried to take down the awning before the wind could tear it to shreds. Rain soaked and refreshed I climbed back into my bunk.

In the morning it was time to start on our homeward voyage. A nice breeze carried us into the Gulf Stream. We headed toward Miami, but allowed the Gulf Stream to take us north, so that we would end up at Fort Pierce. Soon the Bimini Islands disappeared and in early afternoon, the tall buildings from Miami all the way to Palm Beach loomed over the horizon. Sailing before a light wind, we hardly felt the air moving and the sun was fiercely burning down on us.

In the evening there was constant lightning in the distance, well inland. As darkness fell, we identified the light of the Jupiter Lighthouse. Carlos stayed awake with me, taking pleasure in the slightly cooler night air, but Linda fell asleep in the cockpit. I had persuaded her to take Dramamine as precaution against seasickness. The pill had knocked her out.

In the morning, just inside the inlet, we tied up at a semi-private dock. I found a pay phone and reported our return from the Bahamas to Customs. Linda ventured out to find a place for breakfast and she came back with muffins, toast, bacon, scrambled eggs and coffee.

Six hours later we arrived in Stuart. During my absence of three and a half months, Riverpoint Harbor had been renamed Stuart Harbor. A warm welcome awaited us and helping hands took bow and stern lines as *TRITON 3* pulled into her slip.

I had arranged our arrival in Stuart so that Carlos and Linda had a chance to get to know my homeport. They agreed that the old center, Historic Downtown, had a certain charm. Unfortunately, my good friend Michael Mahony had sold his Oyster Bar the year before and moved away. His decision was a loss for his many patrons and friends, and all of Stuart.

The last evening before my New Yorkers had to fly back home, Jon Kreeger joined us on *TRITON 3* for drinks and cigars. We told him about our days in Bimini, and I had plenty to say about my experience in Marathon. We laughed about my suggestion to meet in the middle of the Gulf Stream at midnight of 14 April. My stories about, the Keys, Nassau and Morgan's Bluff whetted Jon's appetite for a cruise of *PEGASUS* and *TRITON 3* together, but I knew it would take a long time and a good deal of persuasion for that to happen. Jon had demonstrated his reluctance clearly enough the year before.

In the morning of Saturday, 22 June, I drove Carlos and Linda to the Palm Beach airport.

TRITON 3, THE COMPLETE CRUISING BOAT

Jon Kreeger asked me, "Will you help me with the design and installation of lazy jacks on PEGASUS?"

"Sure," I said, "if you help me with mine. You know I don't like to climb the mast. I'll do all the splicing and you do the work up on the mast, okay?"

Lazy jacks are basically part of the standing rigging on a boat. Their function is to let the mainsail fold itself when lowered on to the boom instead of coming down unrestrained on the cabin roof or worse, outside the boat into the water. Especially in windy conditions, it is difficult to control the sail when taking it down. Lazy jacks keep it from blowing out and possibly ripping to shreds.

The job on *PEGASUS* done, Jon helped me doing the same on my boat. "Sorry. It's my fear of height," I said. "I'll have to winch you up my mast, too."

"That's okay, I don't mind. Fine view from up there. I'm not good at splicing anyway," and up he went.

I did forty or fifty eye splices that day, until my fingers were swollen and numb.

Someone had once remarked on how I could single-hand a boat without lazy jacks, and occasionally I have had the same thought. Once it had occurred to me when I was struggling with the mainsail in a lumpy sea, trying to fold and tie it down. I clung to the wildly swinging boom, which nearly threw me off the rocking boat. On another occasion, in the thunderstorm near Isaac in June of '92, lazy jacks might have prevented my sail from being torn to pieces.

The device was a success. How easy it was to fold the sail and to put the cover on! I sailed on the St. Lucie and the Indian River, took the sail down in a rough sea, and raised it again. I did that several times and wondered how I had done it all these years without lazy jacks.

August through October, the peak of the hurricane season, Fran, Hortense and Isidore, as well as Tropical Storm Josephine presented a threat to Florida's east Coast, but again Stuart and environs were largely spared.

During those months, and through the winter, I continued making improvements to the boat's appearance. I painted the decks, the lazaret and the pedestal with the beautiful, creamy Hatteras White, and at last I got rid of the shocking maroon color on my toilet seat. I hated the hideous head from the day I had painted it on the beach at Morgan's Bluff.

For a long time I had wanted to change the fabric of the upholstery in the saloon. In January of 1997, I resolved to undertake that enormous project, weary of the dark blue velvety material that gave the cabin a gloomy look. I replaced the foam of couch, settee and my bunk with a firmer quality and bought fabric of a light tan color at a local Calico shop.

After weeks of shaping foam rubber and sewing upholstery fabric, by hand, of course, the interior of *TRITON 3* had changed dramatically for the better. I bought a new indoor-outdoor runner for the cabin sole, leaving enough of the elegant teak and holly wood flooring to show.

Then I turned to more practical things and invented a unique anchor storage system. I installed PVC tubes on the bow pulpit to house the shafts of the main Danforth and the Fortress. The CQR had its place on the bow roller. These anchors were ready to deploy in seconds. The auxiliary anchors were mounted in tubes on the stern rail. This was the best anchor arrangement I have seen on any boat. I brought the Fortress with the bent fluke back to the store where I had bought it in exchange for a new one under the warranty.

The original mainsail, seventeen years old, patched and repaired many times, had outlived its usefulness. Worn and fatigued, it had all but lost its natural shape. Replacement was long overdue. A new sail, ordered from Bacon's of Annapolis, arrived in early spring. Compared with the old fabric, the brand-new material, called 'noisy Dacron', was at first stiff and hard to handle. I soon found out why it was called noisy. Luffing, i.e., flapping in a breeze, the more rigid cloth made quite a racket. It was so tightly woven that hardly any air could escape through the fabric. It was bound to give me excellent service.

The long list of replacements and improvements during the winter months culminated in a Craftsman generator set. With a five horsepower gasoline motor and 2400 amps output, it gave *TRITON 3* complete independence.

I mounted the unit on the cabin roof behind the mast on the cradle that previously held the Winslow life raft. That rubber raft, nearly ten years old, had never been out of its fiberglass container. Life rafts require service at least every two years, something I had completely ignored. I found someone who bought it, regardless of the condition, for ten percent of its original cost.

The cradle served perfectly as base for the power plant. Several layers of rubber from truck inner tubes, between the frame of the generator set and the cradle cushioned the vibrations. I was concerned that neighbors in the marina or in an anchorage might complain about the noise the gasoline engine made, but the noise dissipated a short distance from its source. Of course, I never ran the unit at night. Two hours every morning was sufficient to keep the batteries charged, and I could have my refrigerator/freezer running twenty-four hours a day, independent from shore power.

With that latest addition, *TRITON 3* was comparable to any larger cruising yacht afloat on the Seven Seas, self-contained, compact and complete. One thing, however, was still missing; well, actually, two things: a water maker and air conditioning. The former was on my list for the future, but air conditioning was out of the question. There was just no room for it.

It is said of boat owners that they are forever in the market for a bigger boat. This was definitely not true in my case. The Bristol 27.7 was the ideal boat for me, and with the equipment I carried on board, I could not envision a better one. I was ready for my next excursion, and so was the boat.

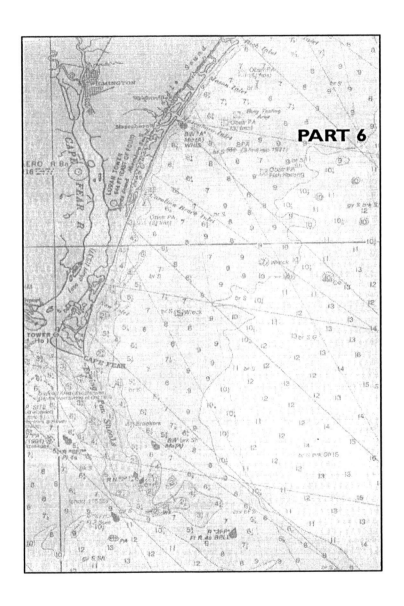

PART 6

PEGASUS AND TRITON 3

Jon Kreeger had once been married. He did not talk much about that and it seemed to have been a long time ago. He had friends, but at this time no intimate female companion that I knew of. In his mid-forties, he began to put on a little weight. His jovial face became more rounded and his still blond hair thinned considerably on the crown of his head.

Jon took great care of his boat. *PEGASUS* finally had a new generator and he no longer had an excuse to sit around at the dock. Yet, he always appeared to be apprehensive when we sat together in the evenings, on his boat or on mine, having a drink and smoking a good cigar. What we talked about was for me real planning; for him it seemed to be more like a dream.

"Cuba, you know... We really should sail to Cuba." I was thinking aloud, to test his reaction. "Sooner or later they'll come to an agreement and lift the general travel ban. Then it will be so overrun, it would no longer be anything special."

"That would be great, sailing into Havana. You think we could do it?"

"Of course," I said. "Many yachts have been to Cuba. People say it's terrific. You know that."

"We should look into it, then." Jon puffed thoughtfully on his Corona.

That was as far as we got that evening, but I was determined to gather all the information needed. I knew we needed a U.S. Coast Guard permit to visit Cuba. I just had to find out how to get one.

"When do you think is a good time to start on our voyage?" I asked him days later. I know patience was not my strongest asset, but if we wanted to go, we had to talk about it. As soon as I became a little more persistent, Jon retracted. One morning on his way to work, varnishing boats, he did not stop to say good morning, as he passed *TRITON 3* in her slip. That was something new. What's the matter with him?

In the evening, as he came home from his job, he walked right by my boat to the end of the dock where *PEGASUS* had her berth. That had never happened. He always stopped to say hello and chat for a moment. Next morning he walked right past me

269

again. What is the matter with him? I knew, he could be moody, but this?

After another day or two, I went over to his boat. "Jon, what is wrong? Do you have a problem?"

"What do you mean, what's wrong?"

"Don't give me that. You know what I'm talking about. Come on, tell me what's the problem?"

Finally I got a reaction from him. "I don't like the way you put the pressure on me. You're always on my back with your planning, the schedule, the when and the where, pushing me. That's the problem, that's what is wrong here." There was real anger in his voice.

"If we want to take a trip together, we've got to talk about it. If that's pushing you, forget it. With or without you, I am shooting for the first of May. You want to come along, fine. Just let me know. Otherwise, I go by myself. Believe me, I'm not gonna push you anymore." I turned around and went back to my boat.

What has gotten into him? How can we plan a trip together without talking about it? Not even an approximate date for departure? To hell with him! I can go it alone.

I remembered the morning I struggled with my new generator, trying to get it on board. He stopped and watched as I winched it up off the dock with the halyard. "That will never work," he said, turned and walked away. Without any help I managed to get it into the cradle on the cabin roof.

Was he jealous because I suddenly got a generator on my boat? Why? This was an adapted piece of machinery mounted on deck, while his was permanently installed in the engine room. *PEGASUS* was a bigger boat than mine.

On 30 March I moved *TRITON 3* from her slip at Stuart Harbor and anchored near the city pier. The evening before I left, I briefly went over to *PEGASUS* and announced to Jon that I was going to anchor out. "I'll still be around here. Shower, laundry, talk to people. So, if you want to get in touch with me, you know where to find me."

"Okay. By the way, May first sounds good to me." If he wanted to say something else, I didn't give him the chance. After the shit he pulled on me, he had to come down to my level. I could very well sail to Cuba on my own.

After our brief conversation, I returned to my boat and in the morning backed *TRITON 3* out of her slip.

I had found a good spot in the not too crowded anchorage where there was enough room to put down three anchors. I used my practical long-term system. All lines came together on one swivel, from which only one line lead to the boat.

The first evening at anchor, a squall came through the anchorage and a boat dragged into *TRITON 3*. The elderly husband and wife crew had a hard time getting their boat clear from my anchor lines. I got into my dinghy and helped repositioning their Bruce anchor. They invited me on board for a glass of wine and I ended up taking them to the supermarket in my car. Out of their purchases the lady gave me a bottle of wine. "You were very nice helping us out," she said.

I had given up the comfort the marina provided for the more nautical life to test my independence from terra firma. I found out that the noise and interference from my generator made watching TV nearly impossible. There goes my favorite program, Jeopardy. Not quite as independent as I thought.

All the other hardships, or inconveniences, I accepted easily. That was my preparation for the anticipated voyage, with or without Jon Kreeger.

Since I had the Harken roller furling system on my boat, I could no longer use the Dolly Parton, the old Genoa or the small jib. My new Genoa was rolled up on the single forestay. For five years the obsolete sails in their individual bags cluttered up precious storage space. The For Sale signs I had posted in various locations brought me one response. I met the man in the park near the anchorage and we spread out the three sails on the lawn for him to inspect. He was interested only in the Genoa, which was actually in pretty good shape, but I managed to sell him the Dolly Parton as well. "If you take both of them, I throw in the jib," I told him. He had brought cash and we were both happy.

On the city pier I met a young fellow who had his sailboat at anchor nearby. He was talking to somebody about Cuba.

I interrupted them. "Did you just say, you had been to Cuba in your boat?"

"Yes Sir, the second time. Spent a week at Marina Hemingway last month." He seemed very proud of himself.

To get the facts from this man, I limited my questions to what's important. "I plan a trip to Cuba in a couple of weeks. Tell me, where do you get the application for the U.S. Coast Guard permit?"

"Miami. Gotta go to Miami. The Commander of the District. Wait, I have a blank form. Not on me right now. Later. I can loan it to you. You make a copy, then give it back to me. You anchored out there? What boat? Ah, that one?" He seemed all business, with his short, no-nonsense sentences, eager to sell his knowledge and his expertise about this Cuba thing.

"Thanks. That'll be good. Meet you here later?" I hoped he would show up and really had what I needed to sail to Cuba.

"No problem," he said.

That afternoon he gave me an almost illegible photostatic copy of a typewritten form.

"This is it?" I asked. "They don't have a printed form for this?" I was skeptical about the unofficial, shoddy, appearance of a document of such importance.

"Yeah, that's it. Government is stingy. But, yeah, believe me, this is what you need. Mail it or fax it, you get it back the next day signed and approved. Take it from me, I know. I've done it. Piece o' cake. There you go. Make copies, as many as you want, then give it back to me."

In my hand I held the document with the title:
ACKNOWLEDGEMENT OF SECURITY ZONE AND
PERMIT TO DEPART DURING A NATIONAL
EMERGENCY

I drove to the supermarket to do some shopping and to use the copy machine. To be on the safe side, I made four copies, in case the application had to be filed in duplicate.

I saw the guy the next morning and gave him back his paper. "Thanks a lot," I said. He was talking to some people, took the paper and paid no more attention to me.

That evening I waited at Stuart Harbor for Jon to come home from work. I was having a beer with some people, when he came walking along the dock. I wondered if I might be pushing him again by showing him the Cuba forms, or even saying something to him about the trip. "Can I talk to you for a minute?" I asked cautiously.

"Suuure," he said, dragging it out most congenially, and I followed him to his boat.

He stepped on board. I remained standing on the dock. "I got these today. You might want to take a look at them," and I handed him two of the copies. "Let me know what you think." With that I turned to walk away and he didn't stop me. Over my shoulder I saw him looking at the papers. Thereafter, I did not hear from him for several days.

The old outboard motor I had bought from Alan Tooley in Samaná, back in 1990, was no longer worth another dime of repair bills. Someone sold me a used two horsepower Johnson. I decorated that little motor with white and red abstract shapes to deter thieves.

One afternoon, as I returned from a short trial sail to my mooring ball, the gearshift linkage broke. Without control over the engine, I shut it off. Close to the neighboring boat *STEEL AWAY*, I called out, "Jack, can you give me a hand?" He stuck his head out the hatch. "Can you take a line to my mooring? I lost my engine."

Steel-Boat Jack, as he was known around the anchorage, understood the problem and came over in his dinghy. I attached the bitter end of a long line to a cleat and handed him the other end. My mooring ball was only a couple of boat lengths away. Jack reached the ball, tied the line to it and I was safe. "Thanks, Jack! I owe you one."

One day a Florida Marine Patrol boat came slowly through the anchorage. The officer on board looked at a few boats, went on board of one, then another, and a third. I observed what was going on and figured she would probably come over to me. I went below to switch the head discharge hose from 'out' to 'holding tank'.

The officer was a shapely and neatly uniformed female. She drove her boat over to *TRITON 3*. "Hi, how y'all doin'? May I come on board?"

"Sure. What can I do for you?" Again I employed my friendly, polite and accommodating attitude that has helped me on several occasions when dealing with the authorities.

"From time to time we do some routine inspections on boats anchored out here, check on safety, see that everything is in order," she drawled pleasantly.

I thought, why isn't she checking those derelict boats? They certainly have no safety or sanitary devices on board. Probably too messy for her. She doesn't want to get her uniform dirty. "Go ahead. Anything you want to see. I make sure to have everything in order and in compliance with the regulations. Life jackets, fire extinguishers, bell, horn, flares. What else?"

"Fine, I see your boat's in top condition. Beautiful. Let me just take a quick look below, if I may."

I knew she was coming to that. "Be my guest. What can I help you with?"

"Where's the head? Just want to check real quick your sanitation arrangement."

I showed her the intricate hose and valve system. "This is the 'Y' valve, marked with the arrows. This hose leads forward to the holding tank. The pump out fitting is on deck."

"Where do you pump out?"

"There's a facility at North Shore Marina." (I didn't say I take the boat there.) "I go offshore a lot and four miles out it's legal to pump out. See, I have the regulations posted here, as required."

"Your valve arrangement is not exactly according to the regulations. It's good enough, I'm not giving you a citation but next time I come by, I'll drop off a pamphlet for you. All the rules are in it." She went up into the cockpit and back onto her boat. "I wish all boats were as neat as yours. Have a real nice day."

"Thank you, officer. You, too." Damn, she's not even going near any of those wrecks at anchor over there. This is what they do to keep the waterways clean? I went below and switched my valve back to 'out'. I never got the pamphlet she was talking about.

The repair of the gearshift cable was not an easy matter. The cable comes up through the pedestal from the shift arm on the transmission, located in the engine compartment under the cockpit sole. All the control cables and the steering chains run up inside the pedestal to the hand levers, the instruments and the helm. The compass sits on top of the pedestal. To make repairs inside the pedestal, I had to remove the compass. The shift cable broke at the very top and there was sufficient length to reconnect the two ends by crimping a sleeve over them. I took advantage of the occasion and checked all the wires and cables, and greased the chains.

Luckily that problem happened when it did. Anything can break or go wrong at any time, according to Murphy's Law. The unpredictable is part of the adventure and there is always a certain amount of luck involved.

Jon continued to be uncooperative and moody. Whenever I saw him at Stuart Harbor, he was reluctant to talk about anything connected with the trip. He tried to evade the subject altogether. I wasn't sure whether we would ever take any voyage together. Did he make preparations? Was he buying provisions? Has he looked at a chart? The last he had said to me about the whole thing was, "May first is fine with me," and that was weeks ago.

I continued with the plan as originally conceived: Okeechobee Waterway to the Gulf Coast, then to Fort Myers, Dry Tortugas and from there to Cuba. The return from Cuba we would do via the Cay Sal Bank and Bimini. All this we had vaguely mentioned when we first started talking about a possible trip together, when Jon did not yet feel 'pressured into something'. He wanted to include a side trip to Bradenton for a couple of days (Jon's mother lived in Bradenton). I worked on my charts and with the cruising guides. I was going to make the trip. I was going to Cuba. With Jon or without him. The only modification, if sailing alone, would be the elimination of Bradenton. There was no incentive to go that far up the Gulf Coast.

I asked a guy to scrape the barnacles off the bottom of TRITON 3. He had done that work on several boats in the marina. I picked him up at Stuart Harbor, he did the job and when I drove him back, Jon came over to me. "Peter, can I ask you something? Would it be all right with you if we postponed our departure to the fifth? I have trouble making it by the first of May."

It was the first positive indication that he planned to go at all. "Sure," I said, surprised at his apologetic demeanor. "What's a couple of days? Make it eight o'clock in the morning?"

"Eight it is, in the morning of the fifth." He was almost cheerful. Scary, those mood swings.

On 3 May, I pulled up my three anchors, which had been in the water for over a month, and docked at the head of the city pier. The lines, green with slimy algae, and the chains encrusted with barnacles, created a horrible mess on the foredeck. Black mud from the incredibly dirty bottom made TRITON 3 look more like a work barge than the neat sailboat she was. I needed several hours cleaning chains and lines before I could store them away and wash down the deck with water and bleach.

I liked my boat to look her best. There were always people coming out to the dock to talk to a sailor and to watch the sunset. The anchored boats on the St. Lucie River, silhouetted against the red fireball, were an often-photographed scene.

In the morning, after some last minute shopping for provisions, I drove my Chevy to the parking lot at Stuart Harbor; the dockmaster allowed me to leave the car there. I told Jon that I would spend the night before our departure at the city dock and that I would cast off my lines at eight a m.

Precisely at eight o'clock in the morning, 5 May, 1997 PEGASUS took a turn past the city dock, at the very moment as I threw off the last of my lines. Jon greeted me, waving his arms enthusiastically. I put my engine in gear and the two boats headed for the South Fork of the St. Lucie River and the Okeechobee Waterway.

THE GULF OF MEXICO

There was a twelve-foot rise at the St. Lucie Lock. After exiting the lock, I set my Genoa, killed the engine and pulled ahead of *PEGASUS*. Jon stopped at the Indiantown Marina for fuel. I slowed my speed by rolling up half of my Genoa for him to catch up.

The lock at Port Mayaca was in the open position. The water level of the lake was the same as in the canal and we powered right through. It was Jon's idea to anchor on Lake Okeechobee.

"I know a good spot to anchor past the lock," Jon called over to me.

The lockmaster advised against it. "No more is traffic coming through until tomorrow morning," he told us over the radio. "You can tie up overnight at the pilings for barges."

We thanked him and spent a quiet night without having to bother with the anchors.

There are two ways of crossing Lake Okeechobee. Route 1 is a straight line across the lake. I had sailed that route in 1992 from Clewiston to Port Mayaca, but Jon favored Route 2, the slower but more scenic Rim Route. We passed Pahokee, a fish camp with no dockage and no fish, and the dreamy town of Bell Glade. At Clewiston in the late afternoon, we left Lake Okeechobee behind. Alligators were lazily floating half submerged in the dark brown water or resting among tree trunks and rocks on the bank. Past the Moorehaven Lock, we spent the second night at the dock of a small, rustic marina.

This kind of traveling was far too slow for me, but I went along with Jon's suggestions. He was not bad company, quite funny and entertaining when in a good mood and we enjoyed pleasant evenings on either his boat or mine.

At noon, 7 May, we reached La Belle by way of the Caloosahatchee Canal, Lake Hipochee and the Ortona Lock, and we tied up at the free town dock.

That afternoon and the next day, Jon worked on his engine. I don't remember what he tried to accomplish, only that he had removed some part, dissembled it, and then had trouble putting it back together.

He flew into a terrible rage, cursed and threw parts and tools around. There was no talking to him; no way I could give him a hand. I was afraid anything I might say or do would cause him to throw the whole thing overboard. At times like this, he was the most miserable fellow to be associated with. I felt sorry for him, that he was so unable to control his temper, that he carried the burden of his own character around with him.

La Belle did not offer much to do or to see. I found a little shop with a wide variety of honeys to sell. There was no sales person in the store. Instead, a sign on the counter read, "Please put the amount shown on the jar in the box. Thank you." An open shoebox next to the sign had some bills and coins in it. I might not have bought any honey, but the simplicity of this approach, the naive trusting in the honesty of humanity, intrigued me. I wanted to participate in this most basic human behavior of being honest. I bought a sixteen-ounce flask of Orange Blossom honey.

After thirty-six hours in La Belle—Jon had put his engine back together—we set out for Fort Myers and anchored at Cape Coral. I would have preferred Fort Myers Beach of which I had such nice memories, but Jon's choice was Cape Coral.

We had crossed Florida from east to west along the Okeechobee Waterway. The following day brought us to Venice. Since this part of Florida's west coast was new to me, I did not object to go as far as Bradenton, just south of Tampa Bay, to visit Jon's mother.

We spent the next night anchored side by side in a cove called Placida Harbor. In the morning, after bringing my CQR on deck, I drifted on to a shoal and was fast aground. Busy, feeding the chain down the deckpipe and rinsing off the deck, I did not notice that the boat was drifting with the slow current to a shallow spot. All my attempts to get afloat failed. I tried to heel the boat over, using both main and Genoa, but there was not enough wind. *PEGASUS* could not come close enough for Jon to throw a line over to me, without the risk of running aground as well.

Concerned for the delay I was causing, I called out to him, "Go ahead, Jon, I'll meet you in Sarasota Bay or in Bradenton. I have to wait for high tide. I won't be able to get underway for nine hours."

"It's not your fault, take all the time you need. You know, I'm not in a great hurry."

"Not my fault? Whose fault is it, then? Of course, it is my fault. My stupidity. Giving priority to washing down the deck, without first making sure I'm in deep water." I was angry with myself.

"Can happen to anyone."

"Yeah, but it happened to me! I'm not letting us lose a whole day because I was such an idiot. I'm calling Boat US." With that I got on the VHF and repeated twice my position in Placida Harbor. My call for help was answered and a powerboat came to my rescue in less than thirty minutes.

The crew consisted of a couple of old men out for a ride on a calm Sunday morning. Not being experienced is one thing, but trying to show off as if they were, that's not helpful. They rejected my suggestion to heel the boat over with a line from the top of the mast. Instead, they tried to pull me off the sandbar, but their craft lacked the power. At last, an hour later, they accepted my advice. By then the keel had buried itself so deeply that it took another half hour to dislodge it. With nearly two hours delay, and after paying Boat US four hundred dollar for the rescue, *TRITON 3* was underway again.

Jon had waited patiently. He seemed to get angry only at his own failures—exactly what I had done. I wished we had chosen Fort Myers Beach. This wouldn't have happened.

We decided to anchor in the spacious anchorage of Little Sarasota Bay, although it was only mid-afternoon. The sky had turned gray, it began to drizzle. My dinghy was stored away in the cockpit locker, but Jon towed his all the time and he rowed over to me. He was in a good mood, funny and witty, trying to cheer me up. I still had not gotten over the mishap of that morning in Placida Harbor.

"What happened this morning could have happened to me," said Jon. "Mistakes are there to be made. We all make them."

"Yeah, thanks. It's embarrassing, though, and it cost me a lot of money."

The weather turned nasty in the night. Dawn brought a cold, light rain. There was no wind, but dense fog. The forecast was for continued rain, but we weighed anchors and headed toward the next bridge. Visibility was two hundred feet at the most. Jon, ahead of me, turned around before we could even see the bridge.

"This isn't worth it. We better go back and stick it out at anchor," he called over to me. I thought he was right, and half an hour later we were back where we just came from, settling down for a leisurely, but cold and miserable day. The rain lasted until four o'clock in the afternoon and then, after a thunderstorm, the sky began to clear.

As darkness fell, I hung the kerosene hurricane lamp out, as I used to do when I anchored my Cape Dory on the Hudson; there had been no electronics on *TRITON II*.

Around ten o'clock, there was a knock on the hull. "Hello! Somebody in there?"

Just about to fall asleep, I pushed the hatch open enough to stick my head out. The night air was cold. "Hello, officer, is there a problem?"

"Is that lamp your anchor light? At first I didn't see it all. Then, as I came within feet of your boat I saw this glimmer." He was a very polite Marine Patrol officer.

"Sorry, I didn't realize I had it set so low." I stepped out into the cockpit and onto the cabin roof. The lamp was hanging from the main halyard just above my head. "I'll turn it up. So, is this better?"

"Are you sure it will burn through the night? Got enough kerosene in it?"

"Oh yes, plenty of fuel. I use the lamp all the time. Saves my battery, you know."

"All right, good night, then."

"Thanks for letting me know, officer. Good night."

Early in the morning of the following day, in fine but much cooler weather, we made our second attempt to get to Bradenton. I turned off the Diesel and sailed in the light breeze, falling far behind *PEGASUS*.

280

Two people in a sailboat with the mast folded down for storage hailed me. They were out of fuel. I helped them with a quart of diesel, enough for them to reach the marina I had just passed. That's stupid, to run out of fuel. Huh, not more stupid than running aground! I reminded myself how easy it is to judge other people and to overlook one's own failures.

After I had stopped to fill a plastic bottle with fuel and handed it to the two guys in need of it, I caught up with *PEGASUS*. At noon we docked at the wooden pier of the Seafood Shack in Cortez right in time for lunch. Bradenton was only a twenty-minute car ride away. Jon called his mother, and in the afternoon the nice little old lady came down to Cortez in her Corolla. It was Tuesday, 13 May 1997.

We did not leave Cortez until Monday, the 19th.

Jon and I had agreed to stay at Cortez for two days, so that he had a chance to visit with his mother. We had dinner at her house in Bradenton. The next morning she came down to the dock, I invited Jon, and Mrs. Kreeger on board for my famous pancakes á la Triton 3. Later, four or five people, family and friends of his family, came to see Jon and we all had lunch at the Seafood Shack.

That afternoon Jon started to remove his large cylindrical water tank, which was located in the portside lazaret. "I've got to find that leak," he explained. Mrs. Kreeger and I sat in the cockpit, while Jon began to get frustrated struggling with the bulky tank. I tried to extricate myself from the situation, but did not get the chance. "Peter, hold this steady for me," or "wrench, that one over there," or "don't tilt the goddamn tank that way, here gimme that fuckin' hose—excuse me, Mom." His asking for help became orders, his language deteriorating into vulgarity.

I hesitated to leave Mrs. Kreeger alone with her son, but I wanted to get off his damn boat. Most of the afternoon the old lady and I watched helplessly as Jon flew from one rage into the next. I don't remember whether he succeeded in fixing the leak.

Jon and I invited his mom to a restaurant on the beach for dinner. I said something about our leaving next morning for Dry Tortugas, when Jon interrupted, "Tomorrow? We aren't leaving tomorrow! I haven't seen all my friends yet. I have friends, you know. They're coming out here this weekend and I'll be damned if I leave before then."

Where the hell did this come from? "We said two days, Jon," I reminded him. "Now you want to stay a week? I don't think I want to pay dockage fee for that many days. You didn't say anything about meeting friends here and all that."

"Well, I am not leaving without seeing them. They are old family friends." His voice was getting louder. "You don't want to stay at the dock, then you can anchor out over there."

"Jon, okay, I don't mind if you want to stay a few more days. Why don't we do this: I go ahead to Fort Myers Beach and wait for..."

He interrupted me. "The hell you will! We take this trip together. If you don't like it at the dock, go and anchor where those other boats are."

I was stunned. Such an outburst I had not expected. Taking the trip together, yes, that was the plan. That it had to be entirely on his terms was not. To stop the argument from going any further I dropped he subject. It could have escalated to an altercation right there at the dinner table in front of Mrs. Kreeger. I resolved to continue our trip together and avoid all disputes and disagreements with Jon. I would tolerate him when he acted normally, and ignore him when he flew off the handle.

The alternative would have been to go back to my boat, untie the docking lines and sail to Cuba, alone. Perhaps that would have made more sense. Our friendship, however, would have ended right then and there. Give it another chance, I thought, and I stayed at the dock in Cortez until Jon was ready to leave.

Twelve noon, Monday, 19 May. Bills paid, Diesel on, dock lines off, waving goodbye to Mrs. Kreeger, we were underway. Was I ever glad to be sailing again! We headed out through the Longboat Pass to open ocean water, the Gulf of Mexico.

There was an excellent sea breeze in the afternoon and we sailed along, often side by side, into the evening. *TRITON 3* was faster in light winds, but in stronger breezes *PEGASUS* pulled ahead. After a short interval of calm, the typical land breeze came on and we made fine progress through the night, passing Venice Inlet, Gasparille Pass and Boca Grande Channel. Toward morning, we had Captiva Pass, Redfish and then the northern tip of Sanibel Island. Changing course at Point Ybel, we approached the channel markers for the Fort Myers Beach inlet.

The anchorage of Ft. Myers Beach was as crowded as I remembered it from my visit there in March of '92. We did, however, find room for both boats near the property of Mr. Wallace.

I didn't mind an extended stay at Ft. Myers Beach. Mr. Wallace still welcomed sailors and allowed us to tie our dinghies to his dock. We signed his guest book, chatted with him and had the convenience of being close to all the fun places. Restaurants, bars, shops, supermarket, the beach—all within easy walking distance.

A Coast Guard patrol disturbed us in the middle of Saturday night. A knock at the hull. "Hey, you've got to move your boat. You're too close to the channel that runs along the shore here."

Why this had to be in the night on a weekend, I don't know. We reanchored both our boats, but basically remained in the same spot. There was nowhere else for us to anchor. The Coast Guard boat cruised through the anchorage, but I did not see it stop at any other boat. The personnel saw us working the anchors and, although we practically did not move the boats, they didn't bother us again.

One day Jon decided to take his outboard motor apart. He did this in his dinghy. I stopped briefly on my way to Mr. Wallace's dock, to see what he was doing and ended up handing him a tool or holding something for him. He became angrier by the minute and started throwing things around. At his first "fuck" and "shit" I feared he would drop the whole motor overboard. I got back into my dinghy, pulled the starter cord and went the short distance over to the dock. I'd pretty much had it with him.

In the morning Jon came over to my boat. "Peter, I really want to complain about the harassment by the Coast Guard the other night. That was uncalled for."

"Yeah, that was pretty mean. But, what do you think they will do about it? Apologize? Fire the guys who did it?"

"I don't care. I just want to let them know, they can't bully me around. I don't take crap like that."

"Okay, we have to go over there anyway, to file the papers for Cuba. I'll go with you. Did you fill yours out?" I no longer cared whether I 'pushed' him or not. If he gets all weird again, I sail alone. I set the rules for myself now.

"I will have them by tomorrow." There it was again, that procrastination.

Next day in the afternoon, "Ready, Peter? Let's go over there. We take my dinghy." At the Coast Guard dock on the other side of the harbor, there were no cleats to tie up the dinghy. I just started to tie the painter to a piling, when Jon ripped the line out of my hands, didn't find a better place for it, and tied up the dinghy exactly as I had begun. In the process, his sunglasses slipped out of his pocket into the water. Why was he so mad again, so violent? Was he aware of his uncontrolled anger? He never mentioned the loss of his sunglasses, which, I knew, he valued highly. Maybe that was pride, or embarrassment. I couldn't help feeling a little sorry for him again.

There were only a few young guys in Coast Guard uniforms at the station. One was sitting at a computer, another looked at a radar screen while talking and laughing with another guy. In an adjacent room, a civilian was on the phone and a Coast Guard man wrote some sort of report on a form. They all seemed happy to have visitors.

"Can I help you?" Asked one of the men who were just standing around.

"We want to apply for a permit to sail to Cuba," I said before Jon could start with his complaint. "We have the applications right here."

"You came to the right place. Let's see, what we've got here." He made a few uhus and uhums, looked over the papers and then, "I'll fax this over to Miami. Should be back by tomorrow. Come by in the afternoon to be sure."

"That's it? Say, are these requests ever denied?" Jon wanted to know.

"Not that I know of. Why should they be?" said another one of the uniformed guys who had joined us. "Anybody can go. You just can't spend any money there. Don't buy anything, don't pay for anything, don't bring any receipts back that show you bought something."

"Okay, see you tomorrow," I said and turned to the door.

"About the other night, when your patrol boat came through the anchorage..." Jon just couldn't let it go. "Was that really necessary, to get us out in the middle of the night, to move the boats?"

"I don't know. You heard about that?" He asked those standing around. Then again to Jon, "some of the young guys here take their jobs real serious. You want to file a complaint?"

I was still standing by the door. "No, of course not," I hurried to answer. "It's just so you know we didn't really like it. But, you know, you guys are all right. I appreciate it. Take it easy. See you tomorrow."

Outside I turned to Jon. "You couldn't keep your mouth shut, eh? Had to harass them."

"You ruined it. Yes, I wanted to file a complaint. They ought to be taught a lesson. I will not be pushed around like that—by nobody."

"I tell you something: what you do is your business. I don't care how you deal with the authorities. But, when I am involved you better behave like a human being." That came out stronger than I intended. But, what the hell. I'd better give him a piece of my mind.

On the way back to our boats he didn't say a word, and later he came over with half a loaf of bread. "I just baked this. It's rye bread. I thought you might like half of it."

I thanked him. He can be such a nice guy, why is he so fucked up?

The next afternoon I asked him, if he wanted to walk over to the Coast Guard. It was not too hot, and I didn't want to ride again with him in his dinghy. He said it was all right, and we went across the high bridge to the station, located on the mainland. Our papers had come back.

"Denied!" said the guard. Then he laughed, "Just kidding! Have a good trip." He handed us our papers.

We were in business and celebrated having dinner at Peter's Place, one of the outdoor restaurants. We had permission to sail to Cuba. Our applications bore a stamp and the signature of the Commander of the USCG. Underneath, handwritten, *By Director of the District* and the date, 25 May 1997.

Besides the identification of our vessels by names, registration numbers and flag of USA, we had given the approximate departure date of 29 May, from Dry Tortugas, and requested entry into Cuban Territorial Sea at the coordinates of 23 degrees 17 min. North latitude, 082 degrees 34 min. West longitude, destination Marina Hemingway.

In light northeast wind, under a sky with thin, high clouds, we weighed anchors in the morning of 30 May and left Fort Myers Beach, Estero Island and the San Carlos Bay for the three small keys of Dry Tortugas, about sixty nautical miles west of Key West. Those are the most remote outposts of the United States.

The sailing was excellent on a broad reach most of the day and through the night with *PEGASUS* and *TRITON 3* often closely side by side. Jon wanted us to be within sight of each other at all times. We made landfall in the afternoon, when we saw the tower on Garden Key. Three hours later, we motored through the narrow channel between Garden Key and Bush Key.

There was plenty of room for dozens of boats in the anchorage. To the south, about half a mile away, seas were breaking constantly over a reef. Bush Key to the east, flat and sandy with sparse growth of shrubs, is home to an infinite variety of birds. Farther away is Loggerhead Key, long and narrow, stretching out in a southerly direction. It is the most removed of the three islets and the site of a functioning lighthouse. Fort Jefferson, a structure of red brick in various stages of disrepair, takes up almost the entire Garden Key. Park Rangers, stationed there, guard the fort, a National Monument.

On the weekend many boats arrived. These small keys, far out in the Gulf of Mexico, are ten to twelve hours away from Key West by sailboat, or a three-hour ride in a fast powerboat. Some visitors came by seaplanes.

Jon and I undertook a walking tour of the immense Fort Jefferson. It was built in the second half of the nineteenth century, but has never been completed. The design called for four hundred guns on three levels, but less than two hundred were actually installed. Strategically the position was perfect—the Gibraltar of the Gulf—but the fortress never saw any action. Later it served as a prison and gradually met with neglect. Some parts of it lie in ruin.

There are a few smaller, nameless keys, some of which cover at high tide. The water depth ranges from forty to ten feet, shoaling toward the reef and the sandy beach of Bush Key.

There seemed to be a great abundance of fish in these waters. One day Jon swam the short distance from his boat to mine and tried to scramble on board in a great hurry. I grabbed him under one arm. With joined effort, he got one knee up on the gunnel. I helped him into the cockpit.

"Barracuda after me," he said catching his breath. We looked over the side. "There he is, motionless, in the shadow under the boat."

The ferocious looking fish was clearly visible under the keel of *TRITON 3*, four or five feet long, slim and slick, with that menacing extended lower jaw. Jon and I were sitting in the cockpit under the awning. From time to time we checked on our uninvited guest.

"He's still there, waiting for you to swim back, Jon. At least you'll have company."

"You think he'll come after me again? They're curious animals, you know. I can make it across in two minutes or less. You'll see."

"Good luck," I said as Jon dove over board and started striking out with powerful arms and working his feet furiously. The barracuda stirred, then followed Jon. The fish kept a distance and was not closing as if in chase of prey. I yelled, "Swim like hell! Get into your dinghy, he's right behind you!" Jon got safely back on board his boat and, in retrospect, the whole affair was great entertainment.

We had our share of stormy weather at Dry Tortugas. The days were stifling hot, and thunderstorms developed every day in the evenings. On Sunday, 1 June, a strong south wind

287

forced seas over the reef, providing us with a spectacular scene. I set a third anchor, a precautionary measure.

Jon and I delayed our departure for Cuba until 3 June. "Today's the day, Jon. The weather seems to have moderated. What do you think?" I proposed to leave at noon. "That will give us plenty of time to arrive at Marina Hemingway tomorrow morning."

Jon looked at the sky, saw some clouds and hesitated. At length, "If you say so, let's go for it."

"Jon, just don't tell me later it was my decision, that I put pressure on you. We decide this together. I just think that we should sail today."

"Let's go. Today or never. Twelve o'clock anchors up. We take the marked channel at Garden Key, then along the east side of Loggerhead." He was determined as if jumping from a tall building.

"Okay. I follow you." I made myself a lunch of pumpernickel and sardines, and at eleven I heaved my first anchor on board. A little later, Jon got busy on the foredeck. At twelve on the dot, we were underway.

Preparing to leave Dry Tortugas

CUBA

On 3 June the weather was fine, some clouds giving respite from the burning rays of the sun. The wind was fairly light out of the southwest. We kept Loggerhead Key to starboard and set our course for Havana, less than ninety nautical miles due south.

PEGASUS and *TRITON 3*, often side by side at shouting distance, moved along at four knots. As we left the lee of Loggerhead and the breeze freshened, Jon rolled out his huge Genoa and pulled ahead.

Two hours out of Dry Tortugas, a beautiful, classic thunderhead formed to the west and moved northward, presenting no threat to us. I saw *PEGASUS* reversing course and coming toward me.

Jon called out to me as the two boats met. "I don't like those clouds. That's going to be trouble. I'm heading back to Dry Tortugas."

"What are you talking about? That weather is tracking north, Jon. Before you reach the anchorage, you'll be in a hell of a mess. We are actually sailing away from it." What was he thinking? Had he lost his sense of direction? "I am going on to Cuba," I yelled back to him. I am no longer putting up with his shenanigans.

After a couple of hundred yards, Jon turned around and followed me. In the early evening I changed my course a few degrees to the east to avoid a cluster of dark clouds, just to be on the safe side.

We had agreed to make contact on the VHF every six hours, starting at 1800. "I put a reef in the mainsail for a leisurely night," I told him in my first call. "Don't want to get there too early. We must be close to the Gulf Stream. Over."

"Yeah, I guess. Nothing to report from here. Talk to you at midnight. Out."

We kept each other in sight, but the light was fading rapidly. Over my port quarter I could see the green light on the masthead of *PEGASUS*. I did not have those tri-color masthead navigation lights on my boat. I still used the old red and green lights in the bow and white in the stern.

There was little freighter traffic in the Florida Straight. I saw the lights of only one ship, far on the horizon. At 2400 sharp Jon's voice was on the VHF. "TRITON 3, how you doing? Over."

"Okay, PEGASUS. You saw the vessel an hour ago due south? Not much traffic out here tonight. Over."

"Yes, I saw it. About four miles ahead. Must be the eastbound shipping lane. I see your port bow light. You're about half a mile behind me. Over."

"Right. We're in the Gulf Stream now, I guess. Watch the GPS, we're being swept along with the Stream. I shook out the reef in my main. Get a better grip on the wind. Over."

"Gotcha. What little wind there is, you mean, huh? I think I can see the glow of Havana. Must be a big city. Over."

"Yeah, that must be it. Either that or a cruise ship. Talk to you 0600. TRITON 3 out."

"Good night. PEGASUS out."

I took up a more southwesterly heading against the effect of the Gulf Stream. The night was mild. I thought of turning on the engine if the wind didn't come back soon. Or I'd end up in Bimini instead of Cuba.

With nothing better to do, I heated water for a Cup-o-Noodles. After dinner I had a beer and lit a cigar, something I rarely did underway. As light as the wind was, it took most of the smoke leaving little for me.

I was bored. If the batteries of my little black and white portable set weren't long dead, I could have watched TV. I did not want to disturb the quiet night with the generator. There was hardly any breeze now. Diesel? Not yet. I like this quietude. Quietude? Quietness? What ever. No Diesel.

I looked up, reached for the binos. There were the lights of Havana. Not the glow, the individual lights, and it was just three in the morning.

As the sky became lighter in the East, the first tall buildings of the Cuban capital rose above the horizon. We were actually approaching this 'forbidden and hostile' territory.

At 0600 Jon and I spoke briefly. I asked him, "if it's all right with you, I make the call to Cuba for both of us, as soon as we are twelve miles off."

He said, "that's okay. I'll listen in."

We approached the waypoint at which we were to enter the Cuban territorial waters. The tall buildings of the Cuban capital materialized out of the smog. At nine a m I tried to establish radio contact with Marina Hemingway on International channel 72, according to Cuban regulations. I called twice in English and received no reply. Then I spoke in Spanish and there was an immediate response, also in Spanish.

I said, two sailing vessels of United States registry were approaching "la costa de la República de Cuba, pidiendo permiso para entrar a la Marina Hemingway." The reply was precise, polite and professional. I identified *PEGASUS* and *TRITON 3* and we received authorization and instructions where to dock once inside the harbor. I told Jon what we had to do and together we headed for the red buoy marking the entrance channel to the marina. Fighting a strong current, we did not make it into the harbor before noon. Uniformed personnel showed us a place at a concrete wall where to tie up. We were in Cuba.

The process of officially entering the Communist Republic of Cuba began immediately. The first person on board was the medical doctor, a sixty-two-year old man in ill-fitting jeans and a threadbare white smock. He filled out some papers and sprayed three short bursts of an insect repellent from a huge spray can into the cabin. He asked me in Spanish, for he spoke no English, if I could spare some cash. I said, "We're not allowed to spend dollars here," He knew that and did not insist but helped himself to a coke; I carried several cases of beer and soft drinks under the saloon table. I offered him a cold one from the refrigerator, so he took them both. "I earn only thirty US dollars and this is my only job," he told me. Thirty dollars a month? A week? I was too embarrassed to ask.

Next, two uniformed men of La Guarda Frontera, the border police, came on board. They sat down in the cockpit, filled out papers, stamped and signed them. Politely they handed me copies of everything, saluted and went back ashore.

After they left, two men, also in uniforms, stepped into my cabin. They were the Immigration officials. More papers and forms passed across the table for signatures, dates and stamps. The stamp they applied to my passport left no more than a hardly visible green smudge.

Then two men from the Guarda Civil, state or local police, came to inspect the boat, but they didn't really know where to look or what to look for.

I wondered how Jon was getting along. It was of much help and advantage to me that I spoke Spanish. All personnel were friendly and polite, but none of them spoke English. All of them commented on how beautiful and neat my boat was, and their inquiries and searches were superficial. Most of the people coming on board had a beer or a coke and asked for money. I told them it was against the law for me to hand out dollars. I offered them bath soap, chewing gum, pens and notebooks, items I knew were in great demand. Flashlight batteries were most welcome.

Two and a half hours had gone by when we were at last allowed to take the boats into the marina, which consisted of four long *canales* ending in a cul de sac. An attendant assigned us a place at the concrete wall of the first canal in this artificial harbor. There were at least thirty-five boats of various kinds and many nationalities. About half of them were US vessels; among the others were many Canadians, one German, a British and a couple of French yachts and a few from various Caribbean nations and Mexico.

Personnel were on hand to help with tying up, connecting electrical cables and water hoses. I am very particular with my lines and cables and wanted to do all that by myself, but they did not allow me. "Ees my yob, meester," one muchacho said.

Then three uniformed men came on board. They were the Customs officials and they proceeded to inspect the vessel. The oldest one was obviously in charge. A little arrogant but polite, he had many questions. "Que carga tiene abordo?"

I had no cargo. They looked everywhere—well, they didn't really know where 'everywhere' was, and I didn't know what they would consider cargo.

292

He explained, "Contrabando? Mercaderia? Armas?"

I had no merchandise, and I never carried a weapon on board. I had nothing to hide.

More papers, stamps, signatures and in the end I had to pay an official fee, for which I got a receipt.

The dockmaster asked permission to come on board. José, neatly dressed in white shirt, tie and blue slacks, explained everything about the facilities of the marina, the restaurants, transportation, security, shopping, prices, supplies, fuel, etc. He spoke some English, had studied Navigation in Bulgaria and had been an instructor at the Escuela Marítima de Cuba for fifteen years. He was in charge of all personnel and the guards in the marina compound.

Police were stationed at various locations on the ample grounds. How these people could wear uniforms, shirts, ties and long pants in this climate was beyond me. I must say they all made a good impression.

The heat of the day was almost unbearable. The twenty-four-hour sail from Dry Tortugas and the five hours of checking in had exhausted me, and still there was more to come. A man and a woman of the Departmento Agrícola showed up to inspect the food we carried on our boats. I had no problem. All my food was canned or non-perishable. I had no fresh meat, eggs or vegetables on board.

As our boats were processed simultaneously, I was unable to assist Jon. Not knowing how to respond or to give explanations, some of his food—eggs, meat, fresh vegetables—were quarantined and sealed in a container.

I had paid a total of thirty-five dollars in fees, given away about ten beers and cokes, as well as some gifts. Jon told me he shelled out over fifty dollars.

PEGASUS & TRITON 3 at Marina Hemingway

At last we were officially cleared to roam around the country. After a shower, we decided we deserved a good dinner. Papa's restaurant on the premises was quite elegant and expensive, but the paella we ordered was not very good. Three musicians with violins and guitars came around and when I asked them to play *Cuando salí de Cuba* (When I left Cuba) they declined. "No no, esto no." That song was not politically correct in Castro's Cuba. I should have known.

The sun rose over the modern hotel EL VIEJO Y EL MAR. The Old Man and the Sea, named after Hemingway's famed novel, ten or twelve stories of luxury, rivaled any five-star hotel anywhere in the world. The lobby was like the glorified foyer of an old-world opera house, with rich carpeting, columns, a waterfall and exquisite paintings on the walls. A wide, curved stairway led to the mezzanine.

Refreshed after a good night's sleep, Jon and I found a taxi to take us into Havana, twelve or fifteen kilometers east of the marina. There were two types of taxis: new European and Japanese models—Mercedes, Volvos, Toyotas—and old American ones, from the 1950s, which were mostly held together by the rust on their bodies. The former were expensive, the latter quite cheap.

We hired one for eight dollars, vintage 1958. The driver said, his father had it, now he and his son drove it. On the way into the city, he pointed out the various embassies we were passing: Iran, Switzerland, Vietnam, Belgium. Most impressive was a tall, tower-like building, the Russian embassy, left over from the days of the former Soviet Union. Well-kept mansions and villas, with elegant and expensive cars on their driveways, housed the headquarters of foreign companies. Between them we saw houses, still showing the splendor of years long past, but neglected and in ruinous state. Some of them seemed to be falling apart, beyond repair.

As the taxi rattled on toward Old Havana, the houses we passed were in worse and worse conditions, yet they were occupied. By the looks of them, they should have been condemned. We came to the Malecón and marveled at this elegant, wide boulevard along the waterfront. There were traffic separations, marked lanes, an underpass at a plaza, like in any glamorous city. However, most of the buildings along this spectacular thoroughfare were in sad conditions. On our left was the ship channel, entrance to the commercial harbor. El Morro, the magnificent old fortress, stood on the far side.

Old Havana and Plaza de la Catedral

We got off at the edge of La Habana Vieja, Old Havana. Central to Old Havana are the Plaza de la Catedral and the park Miguel de Cervantes. The cobblestone streets were narrow, some of them without sidewalks. There were people everywhere. As soon as they saw us as foreigners, they practically hung onto our sleeves. Incredible poverty surrounded us. Men, women and children asked outright for money, not much, una moneda, a coin. A young mother in rags showed us a small, hungry child, pleading. An old man stretched out his bony hand. A woman followed us, crying. Young girls tried to lure us into restaurants or shops where they would get a small reward. Some boys asked if we had a pencil to give them. Men offered cigars of dubious quality from every dilapidated hallway. Women and young girls, in disgustingly revealing clothes, offered themselves for next to nothing; they would go with anyone just for something to eat.

La Bodeguita de Medio, an ancient restaurant in the middle of La Habana Vieja is a must for visitors. Located on a dirty side street, it is a small, crowded vault-like place with low ceilings. We had the typical roast pork with rice and black beans, and the famous Cuban drink, mojito, which consists of rum, lime and a sprig of mint in a tall glass with ice and a lot of water. You can't have just one of those.

Outside the few square blocks of Old Havana, the multitude was less shocking. People dressed better and families strolled by on bicycles or on foot. No longer were we accosted at every step by the wretched populace, to give away money or to buy something.

In the afternoon, thirsty and tired from the meal, the mojito and the heat, we looked for a place to sit down. A very nice looking young mulata, dressed neatly in jeans and a white blouse, stopped us. "I would like to show you the sights," she said in passable English. "My name is Mary. I am not asking for money, just practice to speak English."

We sat under an umbrella of a sidewalk cafe on the Malecón. Jon and I drank Crystal, a local beer, while she took coffee. "Cheaper," she said, very considerate, very respectful. Then she walked with us to the Museo de la Revolucion, a huge white palace that once had been Batista's residence. She showed us the Opera, the Parliament building and, on the plaza in front of it, the boat on which Castro arrived from exile in Mexico.

The time came for us to say goodbye to our tour guide. As we walked away, Jon said, "I am a little suspicious of her. A pretty girl like that, well dressed, educated, a student, asking us many questions, but revealing very little about herself? She could be an agent of some kind, spying on foreigners."

"I don't think so," I said, weighing that possibility.

Jon reminded me of how she did not want to have her picture taken with us. "She covered her face with her hands. 'No pictures, please,' she said. Remember that? We were sitting at the café on the Malecón."

"True, and she avoided all my questions, what her life was like in Cuba. But what would have been the purpose? Arrest us, if we said something stupid?"

"Yeah, like that song you asked for at "Papa's," he laughed

We had arranged with our taxi driver to take us back to the marina. At seven o'clock, the car stopped at the far side of the Malecón. We waited for a green light to cross the multi-laned boulevard. The son of our driver, a friendly young man who spoke some English, drove us back.

On the far side of the marina complex was a large housing project under construction. Every morning several tractors pulling cattle wagons, called camellos, arrived with the workers. They looked like prisoners from a concentration camp to me, being trucked in for forced labor.

A marina attendant explained, however, that they were guajiros, uneducated and illiterate, from the countryside and the mountains, earning one peso an hour—one peso, not one dollar—plus food and lodging in a type of reservation. "They all have the ambition to one day be able to live in Havana," he added. So, I thought, they wanted to join the miserable mass of humanity we had seen there, for a better life?

There were several shops—fashion beachwear and accessories, clothing, cigars, groceries—at the entrance to the marina complex. The grocery store also sold small appliances, radios, binoculars, wine and liquor, all at quite reasonable prices. There were no American goods to be seen anywhere, but the only currency accepted was the U.S. dollar.

In the first-class cigar store at Marina Hemingway I had bought a few cigars, which I smoked in the evenings with newfound friends. Among the variety of brands I sampled was one Partagas. Some of these special cigars, made by the famous cigar maker Ramón Cifuentes, sell for more than thirty dollars a piece. I, of course, bought a much cheaper one and it was awful: harsh, acrid, didn't burn right, fell apart. I was tempted to bring the stub back to the store that prided itself of its elegant decor and refined, sophisticated sales personnel.

The Cuban peso was practically worthless. Even the taxi driver had to pay for his gasoline in dollars. There may have been some stores that sold rice, plantains or beans for pesos. The public transit system of Havana accepted exclusively the Cuban peso. Public transportation was the camellos, substitutes for buses, consisting of farm tractors pulling converted cattle wagons. They were the lowest type of transportation I have ever seen.

A couple of times Jon and I had lunch at one of those little home restaurants called paladares, not far from the marina. The proprietress showed us a menu that pictured the dishes to choose from, usually not more than two or three. It surprised me that, being so close to the ocean, there was never any fish or seafood on the menus.

On Sunday local visitors came out to Marina Hemingway to stroll around, see foreign yachts and talk to people from other countries. It also gave us an opportunity to meet with some Cubans of the middle or upper classes, fashionably dressed, refined and certainly not poor. They did not seem unhappy or oppressed; they referred almost lovingly to their leader as Fidel, who might show up at any time anywhere: a school, a soccer match or a rally of some kind.

Two girls, who had come in a group of fine young people, asked very politely if they might take a photo with me. My beard had grown a little fuller than I usually kept it and was slightly unkempt. They said, I reminded them of "Papa Hemingway", still very much revered by the Cubans.

There was a lot of rain the last days of our stay in Cuba and nothing for us to do but hang out at the marina. Our visit to this 'forbidden' island was coming to an end. A powerful storm named Andres had come across Central America from the Pacific. Torrential rainstorms were pounding Cuba, southern Florida and the Keys.

It was the afternoon of 11 June. We intended to leave in the wake of this weather system, which we hoped would give us good winds from the south and southwest. A thunderstorm in progress made it unsafe to turn on the fuel pumps. We had to wait at the fuel dock until the storm passed. Diesel was more expensive than in the States or the Bahamas, but I did not feel good about leaving with half a tankful and Bimini, our next port, was about three hundred miles away. After fueling, we had to stop at the concrete seawall and go through the formalities of checking out. Less complicated than at our arrival, this procedure nevertheless took an hour and a half.

Shortly before six p m, we finally motored out of Marina Hemingway and waved our goodbyes. The people we left behind on the dock answered likewise, but less fervently so. What might have been in their thoughts? There they go, back into the free world? Most of them had never experienced a free society. Not under Batista, and not under Fidel.

Leaving Havana

CUANDO SALÍ DE CUBA

Advice from the U. S. Coast Guard was not to parallel the coast of Cuba. Their instructions were to promptly head for international waters, which meant we had to sail twelve miles out before we could take up our course for the Cay Sal Bank. Jon and I had planned not to return to the United States directly, but by way of the Bahamas. So, we ignored the instructions, which, we reasoned, did not apply to us. As soon as we reached the sea buoy, we headed east, three or four miles off the Cuban coast.

A patrol boat of the Cuban Navy, underway closer inshore, also headed east. "They are keeping an eye on us," Jon shouted over to me. We were sailing side by side; Jon had set only his Genoa, I was already under full sail.

"That's okay. Makes me feel safe!" I yelled back. "They know who we are. I am sure they asked about us at the marina." The gunboat kept her distance from us, but seemed to keep us under surveillance. As we passed the harbor entrance to Havana, we encountered several freighters, some going in, others leaving the port. I couldn't make out their homeports or nationalities. A gunboat stood in front of El Morro. Jon waved goodbye, but unless they watched through binoculars, they could not have seen it.

In the waning daylight Havana looked fragile, anemic, lifeless. I felt a sadness for the once brilliant capital, the people, the whole country. Gradually we gained distance from the coast. As darkness gathered around us, the lights of the big city became brighter as if saying, "See, I am alive!" Yeah, barely. Parts of you are already dead.

We were sailing through a field of debris. Branches, whole trees and all sorts of flotsam covered the ocean. The recent storms over eastern Cuba had washed entire villages into the sea, as if the Cuban people had to suffer from nature as well as from man. By the time it was fully dark we had come out of this field of debris and Havana disappeared, leaving only the glow. By midnight we were all alone. In the light breeze, *TRITON 3* had pulled ahead of *PEGASUS*. I saw her masthead light following me. Jon and I spoke briefly on the radio and confirmed our course of 070 degrees, directly for Cay Sal and wished each other a good night. "Wake you up at 0600."

The light wind carried the foul odor from a sugar refinery out to us, seven and a half miles away from the coast. Before morning the wind died. In the night I had gone through my paperwork and receipts from the marina and some shopping in Havana. I destroyed all evidence that indicated payments for services or purchases while in the Communist Republic of Cuba. I smoked my last Cuban cigar and, what was left of the excellent Cuban rum, I carefully decanted into an empty Bacardi bottle. All remaining evidence of my visit to Cuba was perfectly legal.

It was common knowledge that visitors to Cuba had to spend some money. Dockage, food and fuel were not free; therefore, without suspicion of wrongdoing, U.S. authorities generally practiced the "don't ask, don't tell" method. Some sailors we had talked to had been in Cuba several times. "If they ask, 'Did you spend any money in Cuba?' just answer, 'No. We were invited guests,' and they'll leave you alone."

U.S. Coast Guard vessels patrolling the Florida Straight have occasionally intercepted boats on the high seas. We have heard of searches that left the interiors of yachts all but destroyed. Those incidents more often than not involved powerboats, sportfishing or speed boats, and usually there was some suspicion of drug trafficking. Even a crumb of some illegal weed, if found, could lead to confiscating the boat.

The morning brought rain and with it a nice breeze. Again we encountered an area of debris. At 0600 I warned Jon of logs, branches and twigs strewn all over the sea. We had both turned off our automatic helms and steered by hand through the debris field. *PEGASUS* had fallen behind during the night, but was catching up with the stronger morning wind. By noontime we were once again side by side. The wind died and left the sea without a ripple on the surface. The heat became almost unbearable. Cay Sal did not appear before us until five thirty in the afternoon. The two or three flat, sandy islets were only a few feet above sea level, and the vegetation consisted of no more than low shrubs and bushes. Only birds inhabited this remote wilderness in the middle of nowhere. Geographically and politically, the Cay Sal Bank belonged to the Bahamas; its location 23 degrees 41 minutes north latitude, 080 degrees 24 minutes west longitude, for those who want to know where it is.

With help from the Gulf Stream, we had covered one hundred eighty nautical miles in twenty-six hours. The shallow water did not allow anchoring close to the largest of the Cays. In open water, exposed to the ocean swells, it became a rolley-polley night. We had anchored at shouting distance and Jon called over, "I'll go around the island, see if I can find calmer water."

"Go ahead," I answered. "I am too tired to move. My anchor is down good. I stay where I am." I just wanted to sleep. Jon then didn't move his boat either.

I prepared a quick supper of macaroni with tuna, drank a beer and went to bed by sundown. The air was still stifling hot. Luckily, and strangely, there were no mosquitoes or flies. I had the luxury of leaving the hatches open without putting up screens. What little air there was could pass freely through the cabin.

Bathed in perspiration, I awoke on Friday, 13 June to a hot and windless morning. The forecast for the Florida Straight was for southerly winds of ten to fifteen knots. If that were true, we could reach Bimini in less than twenty-four hours. Right after breakfast, at eight thirty, we worked our anchors on board and left Cay Sal. With a very light breeze from the south, we pointed our bows in the direction of Bimini.

The forecast was once again wrong, the wind died before noon, but the Gulf Stream carried us at close to three knots. Late in the afternoon, a southeast breeze sprang up and I rolled out my Genoa.

At five minutes past five o'clock—I was below making a cup of coffee—a violent jolt propelled me forward. I lost my balance, hit the table and ended up on the couch; the coffee spilled all over the cabin sole. The bow had struck an object that had to be of enormous size. Immediately another blow followed, this one lifting up the stern. The boat momentarily came to a standstill. In a split second I was in the cockpit. Looking over the transom, I saw a huge tree trunk spring to the surface two feet behind the stern. I had hit the trunk dead on with the leading edge of the keel, then again with the skeg, which protects the propeller and the rudder. I inspected through-hulls, looked into the bilge, tested the rudder. Everything was okay. I looked back again: there was that black monster tree, innocently floating just below the surface, calmly lying there. "You bastard, you almost sank my boat!" I screamed at it.

Then I called Jon on channel sixteen. "PEGASUS, PEGASUS. Over."

"TRITON 3, what's the matter? Over."

"I just hit an enormous tree trunk, that's what's the matter. It all but sank my boat. It was a tremendous shock, first my keel, then the skeg. Over."

"Peter, check for leaks. Are you all right? Over."

"Everything is fine, I'm just shook up. Watch out, Jon. I thought we were out of that debris field. Over."

"Okay. Thanks for the warning. Talk to you at midnight. Out."

I looked again into the bilge. No leaks. What an odd thing, to hit the one log floating in an ocean of thousands of square miles. Boats have hit containers, whales, ships, or were struck by submarines. Shit happens. I was lucky, though. Thanks to the quality and design of the Bristol, I survived what could have been a major disaster for a boat of inferior design. The construction of the keel, molded into the hull and the strong skeg had saved me. Any boat with a bolted-on keel, open propeller and spade rudder might have lost all three and would have been on the bottom of the ocean in minutes.

The night brought a beautiful southeast wind and I had a great time. Freighters and cruise ships crossed my wake far astern.

Jon called at twelve midnight. "TRITON 3, where are you? Over." He sounded frantic.

"PEGASUS, you have a problem? Over."

"Peter, where the hell are you? I want to have you in sight at all times. I scan the horizon, and you're not there. Over."

It was my habit to sail without lights—wrong, but that's me. "PEGASUS, wait, I'll turn on my lights." I switched on everything I had, from anchor light to spreader lights. "Can you see me now? Look over your port side, I'm a mile or so away. Over."

"Yes. I expected you ahead of me. Keep your nav lights on; I want to be able to see you. That incident with the tree stump... you never know what can happen. Over."

"No news is good news. Something happens, you're the first to hear about it, believe me. So, take it easy, man. Talk to you in the morning. TRITON 3 out."

As the sky grew lighter in the east, Cat Cay and Gun Cay came into view on starboard. This was familiar territory to me and Jon had told me he had been to Bimini countless times, although not recently. We found the range markers easily and before noon we arrived in Alicetown.

Jon proceeded to the anchorage. I called out to him as he passed me, "Jon, we have to check in first."

"I anchor first and then take the dinghy in," he answered.

"No, you have to be accessible at the dock. They don't clear you otherwise."

He cut me off with a hand gesture. Maybe he's lucky, maybe I am wrong. He said he knew this place well.

I docked at Weech's marina and walked to Customs and Immigration. After that I anchored *TRITON 3* close to *PEGASUS*. Jon's dinghy was not there.

I was still busy with my second anchor when Jon came rowing back, fuming, screaming and yelling. "They can't do this to me. Who the fuck they think they are? They can take their fuckin' islands and shove'em up their asses. I don't take that kind of shit from them. Where would they be, if not for us?" He kept on spewing more profanities as he rowed past me back to his boat.

"Told you. Its their islands, they can do want they damn well please. We are visitors. They set the rules here."

"I am leaving. I don't stay in their fucking islands." He went on board and pulled up both anchors. Without another word to me he motored out of the anchorage. Is he really leaving? I wondered and watched him. *PEGASUS* pulled over to the dock at Weech's. In little more than an hour he brought his boat back and anchored where he had been before.

He did not talk to me that day, the next and the one after that.

On the third day he came over in his dinghy to drop off a loaf of bread he had baked. "Here. I thought you might like some bread," he said and before I could say more than "thanks", he rowed back to his boat. He did not go ashore, sat in his cockpit, busied himself with this or that on deck, but most of the time he spent below, out of sight. I went ashore every day, for lunch, for some beers, for provisioning. Jon did not leave his boat.

I was no longer willing to cater to his weird behavior. We did Cuba together and that was the main purpose of the trip. We had planned a continuation through the Bahamas, but under the circumstances, I was not looking forward to that. He could be good company, funny and entertaining, but he could at any time fly into a rage and then the fun was over.

On the fourth day of our arrival in Bimini, I prepared to sail to Nassau, or wherever else I felt like going. In the night there had been a big thunderstorm, but the morning looked good to me. In the afternoon, without having spoken another word with Jon, I went to work on my first anchor. He must have heard my anchor chain rattling, but he didn't come out of his cabin to see what was happening. With the second anchor on deck, and the Diesel running, I slowly passed by him and called out, "PEGASUS!" He appeared in the companionway, surprised to see me underway. "I am leaving," I said. "For Nassau. You coming?"

Still incredulous, he just said, "Have a good trip." From the way he sounded, I knew that he had not expected me to leave just like that. Had he said, "Wait, I come with you," or something like that, I would have waited. He might have been short on money, but we could have talked about that, too.

I had mixed feelings. Was it right for me to end our cruise like this? Throughout the voyage he has often enough acted like an idiot. Then again, we also had some good times together. What the hell, I've had plenty of reasons to take off by myself, but I stuck it out. Enough is enough.

As soon as I left the range behind, I set my sails and headed for North Rock. On the Bank, the wind allowed me to steer a course north of Mackie Shoal. A small Bahamian freighter came up from behind and passed me. I followed in his wake to be sure not to strike the wreck that was marked on my chart, but without indication of its depth. There was constant lightning in the west. Some dark clouds overtook me, bringing with them a fine, cool breeze.

On a beautiful broad reach, I sailed past Northwest Channel Light at seven thirty in the morning, and ten minutes later I hit something. It was not a hard object, like the big log between Cay Sal and Bimini. This was more like a thump, not a terrifying jolt. I had just left the Bank and was already in deep water. Looking over the stern, I saw in my wake a bluish-gray, silvery creature following me. A dolphin? A shark? Barracuda? They all are such great navigators, so how could this happen? Must have been asleep just below the surface, poor thing.

I guess I was in deep thought, either about this whole thing with Jon, or perhaps about the dolphin or whatever it was, when I came close to making a disastrous mistake. In my GPS I had two waypoints for the approach to Chub, one to be used coming from Nassau, the other from the Bank. I had punched in the wrong one and headed straight for the reef that extended from Mama Rhoda Rock.

Through the clear water I noticed big boulders on the bottom, boulders that weren't supposed to be there. The quickest way to reverse course under sail is to jibe, i. e., turn the boat around so that the stern passes through the wind—not an easy operation for a singlehander. I spun the wheel around, took care of the mainsail and worried about the Genoa later. It was not an elegant maneuver, but it got me out of trouble. I retraced my course until I was sure I could round Mama Rhoda safely. What a great instrument, the GPS—if used correctly!

I anchored near the white beach in the calm bay, shaped like a crescent moon and stayed for two days. Totally relaxed, I wrote down in my notebook the recent experiences while they were fresh in my memory. Light breezes and the awning over the cockpit made life comfortable. I swam in the perfectly clean water around the boat, scraped barnacles off the hull and enjoyed my sundowners at the end of the day. I had no worry in the world. Two or three other boats came and left and I must admit that I caught myself thinking of *PEGASUS* whenever a sail appeared from behind Mama Rhoda Rock.

Early on the third morning I sailed out of Chub and headed for Nassau. The wind was light, but on a pleasant close-hauled course I was able to make the harbor entrance with the last of daylight. Passing the huge, gleaming white cruise ships at the Prince George Wharf, I once again became aware of the tiny speck my boat was next to these giants.

At the Yacht Basin in East Bay, I treated myself to the luxury of a slip in the marina. No mess with the anchors, no worries about boats dragging, no need to inflate the dinghy. Instead, I had the convenience of fuel, water and showers on the premises. I registered with the dock master and received a key for the security gate. Only boat owners, their crew and guests had access to the dock.

I did not forget to report my arrival to Harbor Control, before taking a shower and dressing in respectable shore clothes, the first time since Cuba. It was after ten o'clock when I entered the Hammerhead Bar. The young women with whom I hoped to play a game of Dominos were not there. Only a few people, mostly sailors from boats in the anchorage, were at the bar. No real conversation developed beyond "Hi, how you doin'?" " Just got in from Chub." "I'm leavin' tomorrow for Highborne." "Weather today not too good in the Straight." Things like that. I had two Kaliks and went home.

During the two days I spent in Nassau, I wandered through the familiar streets, had lunch at the Peking Garden and enjoyed my favorite conch salad at Potter Cay. In a crowded souvenir shop I bought a set of Dominos. A duty free liquor store advertised a two-liter bottle of Coke free with purchase of Baccardi rum 151. That's 75.5% alcohol! I couldn't resist that offer. The bottle came with its own flame arrest cap. I brought my treasures home and tasted the rum. Smooth, almost evaporating on the tongue, I inhaled the fragrant fumes rather than swallowing liquid. More a sensation than drinking. Too good to mix with the free Coca Cola.

At the small rustic grocery store opposite the post office I bought bread, meat and some canned juices. I was ready to return to Stuart, via Chub Cay and Bimini.

The night at Chub was turbulent with thunderstorms into the morning hours. In the afternoon I pulled up my two anchors and sailed out of the anchorage. In perfect wind, I flew past Northwest Channel Light by evening and Mackie Shoal at midnight. Long before daybreak my GPS told me I was at North Rock, but the light on top of the thin, spidery legs was not working and I could not find it. I had experiences with erroneous charts and recently made a mistake at Mama Rhoda Rock. Passing the pile of rocks without visual identification seemed foolish to me. For a while I sailed in a holding pattern, airplane style, and waited for daybreak. To the west, the shape of Bimini rose out of the early dawn, but still no North Rock. Then, suddenly, the heap of rocks with the thin stake on top was right where it's supposed to be. Why don't they fix the damn lights? How much longer will it take them to fix Northwest Channel Light? It's been years. And now this one...

When I arrived in the anchorage of Alicetown, I was surprised to find *PEGASUS* still at anchor in the same spot. Jon's dinghy, tied to the transom, indicated that he was on board. I called out, "Hey, PEGASUS, I am back!" His hatches and companionway were open. He must have heard me, but did not respond.

There were only a few boats in the anchorage. I anchored where I had been the week before, close to Jon's boat. After the night sail, and with little rest the night before at Chub Cay, I was tired and stayed on board under the awning, out of the direct sun. The heat was bearable, although there was not even as much as a breath of air.

In the afternoon Jon came out of his cabin and began to pull up an anchor. At first I thought he was just checking or replacing his CQR, but then he started working on his second anchor. Still no word from him and not a glance over to me. What a strange man.

Both anchors on board, he took one turn around *TRITON 3*. "I am leaving for Fort Lauderdale," Jon called out. "I'll talk to you on channel sixteen as soon as I am outside the range."

"Have a good trip," I said, as he had replied to me the day I left for Nassau. What a strange man, I repeated to myself. Why wouldn't he talk to me? Why did it have to be on the radio after he left? Why was he still here, only to leave the very day I came back?

He did call me on the VHF. "I wanted to leave a few days ago," he said. "I was just waiting for the right weather. I have to be back in Bradenton, take care of something."

"Well, have a good trip," I said again and wondered what he considered the right weather. Today there's hardly any wind. Is that what he had waited for? How very, very weird.

I stayed in Bimini for two more days and enjoyed the slow passage of time. In Bimini nobody is in a hurry, ever. The few cars and mopeds in Alicetown never go over fifteen miles an hour. Island folk stand around a lot, and when they walk, it's a slow shuffle, barely lifting the feet, barely raising an arm in greeting. "Okay, mon. No problem". I almost got myself in trouble, though, when I yelled at a boy who threw stones at a dog. The poor stray animal tried to scavenge something to eat from a pile of garbage. People gathered around, and I knew they weren't taking the dog's side—or mine.

I made my exit from the scene and went to the plaza next to the Customs House. Some sort of celebration was going on—Bahamian Independence or something. Vendors had set up their tables. Tarps hanging on poles protected some of them from the sun. There was food on portable grills, the smell of roast pork and chicken in the air. Women and children offered T-shirts and souvenirs, although the tourists did not come out until the sun went lower in the sky and the temperatures became tolerable. I bought myself a conch salad and stood around on the dusty soil in the crowd of local revelers while I ate. Then I started on the long trek back to my dinghy.

I had almost reached the place where my dinghy was tied up, when I felt in my pocket that something was missing. My gold money clasp the shape of a large paperclip, a gift from The Cat, many years ago. I couldn't bear to lose it.

Slowly I retraced my way, eyes glued to the ground before me, crossed over where I had before to stay in the shade. I remembered where I bought the conch salad. That's where I must have dropped it. I pushed my way through the crowd to that stand. What are my chances to find it? There's no hope, yet I have to try.

Stepped on and half buried in the dirt, between feet, some bare, others shod in sandals or sneakers, something glittered yellow golden. I bent down and picked it up. My money clip! Nobody had seen it? Nobody thought it more than a measly paper clip? For me the value of this lost and found revered object became tenfold. It had been with me for twenty years, in good times and bad, through storms and shipwrecks. I must tell The Cat about this.

Back on *TRITON 3*, I did not know that it would be my last night, my last time in Bimini.

RETURN TO TERRA FIRMA

My last time in Bimini... At that time I did not know how true that was.

I motored out of Alicetown. The wind was light. I set the sails, but I was in no hurry. Let the Gulf Stream take me along. I don't want to arrive at Fort Pierce before daylight anyway.

With Bimini out of sight before noon, a strange feeling of nostalgia took possession of my psyche. At the latitude of Isaac Light, memories played in my mind. Isaac was not in sight, but the mere thought of it conjured up the night I had anchored there after fifty-nine sleepless hours. Then I thought of the time Carlos and Linda had been with me at Isaac and how happy I was to see them having so much fun. Why does that memory depress me now?

The wind remained light throughout the day, while the Stream carried me northward. The midday heat was bearing down on me. There were only a few clouds in the sky. "Dad, don't drink all that beer," I heard Carlos saying. I reached for a lemonade.

In the evening I could see the buildings along the Florida coast from Palm Beach to Jupiter. From time to time I had to run the Diesel in order to keep my course for the Fort Pierce Inlet.

During the night there was a lot of traffic in the shipping lane. One southbound container ship came at me at eighteen or twenty knots. The Gulf Stream carried me toward the vessel. I tried to make radio contact to make sure they saw me, but received no answer. I pushed the engine speed up to 2600 rpms.

Distances on the ocean are difficult to judge, especially in the dark. When at last the freighter's range lights separated and I saw the green running light, I became aware of how tightly I had held onto the wheel. I relaxed my grip and throttled back to cruising speed of 1900 rpms as the big ship plowed past my stern at only a hundred yards distance.

That might not seem dangerously close. Two cars may pass each other on a highway with a couple of feet separating them, but comparing the wide ocean with a narrow highway, a hundred yards isn't all that much. That became even more exacerbated as the ship's engines and the churning propellers drummed in my ears and the peculiar smell of diesel exhaust stung my nostrils.

This close encounter behind me, I dropped back into my reverie. I have sailed many nights and many miles alone, and often I have felt loneliness closing in on me. In the end, my enthusiasm always prevailed. My first solo voyage from Samaná through the Bahamas, the solitary months in Graham's Harbor, the eerie, dark night in Hawksnest Creek of Cat Island—I had never thought seriously of living any other way. *TRITON 3* was my home, my only home.

At two in the morning I lost the effect of the Gulf Stream and steered directly for the sea buoy of Fort Pierce, which appeared before dawn. Against the ebbing tide and a horde of sport fishing boats of all sizes, I fought my way into the inlet. From my cell phone, making believe I was at the dock of Pelican Yacht Club, I called Customs and got my clearance. Wanting to end the trip more than anything, more than ever before, I turned without stopping into the Intracoastal Waterway and headed for Stuart. I did not quite understand this urge, this need to end the voyage.

At the Indian River Bridge the bridge tender advised me to give the right-of-way to a tug and tow, coming from the opposite direction. A tugboat, pulling a barge with an entire house mounted on it, narrowly made it through the opened drawbridge. Some historic landmark or national treasure was underway to a new site. With its balconies, porches and intricate gables, built of wood except for the chimneys, the structure looked like an oversized birdhouse.

It was Saturday, 28 June. Early in the afternoon I pulled into my slip at Stuart Harbor. Many helping hands were at the dock, guiding me in and taking my lines. Bo and Debbie, special friends of mine who lived on their boat *MOOREA*, welcomed me home with a generous glass of rum.

Everybody wanted to know about the trip. "How did it go?" "Where did you lose *PEGASUS*?" "Did you go to Cuba?" "Did you come straight back from Cuba?" I had to put off answering those questions. Underway from Bimini for almost thirty hours, I was tired and in a strange, somber mood, which I could not explain to myself.

"Thanks for your help, guys, but let me get a few hours of sleep. Yes, we were in Cuba, Jon went back to the Gulf Coast. I just came back from Bimini." Later, guys, later. I'm not in the mood right now... "I am really tired. Thirty hours..." I went below and stretched out on the couch.

Half asleep, I tried to comprehend my weird state of mind. I was tired, but that could not be the reason. Had something happened that made me feel uncertain, troubled? Jon's strange behavior? No, that couldn't be it. Or Graham's Harbor, when I decided against the Caribbean and returned to the States? I had no problem with that. Something deeper, more drastic was clouding my mind. But why? What had changed? Why this unrest, this feeling? Will it pass?

I have been to Cuba, perhaps the crown of my sailing exploits. Oh, there is much I haven't done: cross the Atlantic, sail round Cape Horn, circumnavigated the globe.

Eleven years afloat on *TRITON 3*, I mused and looked around as I lay on the couch in my cabin. It is comfortable, it is cozy, but it also is small and without air conditioning. I am sixty-nine years old. Do I want to live like this? What do I want?

I could not sleep. Maybe a shower would clear my mind. I had a bagful of laundry to do and put it into the washing machine in the little green building on the premises of the marina. While the machine was running, I took a shower in the adjacent bathroom.

Someone was at the door, tried the handle. "I am in here, give me five minutes!" I yelled at whoever was trying to get in.

That was it. Suddenly it became clear to me. A public bathroom... A public, coin-operated Laundromat... This was home? No heat in the winter, no air conditioning in the summer—who lives like that? Vagabonds, bums, the homeless, that's who. It hit me like a powerful shock. I felt oppressed, deprived of the very necessities of life, brought down upon me by myself.

I drove to Jacksonville, partly to be away from the boat and the marina for a day or two, and partly to see how Julia was getting along, but her spacious home in a fine neighborhood depressed me. I lived in a space twenty-seven by ten.

I can't stand it, I have to get out of here, I have to do something, I have to... I returned to Stuart the very next day. During the four-hour drive back, a decision matured in my mind.

The process of transforming an idea into a firm resolution was never difficult for me. Once I had focused on an idea, the jump to its realization was swift—a consequence of my impatient nature. Luckily, I also had the ability to accept the results of sudden actions without looking back. What's done is done. No regrets.

During the Fourth of July weekend I explored the possibility of buying a house. Unlike the selection of a boat, which became my home for eleven years, the choice of a house presented no problem for me. I had seen at least two dozen boats, before I found the *SHADOWFAX* and decided to buy her. I saw one house, pictured in a leaflet, and that was enough. Obviously, the boat had been much more important to me than a house.

Accompanied by a real estate agent, I went to see the house, located in a subdivision of Stuart, called Fishermen's Cove. The nautical sound of it seemed to confirm that my choice was a good one. To my surprise, I was able to come up with sufficient cash for the down payment. There was no immediate need to sell *TRITON 3*.

I closed the deal on the house on 18 August, 1997 and that same day I moved from the boat into my new home. The money I had left allowed for no more than the bare essentials: a bed, a dresser, a table and some chairs.

I never slept another night on *TRITON 3*.

THE SALE OF TRITON 3

TRITON 3 was for sale. When I put the For Sale sign on her bow pulpit, she was in the same flawless condition as when I bought her, exactly eleven years earlier. I advertised the boat, including all the equipment and accessories I had added over the years, at the same price I had paid, $27,500.

While I was still living on board, I did some cosmetic work to make the boat even more appealing. I oiled the teak, polished the stainless steel rails and painted the pedestal. I washed and waxed the topsides, and my friend Bo Gidlof helped me with some of the mechanical maintenance and improvements.

The day I moved from *TRITON 3* into the house, I started with the removal of my personal property. This consisted mainly of my clothes and the galley utensils, dishes, pots and pans. My tools, useful in any environment, I also considered personal property. All other items, for which I would have no use in my new life, I had decided to sell with the boat. Not that I expected to get more money that way, but I believed that a complete sail-away boat would be more attractive to potential buyers.

The last items I removed were mementos of nostalgia. My courtesy flags, the small US ensign, which I had flown on the transom of *TRITON II*, a pair of binoculars, my favorite hand-held bearing compass and the brass horn, a gift from my children. I also took with me a few of my charts, the ones, which had a special meaning for me.

I listed *TRITON 3* with a yacht brokerage firm and on 31 October I brought the boat to Stuart Yacht Sales at the South Fork of the St. Lucie River. As I maneuvered carefully into the assigned slip, it was not a dock attendant, but my good friend Ingo who stood there to take my bowline and assist me with the docking. Ingo and Carole? From Cruz Bay, St. John? What are they doing here? And how did they know where to find me?

"What are you doing here, and how did you know I would come here?" I had last seen them more than seven years ago, when I left the paradise of the Virgin Islands. We had stayed in touch through an occasional letter or a postcard.

Carole came up and gave me a hug. "Peter, so good to see you! We checked at your marina and learned you had just left for Stuart Yacht. You are selling your boat? I can't believe it."

The last pictures of TRITON 3

"That was a quick decision, although it must have been brewing in the remote folds of my brain for some time. After all these years, I am longing for a more comfortable life. I bought a house, you know."

"We were so surprised to hear that when we asked for you at your old marina," Ingo said. Then, as if it were a confession, "Peter, we did the same thing. We bought a little house on Culebra."

"You did not!" I blurted out. "What happened to *SEPTEMBER SONG*?"

"Oh, we still have the boat," Carole hastened to explain. Then she added, "haven't sailed since we moved into the house, though. She is for sale, too." There seemed to be a slight undertone of misgiving or sadness in her last words.

The similarities of events in our lives were astonishing. I had never thought that they would give up their floating life style, as they had not imagined that I would.

We had lunch at a local Cuban restaurant. Carole and Ingo told me how they had sailed less and less in the British and U.S. Virgin Islands. During the hurricane seasons of the last years, they had taken their boat into the mangroves at the little island of Culebra. Eventually, they decided to make Culebra their home.

I told them of my odyssey from the Virgin Islands back to the States via the Dominican Republic and the Bahamas and my later exploits, including Cuba. Before they drove back to Fort Pierce, where they stayed for a few days at the home of Ingo's father, we promised each other to stay in touch more closely.

Within a month my broker had found a prospective buyer for *TRITON 3*. A young man had made an offer of $20,000. After some negotiations, we reached an agreement at the still disappointing price of $23,300. I did not want to lengthen the agony of selling my beloved boat. I was not exactly happy with the outcome, but, considering the used boat market at the time, I had obtained a reasonable conclusion of the transaction.

On 4 December, a cold and rainy morning, we went out for the sea trial. Sean Mackinaw, the buyer, arrived at Stuart Yacht Sales with his agent and the surveyor. Still the owner and the skipper, I steered the *TRITON 3* out through the narrow channel into the St. Lucie River. The agent had scheduled haul out at Northside Marina for eleven o'clock. All the way under power, we arrived on time. The inspection of the hull showed no flaws. The boat back in the water, Sean wanted a demonstration of the boat under sail. It was a nasty day. We were cold and wet.

"In this weather?" I said. "Okay, you're entitled to see her perform, but you take care of folding the wet sails afterwards. Help me take off the sail cover, I'll hoist the main and roll out the Genoa." There wasn't much wind, but I could show off my still new mainsail, the fine Harken roller-furling system and the advantage of the lazy jacks. I am sure they were impressed, but they didn't say so. *TRITON 3* behaved well in the light wind, and after half an hour we took down the sails. It was almost five o'clock by the time we tied up again at Stuart Yacht.

During the entire sea trial, the rather unfriendly surveyor was busy looking for defects in every conceivable place: forward, amidships, in the engine room, behind the cupboards, under the cabin sole, in the bilge. From time to time he conferred in a low voice with Sean. This annoyed me, but I was not concerned. As soon as we had docked, they left with the buyer's agent, who had driven them down in the morning.

Two days later, my broker called me. The surveyor had sent him a list of defects and necessary repairs on the vessel, before final acceptance by his client. When I saw that list, I had the feeling that an amateur had prepared it. Most of the flaws listed were so insignificant that I could correct them without difficulty. Others were regular routine maintenance on any boat and the new owner's responsibility.

The only item in need of repair, and my responsibility, was one of the backing plates under the cleats on the foredeck. I thought of the day in Bimini, when I forced my anchor out from under a rock and remembered how the boat's bow went down before springing up as the anchor broke free from the bottom. The cleat had held, but the backing plate had suffered in the process. I asked my friend Bo to help me with the repair.

Then I wrote a letter to the surveyor, stating that I had corrected the few defects, rejecting all other ridiculous demands. I pointed out "TRITON 3 is seventeen years old and in better condition than most newer boats." We finalized the transaction on 9 December at the bank where I had my account.

Sean Mackinaw intended to sail the boat in the winter months between Florida and the Bahamas, and possibly in the Caribbean. During the summer months, Sean resided in Switzerland where he operated a hot air balloon enterprise. After conclusion of the business at the bank, I returned with Sean to the boat to retrieve the last few items of mine: a pair of boat shoes, my foul-weather suit and my watch cap. Sean and I toasted the successful transaction with a glass of rum and I wished him smooth sailing.

In the morning, I drove to a spot near the St. Lucie Inlet. I knew he was going to sail the boat to Fort Lauderdale. *TRITON 3*, no longer mine, sailed past me into the ocean. She was a beautiful sight. The mainsail was up, the Genoa unfurled but the engine was driving the boat on this calm morning. Sean and a friend of his were on board. I did not let them see me. When the top of the white sail disappeared behind the jetty, I turned around and went back to my car. I was surprised that not a single tear came to my eyes.

Sean had asked me, if I didn't mind, he would like to keep the name *TRITON*. I didn't mind. I felt honored.

EPILOGUE

Bo Gidlof was a tall, gentle and soft-spoken man in his mid-forties. He was building a racing sloop in the backyard at a friend's house and I sometimes gave him a hand with fiber glassing and painting. He had designed and built boats in his home country, Sweden.

Debbie and Bo lived at Stuart Harbor on their ketch MOOREA, a forty-two foot Sparkman & Stephens design. The MOOREA was registered in Debbie's name, and a bank held a considerable mortgage on the boat. Bo was not a citizen of the United States.

When the couple divorced, Bo temporarily moved in with me at Fishermen's Cove. On the weekends we usually worked together on the boat he was building. In April of 1998, when the twenty-four foot hull was finished, we put it on a trailer and, with Bo's truck, towed it to Jacksonville. There we loaded it onto a freighter for shipment to Sweden.

Bo and I contemplated sailing MOOREA to Sweden. Debbie at first agreed with our plan. The boat would sell for a much better price in Europe. Although the ketch was in good condition, a lot of preparations had to be made for a trans-Atlantic crossing. Bo overhauled and upgraded the rigging, thoroughly inspected the Diesel engine and replaced worn parts. We bought and installed new belts, through-hull fittings and pumps. When everything was in top condition, Bo arranged to haul the boat out at a yard in Fort Pierce for two coats of bottom paint.

The questions of ownership, title, mortgage and insurance became obstacles. We could not legally remove the boat from U.S. waters without the bank's approval and insurance coverage in the amount of the mortgage. We could not afford the high insurance premium, much less payment in full of the $80,000 mortgage the bank was still holding.

Bo and I were frustrated, our dream shattered. Bo, an experienced sailor, had yet to cross the Atlantic. I would have at least partially satisfied my early aspiration to sail around the world. We had accumulated charts and books, together spent hundreds of dollars to prepare the boat and ourselves. This voyage would have meant so much to us.

It occurred to us to sail uninsured and without the bank's knowledge. Bo tried desperately to find a way. "What about this? In Sweden I can sell the boat quickly. The bank gets the money and nobody is the wiser."

We were sitting in *MOOREA*'s saloon. "We might get away with it," I pondered. "We don't tell anybody where we're going. Who the hell would give a damn? The boat's insured for coastal cruising, isn't it?" I was clinging to the idea Bo had put forward.

He opened a couple of beers. "Yes," he said. "The trouble is, too many people already know that we are planning to sail across."

"I know, but before word spreads around, we're halfway on the other side."

"What are you talking about?" Debbie came down the companionway.

"We're just thinking out aloud. Isn't there still a way, we can make this happen?" Bo asked her. He and Debbie had remained on good terms after their divorce.

"Not without insurance or paying off the bank," said Debbie. "I have tried to borrow some more money from my mother, but she doesn't have it right now."

"So I guess, that's it."

"I don't know how you guys can even think of sailing to Sweden like that." Debbie tried to make it clear to us that, legal consequences aside, she would have the financial burden, if something happened to the boat. "The moment they find out the boat isn't here anymore, they'll hit me with an eighty-thousand-dollar law suit, long before you reach Sweden, let alone sell the boat and mail me the money."

Of course, we knew she was right. "I know, Debbie," I said. "We were just talking, that's all. It is such a disappointment." I got up and climbed out the companionway. "See you later," I muttered back over my shoulder. I drove home.

Bo came an hour later. We had nothing to say. We each dealt with our disappointment in our own ways.

Bo returned to Sweden. Half a year later I received the announcement that he had married a young Swedish woman. The following year I met Bo and his new bride in Berlin. We traveled together through Germany and Denmark to their home in Sweden, where I stayed with them for a week.

I did not remain in touch with Debbie, but learned that she and her *MOOREA* had moved away from the area, presumably to California.

During the first months after selling my boat, I returned sometimes to Stuart Harbor to chat with old friends, but there were fewer of them as time went by. Jon Kreeger did not return to Stuart. He had taken a job as captain on a sport fishing boat and moved away.

My friend Frank Gallardo had settled in Germany. He shipped his CIN CIN to Amsterdam and sailed her from there to the island of Föhr in the North Sea, where he and his new family took up residence. I see him every time I travel to Germany.

My life had begun in Rostock, the old Hanseatic City by the Sea. The love for the ocean, boats and sailing was bred into me with the scream of the sea gulls, the wailful howl of a foghorn at night and the distant thumping of fishing boat engines.

The cool Baltic storm winds of my youth mixed in my later years with the steady tropical breezes and made my life complete.

CPSIA information can be obtained at www.ICGtesting.com
Printed in the USA
LVOW071518010313

322221LV00001B/7/P